CONTENTS

INTRODUCTION

The M1 Garand is now a historical and collectible item, as well as a durable rifle, well-suited to hard use. While it's not as historical as a Roman Gladius, or a crusader sword, it's still fully capable of performing as expected. General Patton named it "The finest battle implement ever devised." The Garand was used to win one war, fight a police action to a standstill, arm much of the free world for a couple of decades, and was the basis on which, and the yardstick to be measured by, the next generation of battle rifles outside of communist countries.

The North Koreans invaded South Korea and were driven back. When we approached the Yalu River, the Chinese took that as a provocation, crossed the river, and the Marines fought their way back — using Garands.

We now see it as heavy, powerful, intricately machined and just a bit quaint. In its time, though, it was the space-age tool made by the finest methods possible, a handy and highly reliable weapon, and *the* rifle to depend on by a generation of men who saved the world.

The tales of the Garand, at times, hardly seem credible. And it has even been the center point in movies. Who can forget the movie "Uncommon Valor," where having been denied the "modern" small arms they need for their mission, our intrepid band finds they are "stuck" with a storage trunk jammed full of dusty WWII castoffs, such as the BAR, Thompson, and Garand? That was in 1982. Imagine the surprise on everyone's faces (except those in the know, of course) when much the same happened on Guadalcanal. The locals, the traditional inhabitants, had found themselves economically disadvantaged by the newcomers, so they were starting to be a problem. When it came to blows, the newcomers had the money to buy new firearms: M16s, AKs, and the like. The locals went into the jungle, opened the bunkers they had filled with salvaged, cast-off, or battlefield WWII pickups, and came back to fight. After a few dustups where the newcomers had to face Garands, Thompsons, BARs, and M1919A6s, they decided that talking would be better.

When asked about the incident by reporters, incredulous about then-60-plus-year-old small arms and ammunition still working, one of the locals remarked, "Of course they worked. They were made in America." (So long as we hold to that standard, we will be able to keep our enemies at bay. If we abandon it, we are lost.)

I've read accounts of the Garand that make you blink, slack-jawed. One, a Marine in Korea, who stalled a Chinese advance along a narrow road, holding his position and firing his Garand until it was so hot the charred wood could not be held, then picking up another to repeat the experience until the Chinese decided to stop running straight at him and getting shot for their efforts.

Adopted in 1936 and supposed to be replaced by the M14 before the end of the 1950s, the Garand was still in frontline use in the U.S. military in the early 1960s. We'll review the fumbled replacement of the Garand with the M14 in this book.

But even when it was replaced, it hung on. You see, there was this little thing called the National Matches, aka Camp Perry. In the Service Rifle category, when the M14 was adopted, it was to be the new thing, and everyone who competed in the Service Rifle category used one. But the M14 was a machine gun (select fire, even if you took the parts out, they could still be re-installed) and thus a tightly controlled inventory item. While you might have been able to shoot in a match where you'd be issued an M14 and ammo and then turn it back in once the match ended, you could not buy one of your own. At least, not easily.

So for an entire generation after the adoption of the M14, the M1 Garand was still the only Service Rifle available to be purchased, the only choice available to many competitors. Thus, many continued to use it in the matches. And it was fully capable of doing that job. Since M14s were off the table, the DCM, Department of Civilian Marksmanship, hosted matches where you could, for your entry fee, draw a Garand out of the rack and shoot a match. (Went there, did that.) After posting a score and qualifying for purchase, you could buy a Garand from the DCM inventory. (Having qualified, I did so and bought one.)

The DCM was later changed to the CMP, the Civilian Marksmanship Program, and that policy continued for a long time until the supply of Garands dried up. Yes, dried up. Even a rifle made in the millions has a limited supply if you keep using and selling them for a long enough time.

The Garand was the apex of technology of its time and was designed and built almost a century ago. There are details about it, its ammunition, its maintenance, and points of inspection that do not correspond to the rifles used by the current generation. They are not always obvious and may even be head-scratchingly peculiar.

THE GARAND WAS THE APEX OF TECHNOLOGY OF ITS TIME AND WAS DESIGNED AND BUILT ALMOST A CENTURY AGO.

The generations who grew up with or were familiar with the Garand are now getting long in the tooth. Collectors have increased the price and diminished the supply outside of collections, but it's still a sought-after rifle. I'll provide the background and the basics to run one in this book. Also, the history that we had to dig out of books (now long out of print), magazine articles (long-ago tossed, pulped, recycled, or forgotten), plus the trips, tricks, do's and don'ts of safely running a Garand.

The current generation of practicing riflemen is intimately familiar with the AR-15. That's good, but almost none of that knowledge will be useful when it comes time to inspect, buy, maintain, fix, load for, sight-in or shoot a Garand. It's like — but not as bad as — being the guy who knows how to program every digital device in existence, now being faced with tuning the engine in a 1970s muscle car. A carburetor? What's that? Alternator? Gapping spark plugs?

The Garand is, in many regards, a different animal

than the AR-15, and you need to be aware of that.

So, don't be alarmed or annoyed that I make comparisons to the AR-15 regularly in this book. The AR is the rifle with which most shooters and gun owners are familiar. Using it as the yardstick to explain everything Garand will give a perspective, background, and information that would otherwise require much more explanation. As we go along, there will be comparisons to the AK, the FAL, and who-knows-what.

There are collecting books that will tell you not just how many Garands this or that manufacturer made but break it down by monthly production and serial number lists. They'll tell you which parts were modified and when they went into production. This isn't a book like that. Some collectors will shoot the rifles they own. Some won't shoot them and handle them only with gloved hands. I'm assuming you're like me, and you own firearms to use them, and I'll spend much time giving you that info.

Now, don't get me wrong. I had a chance to handle a Garand during my research and photography for this book, which was not just like-new but unfired except for the test firing when it was made. The original shipping grease was packed in the bolt lug and locking slots. When I picked it up, I automatically racked the bolt back to check the chamber, then realizing what I had done, I apologized to the owner. He wasn't bothered.

"I did the same thing myself," he said.

Checking the chamber is a reflex requiring a Herculean effort of will to resist.

Let's start with John Garand himself. John Cantius Garand is the embodiment of the American dream and aspiration. Born in 1888 in Quebec, Canada, he learned to be a machinist and toolmaker, moved to America, proved his design advances, became an American citizen, developed the iconic rifle of WWII, and lived a long and prosperous life. We think of him as the designer of the M1 Garand, but he was more than that, as it took him more than a decade of fighting the system (another American trait) to see his design come to fruition. In this age of "developing an app" and becoming rich overnight, by comparison, his struggles were borderline *Sisyphean*, that is, arduous.

The family moved to the U.S. in the 1880s, and John learned his basic machinist skills while working in a local clothing mill. He also learned to shoot in the local gallery

Some of the Garands the author looked over, inspected, and photographed from the collection of a serious Garand collector. No, this is not all of them. He just brought the ones of most interest.

and immensely enjoyed it. That situation is no longer found in the U.S. or perhaps anywhere. It was possible back a century-plus ago to walk into an establishment in a city, plunk down some money, be handed a rifle and ammo, and shoot at targets. There would be competitions, shooting leagues, and fun had by all. All in a downtown shooting range. Imagine that. Yes, there are indoor ranges today, and you can rent firearms, but try doing that in downtown Manhattan, for example. Even the biggest cities had shooting parlors.

In 1909, he was accepted as a machinist at Browne & Sharpe in Providence, Rhode Island — the premier tool-making firm in the U.S. At that time, tool making was the apex machinists' work and kind of like the prehistoric predecessors to the CNC machining stations of today.

THE AR IS THE RIFLE WITH WHICH MOST SHOOTERS AND GUN OWNERS ARE FAMILIAR. USING IT AS THE YARDSTICK TO EXPLAIN EVERYTHING GARAND WILL GIVE A PERSPECTIVE, BACKGROUND, AND INFORMATION THAT WOULD OTHERWISE REQUIRE MUCH MORE EXPLANATION.

In the latter half of the 19th century, the United States was *the* world's high-tech machine tool industry leader. Great Britain did heavy industry, but America was where you came for precision. Known as "The American Method," the process of defining terms, establishing standards, and getting the entire industry to accept the standards, was the desire of all who wanted to catch up to the U.S. This was more than "what size is a 6x48 threaded screw?" It meant fixtures to hold parts, inspection gauges to measure Go or No Go, and tight tolerances, but not exact ones. An illustration might be helpful.

In the British gun-making industry, gunsmiths underwent a long apprenticeship. One of the tests was to hand file a chunk of mild steel into a cube that was one inch, exactly, in all dimensions. That is, once done, it didn't matter where on the cube you placed your micrometer; it would measure 1.000 inches.

That was fine if your business made bespoke shotguns for the landed gentry. If they needed a new shotgun, or a better one, having it sometime before the next shooting season was good enough. But if you were making an industrial fill-in-the-blank, you didn't need one-inch cubes of exact dimension. And you needed a hundred or a thousand of them at a time, close enough to one inch for your needs, by a set deadline, or the contract you were working under would penalize your supplier who could not deliver. So, you had specialized companies that were tool makers. They made a fixture to hold the steel, machining them as close to specs as possible, but they made 10, 20, or 50 fixtures. Each fixture would be locked into a milling machine, and the operator would clamp the steel in place, run the machine to cut, pull the steel out, and set it back in the rack. The racks would go from row to row of milling machines, each row performing one cut until there was a finished cube.

Inspectors would use the gauges marked "Go" and "No-Go" to check the cubes. (Why a company would need a figurative ton of one-inch cubes is beside the point.) The gauges would reflect the acceptable standard the customer had ordered. So, our one-inch cubes in this fictitious example can be as small as .950 inch or as large as 1.050 inches. The inspectors' gauges would be those sizes, exactly. If it would not fit into the 1.050 inches, it was too big, requiring you to correct the tooling. Similarly, if it would fit into the .950-inch gauge, it would be too small. Correct that machine.

If this sounds suspiciously like the standard for headspace, where you have a maximum and a minimum, you have been paying attention. No one could afford perfect ammunition in every cartridge, but ammo made within acceptable tolerances was good enough, reliable, and inexpensive.

Browne & Sharpe was not only one of, but perhaps *the* premier tool-making firm in the U.S., and it established

The Garand has long since been replaced by the M14 and the M14 by the M16. The latest iteration of that is the M27, a piston-driven M16, and soon, apparently, they will all go the way of old gear and be replaced.

industry standards that for a long time (and still, in engineering circles) are named after it, like the dimensions and tolerances for gears, wire gauges, and machine tool tapers. Being an inventor who was also an experienced tool maker gave Garand a big leg up when it came time, decades later, to see his design manufactured.

During The Great War or WWI, the War Department put out a request for light machine gun (LMG) designs. At the start of the conflict, the U.S. Army was woefully deficient in machine guns. Even by the day's standards, it didn't have many but a mixture of various types. It didn't have a dedicated machine gun branch, and even if it had wanted one, there was no money for such a thing. Well, as was the usual result when John Moses Browning got involved, his design won. But Garand's design was so promising that he was hired as a designer, tool maker, and engineer at the Springfield Arsenal, where America's military rifles were produced.

That was where he worked for the next couple of decades. But let's get familiar with the rifle before we set the stage that leads up to his hiring and his work on the rifle we all know as the M1 Garand.

(Oh, and the pronunciation? The family pronunciation rhymes with "errand," with a hard "G" at the start, *G-errand*. Millions of GIs, in WWII, Korea, and after, pronounced it emphasizing the front end; *Ga-rand* or *Guh-rand*. Which is correct? It depends on whom you are trying to impress. Yes, the family pronounced it the first way, but my father and millions like him pronounced it the second way, so that's how I pronounce it.)

PARTS AND NOMENCLATURE

Let's start by pointing out and naming the various parts of the Garand so we all know what we're talking about. First, some brief entertainment trivia: did you know that while he was doing his iconic Detective Joe Friday on weekly television, Jack Webb did a movie in 1957 called "The D.I."? He played Drill Sergeant Jim Moore on Parris Island, and the movie followed a group of draftees he trained. In one scene, the boots have their Garands in parts behind them on their bunks, and when he points to them, they have to reach behind, grab a part, pull it out and name it. To add to the pressure, he instructs them not to name a part someone else has already named.

One draftee names the same part the previous chose, and Gunnery Sergeant Moore's reply is, "Maybe in the Russian navy they have rifles with two bolts, two operating rods and two trigger housings, but not in the United States Marine Corps."

So, let's not be like the Russian navy.

The Garand has a wood stock. The originals were walnut; later, other woods were substituted as wartime production required, but the stock is wood. Modern stocks can be laminated, as competition shooters are not required to be historically exacting when it comes to stocks. The stock has a steel buttplate with a stamped checkered pattern impressed into the steel. The buttplate has a trap door, and inside of that door, it's been bored out. This was done partly to adjust the rifle's balance, partly to take a small amount of overall weight out, and to provide storage for a cleaning rod and other essentials.

The stock has sling swivel loops for carrying or bracing while aiming. There is no pistol grip. No provisions for lights, lasers, grenade launchers, bipods, or anything else you might have added to your AR-15.

The buttplate is another multi-purpose part. It protects the end of the stock from impact with the ground, mud, and the heads or helmets of those who got butt-stroked with your Garand. (This was a combat tool, after all.)

Now, I will give you a small peek into the mindset of collectors and purists. The size and pattern of the impressed checkering of the buttplate vary from one maker to the next. As long as it was close enough and fitted all the rifles, the War Department didn't care about exactitude on that detail. However, it is known which makers used which pattern on their rifles. And so someone who is (because they make the chiding so easy) attempting to own a fully Winchester Garand will replace a non-Winchester pattern buttplate on a stock if that stock goes on a Winchester receiver. I kid you not.

Did they care in WWII when they were making rifles as fast as they could? No. But today, collectors do, and they will rebuild rifles to make them the "correct" pattern, even if that particular rifle was not built initially on that cold day in November 1943, to what is deemed the "correct" pattern. Sigh.

THE GARAND USES AN APERTURE CLOSE TO THE SHOOTER'S FACE (FINALLY! SOMETHING FAMILIAR TO THE AR-15 USER WHO KNOWS HOW TO USE IRON SIGHTS!) FOR FAST AND PRECISE AIMING. AND IT IS USER-ADJUSTABLE.

The stock is a single piece of wood and extends up to the front sling swivel. The Garand retains two other pieces of wood furniture — the rear handguard and the front handguard. They are fixed in place. The rear handguard is clipped to the barrel, while the front is held in place by the gas cylinder when installed on the barrel. These protect your hand from the hot barrel during extended firing. The Garand was meant to be used as much as it needed to be used, without failure and without injuring the user. If you run through all the ammunition you have on you in one extended shooting session (human wave attacks in the Pacific or Korea come to mind), the barrel will become very hot — hot enough to burn you if you touch the exposed barrel. So, the barrel was wrapped in wood.

The front handguard also encloses and protects the operating rod (henceforth to be known, as everyone calls it, the op rod). If something were to press against the rod — lacking the front handguard — it might create enough drag to prevent proper function.

Since we're near the muzzle, the barrel protrudes from the front handguard, and below it is the gas cylinder. The gas cylinder does four things. First, it provides a base for the front sight to be attached. The top of the gas cylinder has a reverse dovetail bar across the top, and the front sight has a dovetail machined into its base. The front sight is attached by sliding it onto the gas cylinder base, centering it, and tightening the screw that holds it in place. Second, the gas cylinder has a rectangular boss, the bayonet lock lug. The bayonet has a spring-loaded catch in the handle. To install a bayonet, slide the bayonet loop over the barrel muzzle and slide the handle back onto the bayonet lug until it clicks in place. To remove the bayonet, press the spring-loaded button and slide the bayonet forward.

At the base of the gas cylinder is a loop. Some might assume this to be an alternate sling swivel loop, but it is actually a curious device known as a stacking swivel. For a long time before WWII, battles had been fought in locations that did not have convenient rifle racks or places to put a rifle when it wasn't being used. If a unit of soldiers were engaged in a task that did not require rifles (digging trenches, for example), they had to put them someplace. The stacking swivel on each rifle allowed them to create a tripod of swivel-connected rifles that stood on their buttplates and were not lying on the ground.

The fourth and most crucial task of the gas cylinder is to guide the gas from the gas port to the op rod and operate the action.

The gas cylinder fits onto the barrel as a snug fit and stays correctly oriented by three splines. This involves three square-bottomed grooves machined in the barrel and three projecting studs in the front loop of the gas cylinder. The gas cylinder slides onto the barrel and locks threads onto the threaded muzzle to press the gas cylinder into place. Finally, the gas cylinder screw passes through the gas cylinder lock and threads into the front of the gas cylinder, locking everything together.

That complex assembly of parts is one you will only sometimes need to take apart, as the gas cylinder is made

The Garand is well-balanced, and as a result, it is used as a parade rifle and a blank-firing gun at interment ceremonies. The author's late sister was the flag recipient, and the blanks were fired at their father's interment.

of stainless steel, and unless you score some corrosive surplus ammo, it will not need to be removed for cleaning.

OK, back to the rear. On top, we have the receiver. This part is the heart of the Garand and supports the rear sight and bolt assembly. The Garand's sight was a breakthrough, as until that time, military rifle sights were of two types, both marginal for use. One was the open notch and blade, like the Mauser, Enfield or 1903 Springfield, which are not user-adjustable. If a rifle was "off," there was nothing a soldier could do except complain and turn it in or learn the Kentucky windage needed to account for the point of impact. The other type was found on the '03

Springfield as a long-range sight. It was a ladder type that could be stood up, and the panel adjusted for distance. The soldier used the small aperture in the panel, a foot from his face, to aim.

The first method was coarse and not adjustable. The second was precise but slow.

The Garand uses an aperture close to the shooter's face (Finally! Something familiar to the AR-15 user who knows how to use iron sights!) for fast and precise aiming. And it is user-adjustable. We see this in use in the movie *Uncommon Valor* (1983) when Gene Hackman is zeroing his Garand, and when he hears the target impact point called the same several times, he stops, adjusts, and continues.

The rear sight has two adjustment knobs, one on each side of the assembly. The left-hand one is for elevation, and the right is for windage. When you adjust the right-hand knob, it moves the entire assembly to the right or left, changing the point of impact in the opposite direction. Yes, move the rear to the right, and the bullet impact moves to the left, and vice-versa.

You may notice that some right-hand knobs have a rectangular bar across them, and some do not. The original design did not have a bar. These had the assembly screw flush with the locking nut staked together. Well, this proved to be just fine in pre-war manufacture and assembly. However, with the simplification of the design, the "flush nut" did not hold its attachment. It could come loose with adjustment or loosen during use and abuse. Once loose, it could cause the sight assembly to disassemble. So, the locking bar design was a stop-gap, wartime measure. It replaced the flush nut, and unlike the flush nut, which required a special tool to re-tighten and secure it, the locking bar could be tightened by hand or with a pair of pliers.

The locking bar went through three types, known (you guessed it) as Type 1, Type 2, and Type 3. Those looking to build or re-build their Garand to the period-correct version will have to track down the time and location of manufacture and then compare that with the use of the Type 1, 2, or 3 locking bar to make it genuine. Incidentally, that problem was finally solved after WWII with the T105 pinion and knob, which did away with

The Garand's balance allows complex acrobatics, and here the USAF is demonstrating some, with bayonets attached. So, throwing almost 10-pound rifles with knives attached isn't exciting enough for you?

the need for a locking bar. Many Garands being arsenal rebuilt post-war would have had the old locking bar sight replaced or rebuilt with the T105 pinion.

Moreover, the T105 pinion and rear sight assembly was used in the M14 and is the only assembly carried over from the Garand to the M14. A few parts from the Garand were used in the M14, some from the trigger assembly (but not all) and the extractor, spring, and plunger.

On the top of the receiver, you'll find the bolt. It has a pair of locking lugs, right and left, with the right-hand lug machined to accept the extractor, its spring and plunger. You'll look at this and think, "there's a bunch of steel that Garand carved out of that locking lug to make room for the extractor." Yep, you're right. But despite that, it holds up to use. It also fails when subjected to abuse or overload, providing a path away from the shooter should that happen. Good thing for us that rarely happens, and when it does, it's usually owner/shooter induced.

IF YOU'RE GOING TO RUN A GARAND AND WANT TO DO IT PROPERLY, YOU HAVE TO STICK YOUR TRIGGER FINGER INSIDE THE TRIGGERGUARD AND PRESS THE SAFETY FORWARD. THERE'S JUST NO WAY AROUND IT. HOWEVER, WHEN YOU DO IT, KEEP YOUR TRIGGER FINGER AWAY FROM THE TRIGGER UNTIL YOU ARE GOING TO SHOOT.

The op rod is connected to the right side of the bolt. Pulling it to the rear rotates the bolt to unlock it and moves the bolt to the rear to open the action. If there is a round in the chamber, moving the op rod extracts the cartridge, and once the round clears the chamber, the spring-loaded ejector, pushing from the bolt face, pitches it clear. If the last round or no clip was in the action before you drew the operating rod back, the action would lock open once the bolt is pulled entirely to the rear.

OK, time for the first warning concerning the Garand: It is possible to retract the bolt, but not entirely, and have it *appear to lock open*. However, it isn't fully locked: The follower has lifted high enough that the follower slide is binding against the bottom of the bolt. Again: *It is not locked open*. The bolt will snap shut if you bump, jostle, or disturb the binding engagement. The usual occurrence is when a finger or something else is in the bolt's path (usually while bumping into the lifter, which releases the pressure on the bolt), and the bolt slams shut on the said finger. This is followed by cursing, struggling, juggling the rifle, and perhaps damage to the rifle if dropped.

When you watch someone familiar with a Garand open the action, you will see them briskly bring the op rod fully to the rear. There is no hesitation, and some will even give the op rod a second tug to the rear to lock it open.

There's also a stylistic component to the Garand and opening the bolt. For reasons perhaps mechanical, physiological, or just historical, the experienced Garand operator, while opening the bolt, will do so with the thumb of their hand. They'll reach down to the receiver with their right, hook their thumb across the front of the op-rod hook, curl their fingers, and quickly snap the op rod back. New Garand owners typically reach under, hook the last finger on the op rod, and pull it back.

Why? I don't know. That's how I was shown, and I've done it since.

The clip latch is the last external part before we turn to the trigger housing. This part is the flat bar on the left side with a rectangular tab. You use it to unload. The procedure here is simple: First, ensure the safety is on. Pull the op rod back with one hand (usually the right) and hold it back. The chambered round will be ejected. Now press the tab on the clip latch. The rest of the rounds, and the clip, will be ejected as one. Yes, your ammo is now tossed out onto the ground. But that's how you unload, not cycling the op rod repeatedly until you have tossed the rounds out one at a time. Why do it this way? Garand's design doesn't allow the user to "top up" the magazine or clip. You stuff eight in, and if you've shot a few but want to reload to eight, you must eject the ones in there and shove in a new clip.

This detail was something my father explained to me as an unavoidable detail of the Garand.

On the bottom of the stock, we have the triggerguard, the trigger, and a big steel plate, the un-named part of the trigger assembly. The safety is the flat steel piece with a hole that protrudes into the trigger housing. When you press the safety to the rear, it's inside the trigger loop and can be felt with a finger.

OK, stick with me for a moment here. Those raised in the late 20th- and early 21st-century safety protocols are now having an attack of the willies. "Finger inside the triggerguard? That's not safe." Times were different then, and the procedure was also different. If you're going to run a Garand and want to do it properly, you have to stick your trigger finger inside the triggerguard and press the safety forward. There's just no way around it. However, when you do it, keep your trigger finger away from the trigger until you are going to shoot. You can even press the safety to the fire position and get your finger out of the triggerguard until you need it to shoot a few seconds later.

If you look closely at photographs from WWII, you will see lots of GIs and Marines with their fingers firmly inside triggerguards. As I said, times were different. And, there was a war on.

What seems like a long time ago, I was a consultant and instructor on the movie "Public Enemies." My job was to teach Stephen Lang how to run a lever-action shotgun (he played Charles Winstead). When I arrived, talking with the Armorer and Lang, I said, "Times were different then. Are we going for verisimilitude or modern safety?" The armorer knew precisely what I was asking and, even as he turned pale, said, "Modern." I said, "OK, Stephen, keep your finger outside the triggerguard at all times."

With a Garand, you must have your finger inside to work the safety. To press the safety to Safe, loop your finger in front of the triggerguard, and press the tab back. It will slide into the triggerguard and, with a click, lock in place.

If you've been instructed in the modern world, you'll be told to the point of being fitted with an electric shock collar, "Do not put your finger inside the triggerguard until you plan to shoot." What can I say? Times were different in the 1930s. It will take some getting used to.

So, with that brief introduction, let's jump right in, shall we? •

In World War II, and before the modern era of gun handling, keeping a finger inside the triggerguard while adjusting the sights was normal. It isn't normal today, but you still must poko your finger inside the triggerguard to work the Garand's safety.

SECTION I

HISTORY AND ESSENTIAL INFO

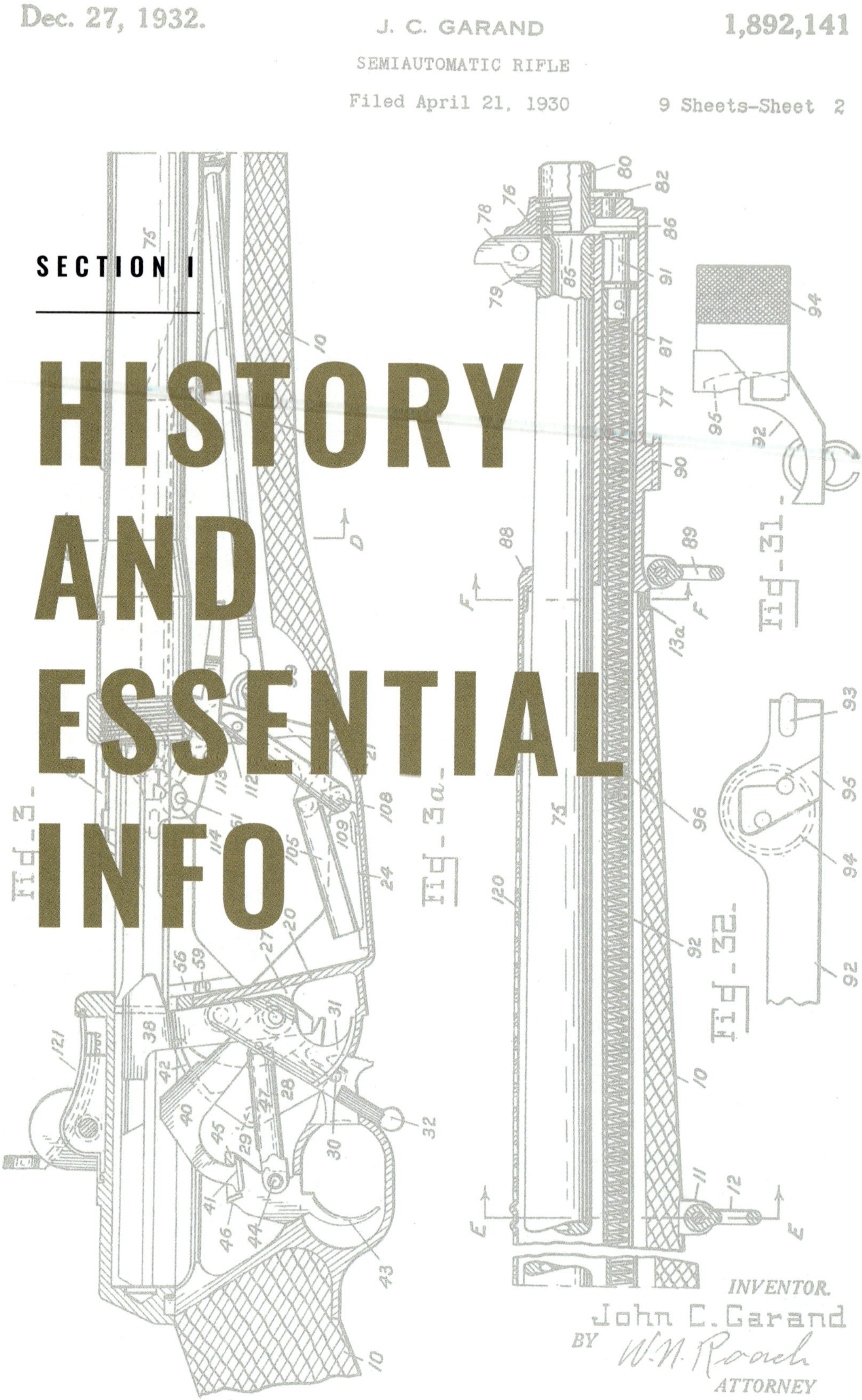

CHAPTER 1

DESIGNS THAT INSPIRED THE GARAND

The Garand grew out of the combat experiences of the veterans of The Great War (or World War I, as referred to by people before WWII). Before the war, few armies had many machine guns. Germany's military had more than most because it was simply more organized than most armies.

Even as late as the first decade of the 20th century, Napoleon's military tactics were the organizing principles of army strategy. This was partly due to the few changes in military equipment and capabilities from 1815 to 1890s. The primary pursuit of a commanding officer in a big battle was maneuver — to box in your opponent: he had the choice of attacking towards artillery or retreating from the field.

Some lessons had been learned, but not by all parties. One learned by the American Army was that firepower mattered. Using lessons learned from the Civil War, the American Army was not interested in massed assaults on fixed positions once the maneuvering was over. Of course, the experience of the frontier was also part of that. Small cavalry units over long distances patrolled the American frontier. The experience of the Spanish-American War in 1898 didn't change that much. So, at the outset of The Great War, in 1914, even the most senior American commanders had little or no experience in com-

Founded in 1777, Springfield Armory supplied the newly declared America with the weapons to fight for independence and stood as the production facility of the country until its closing in 1968. Now a museum, you can see the production history of modern firearms and some of the rifles we discuss in the book.

manding large units in the field. You could be a General in the U.S. Army in 1910, and your last field command might have been a Company (maybe 150 cavalry troopers) on a campaign in Montana in 1881. Since then, any larger group you commanded was in garrison, in a fixed base, someplace not in the middle of the western emptiness.

In Europe, things were different. Europe was settled, civilized, and organized. Let's take the German army as an example. Many years of staff work had developed detailed, extensive mobilization plans for war. Let's say, just as an example, that the War Ministry wanted the German army to invade France. It had timetables already drawn up for

This Maxim dates from the Boer War, but the mechanism was the same through WWI. Take this, dig a pit, put sandbags on the sides, and cover the top with timbers and more sandbags. Short of rifle fire directly into the firing port or a direct hit from a shell, the crew manning a gun like this was safe from the enemy.

The French 75 was a fast-firing direct-fire artillery piece that was quick to move but not what you wanted for supporting artillery fire. Still, the French stuck with it because it worked. And they made plenty of them.

everything. The schedule, starting from Day One, would be pre-planned for each unit to be mobilized, transported to the rail lines, sent to the staging areas, delivered to the border and then marched off to battle. What trains would proceed along which routes and then drop off their troops and return was worked out. The supply system had similar schedules to deliver food, ammunition, blankets, tents, artillery shells, and even forage for the horses pulling the wagons and artillery once everyone was off the trains.

The French had the same setup. I'm sure the Russians had similar aspirations, but just how well-organized their system was, we're not entirely sure, as in the long run, things didn't work as well for them.

Why this organization? Because the European armies were a mix of small professional cadre, local semi-pro units (each German duchies had its own military, subordinate to the Imperial organization, but fiercely their own) and the Reserves. The European militaries had fought against each other, knew modern warfare, and would not be caught unprepared. The Reserve units had a similar timetable and schedule. Still, it included the time needed to call the Reserves, issue them their equipment, and give them a refresher training period. The British had none of this. The British had a small, entirely professional army, ready to go at a moment's notice but with a remarkably small logistical tail. The British had ruled an empire, which meant local bandits and military organizations that were a generation or century behind in equipment, training, and organization. The American experience spread across the entire world.

The French and German armies had a complete supply system planned, staffed and organized. The British were much like the Americans in fielding small units to far-flung locations. Once there, those units would resupply locally, except for replacements and ammunition. A U.S. Army post in the Montana Territories would not get supply trains delivering food from the East. They'd be given a budget (not much) and buy locally. What came from the East were replacements, recruits, equipment, and ammunition.

They were all remarkably similar in how they would fight a war. As mentioned, it was going to be a war of maneuver. The Cavalry was going to go first, scout, patrol, find the enemy, harass and fix them in position, and screen the enemy Cavalry out of place, so the Infantry could march in and do the heavy lifting. The Infantry, walking there, would pin the enemy in position, flank, assault, and overwhelm. If a position proved tough, the artillery, following behind, horse-drawn, would set up shop close by, pummel the position, and then the infantry would take it. Meanwhile, the cavalry would still be screening the enemy cavalry from this operation and also finding the next enemy concentration for the infantry to overwhelm.

In a war of maneuver, each rifle company (let's call it about 150 men) was on its own. The Company Commander would receive his basic orders from the Battalion Commander or higher at a briefing. "We will advance along this line of approach, and if the enemy does not offer resistance, take the bridge to enter the city." Warfare was in open ground, empty territory, not cities, suburbs, etc. In the 1890s, the population of Europe was in the range of 150 million. There was lots of empty space, well, farmland, but armies viewed farmland the same as empty land: maneuvering space.

A RIFLE COMPANY RUNNING INTO AN ENEMY UNIT DID NOT HAVE MACHINE GUNS, ARTILLERY, RADIOS, AIR SUPPORT, OR ANYTHING LIKE THAT. THEY MIGHT NOT HAVE ANOTHER COMPANY OF THEIR ARMY ON THEIR FLANK. THEY COULD BE ESSENTIALLY ALONE, DETACHED FROM THE LINE, AND HAVE TO SOLVE THE PROBLEM BY THEMSELVES.

A rifle company running into an enemy unit did not have machine guns, artillery, radios, air support, or anything like that. They might not have another Company of their army on their flank. They could be essentially alone, detached from the line, and have to solve the problem by themselves. So, the various platoons and squads would be ordered to direct their rifle fire to specific problems. A rifle squad might be detailed, "Take care of the soldiers at that farmhouse on the left flank." The Lieutenant would turn to his Sergeant, who would then send a squad here, another there, and probably hold one in reserve. The squad would be told, "Farmhouse, 800 yards, right side, one magazine suppressive fire." Each soldier would hit the ground, stand his sight up to 800 yards, use a stripper clip to shove five rounds in the magazine, and then aim and fire. The clever Company Commander would have another unit maneuvering to get closer, and the various sections would leapfrog to the farmhouse, each providing covering fire to the other in turn, until the farmhouse could be assaulted, taken, and then regroup and move on. The officers and NCOs would direct the fire of the units or soldiers under their command until the problem was resolved, pick up and continue the advance.

When possible, communications to and from higher command would happen by runners or horsemen. When enemy resistance was strong or numerous enough, the rifle companies would be in direct contact with each other and not work independently. At this point, cavalry went off to find other approaches or to screen off enemy cavalry and prevent the enemy from knowing your disposition of assets.

Two things made a mockery of this approach: machine guns and lightweight, direct-fire artillery. The Maxim gun is the exemplar machine gun here, and the French 75 is the artillery piece. The Maxim was heavy by any standard. The gun itself weighed 60 pounds. It was water-cooled, and the water jacket took another 15 pounds of water to fill it. (It boiled off when heated, and had to be refilled, adding to the gun crew's workload.) It used a short-recoil mechanism, so only the bore and the breech parts were exposed to the corrosive powder residues. Swapping barrels was not easy, but since the barrel rarely overheated, that was not needed often. The original German mount, referred to as the sledge mount due to its shape, was heavier than the gun, even with the water jacket filled.

Full up, excluding the steel shield that someone no doubt thought was a good idea, a Maxim gun ran 140 pounds. Transporting this and the ammunition to keep it going, a Maxim team could be a squad of men. It took four men just to run the gun, but four men could not transport it and the ammunition. Today, a machine gunner is one man, with an assistant, and a support Fire Team, depending on how the military organizes its squads. A Maxim team could be a dozen men. With a dozen men on a team, you can very quickly "dig in." That is, dig a pit in the ground, fill sandbags and make a protective wall, stake down the sledge mount, and set up a stable firing position, one protected from incoming fire. Then, a bit more work, and you have similar protected positions for the squad, the stored ammunition, and the firing positions for the squad who protect the Maxim gun.

Cavalry stood no chance against a dug-in machine gun manned by a crew with minimal skill. A Maxim gun, once machine gunners had the range, could put paid to the careers of a cavalry troop at a thousand yards in less than five minutes. A single dug-in Maxim could thwart the assault of a rifle company if the Maxim gun commander had selected a suitable spot and the rifle company commander wasn't up to the task. And when adopted by the Germans, the Maxim was slightly modified, and they designated it the *Maschinengewehr 08*, or MG08, the machine gun of 1908. The pedants among you will want me to refer to it from now on as the "MG08," but since it was a Maxim design, I'm going to call it a Maxim.

Yes, the U.S. Army had maxim guns though only a few, and it lacked real organizing principles on how to use them. The Army was, in the 19th century, mostly a wilderness scouting and patrolling organization and not what we'd today call a "neer-peer" focused combat arm.

The French 75 was a similar sort of situation. The field piece was small and light enough to be drawn by a four-horse team, and the gun, its shell supply and crew were a self-contained group. It would take a couple of minutes (less with a skilled and trained crew) for the crew to arrive at a location, unlimber (the shell cart was called a "cassion" and the assembled gun on its carriage and the cassion when ready to move was called a limber, hence the term "unlimber") and be firing. The previous generation of artillery had a firing rate of a couple of shells a minute. And the aiming apparatus was still primitive. Previously, a skilled crew would set up, fire a ranging shot,

The U.S. Army had machine guns before WWI, but only a few and no real training or organization on how to use them. Still, in the experimental (and "do we need this?") phase, they were bought in ones and twos, tens and twenties, not hundreds and hundreds, like Germany. And an Infantry company could not readily transport this. It was too heavy.

adjust, fire again, and then get to work. If they had to shift to another target, they would have to re-range and start work. The reason was: recoil. When the previous designs were fired, the gun would roll on its wheels in recoil and then have to be manhandled back into position, re-aimed, loaded and fired.

The French 75 had a hydraulic recoil system. The mount did not move during recoil; the barrel and breech would surge back in recoil, controlled by the hydraulics, and then be pushed back by the hydraulic system to the start position. So, no manhandling once set up. The ammunition was "fixed." The brass shell, projectile, and powder charge were all one piece, like a scaled-up rifle cartridge. Previous generations had used semi-fixed (shell with powder, loaded behind a separate powder-holding cartridge) or bagged (shell goes in, bags of powder get shoved in, breech closed, and fire), and those were slower to load.

The design, and the possibilities it offered, were so revolutionary that the French kept it a secret. So secret that when the design was being developed, there were no written reports on the progress. The money to develop it wasn't officially approved but diverted from funds earmarked for property acquisition for the French army.

You can see how miserable trench conditions could be and how much exposure to dust, dirt, mud and rain the rifles would be subjected to. Oh, and the soldiers, too.

Once fielded, the recoil system was kept so secret that even the officers commanding the guns didn't know the details inside the hydraulic system.

Now, the fixed cartridge is less flexible or adaptable. Even if you don't need the full powder charge for the distance you need to shoot, you are firing it anyway, every time. But, in a war of maneuver, the volume of fire a fixed shell offers is more important than adaptability.

The French 75 was a rapid-firing direct-fire artillery piece, not meant for siege or indirect fire. But when used correctly, it owned the battlefield.

But wait, it gets better. The 75's breech was fast to open and quick to close. Instead of multiple-thread breeches, the 75 had a rotating plate or block. A skilled team could open the breech as the barrel and breech were moving forward to the start point in recoil. The loader could shove in the following shell and close the breech smoothly. The best part was the aiming apparatus, which was built onto each gun, and was essentially a riflescope calibrated to the shell. If the gunner had orders from the gun Captain to keep firing, he could trigger a shot every time he felt or heard the breech slam shut and the barrel stop at its forward position. (It was the loader's responsibility to get out of the way.) A trained and experienced gunner would adjust his aim for each shot, following the Captain's general order.

A French 75 could fire leisurely at ten shots a minute, while a skilled crew could exceed 20 shots a minute until the gun was too hot to operate. No cavalry or infantry unit could stand up to that. Depending on who found the range first, it was a quick-draw duel to the death between a French 75 and a Maxim gun crew. Everyone else on the battlefield was toast. A four-gun 75 battery could quickly put 80 shells into an area, or on the spot, in a minute. One explosive shell per second arriving in your immediate area is a disaster. And more than a few German infantry and Cavalry units had that experience before the trenches got built.

Things grew from one Maxim position to two linked together to provide mutual support. As soon as the maneuvering space ran out, and one side or the other had locked itself down into a position that could not be taken by assault, the battle turned into trench warfare and a war of attrition. Once those two Maxim locations had been found and held, it was then essential to dig trenches between them for travel, communication and observation positions, so they could not be flanked. The result was an unbroken trench line from the North Sea to Switzerland.

With me so far?

At first, the armies on both sides tried to break through the enemy lines by mass and effort. Huge assaults were tried, and massive losses resulted. Sending troops "over the top" to walk or run straight toward the enemy made them targets for massed and interlocking Maxim fire and suppressive artillery. After a year of this, the Germans tried a different approach. They tried to lure the French until defending a strong point in the line, Verdun, and in so doing, ground the French army into nothing. The Germans ended up grinding themselves up as much as the French.

Rifles with a 1,000-yard aiming capability are of no use in trench warfare. A thousand yards from your trench is the enemy's supply depot, a target for longer-range machine guns or short-range artillery fire. The enemy trench might be 100 yards away or closer (or farther), but there were no longer long-range rifle duels to be done. But, the military organizations had to use their equipment, which meant bolt-action rifles were still manufactured in enormous quantities and issued. As the war evolved, trench raids became the norm. The idea was simple: go over the top at night with a team, slide into an enemy trench, wreak mayhem and even grab a prisoner or two, and get back. If all you wanted to do was make sure the other guys didn't get much sleep and grab the occasional prisoner, this worked fine. The Germans then evolved the process.

They selected leaders who were good at it. They trained and equipped soldiers to do it and developed equipment and tactics. In due time, they were going to develop a system where an entire section of a trench line could be taken overnight by trench assault and then reinforced the next night — no need to run straight at machine guns.

Then the Americans came.

The Commander of the American Expeditionary Force, the AEF, was one General Pershing. He was not an old-line General. He had been promoted over officers much his senior to make General. In the late 19th century, promotion in the U.S. Army was strictly by seniority. You didn't move up until everyone more senior had been promoted, and there was a slot for you at your new rank. To give you an example of how long this could take, Pershing graduated from West Point in 1886. He was promoted to 1st Lieutenant in 1892. In 1895, he was assigned to the 10th Cavalry, a "Buffalo soldier" unit of Black soldiers. His nickname "Black Jack" Pershing came from this command. (Yes, it was a term from a lot less polite society.)

His bravery and calm command during the Spanish-American War and the Philippine Insurrection got him noticed. The President of the United States, Theodore Roosevelt, asked the War Department that this promising young officer be promoted from Captain (yes, in

The helmet was copied from the British, but the rifle was American. Note the rear sight ahead of the bolt, with an elaborate arrangement of range selections.

1903, with combat experience and having spent a couple of years fighting a guerilla war, he was still a Captain) to Colonel. Everyone agreed such a promotion was warranted, but the Army did not promote him, sticking with the seniority system.

Captain Pershing became the Military Attaché in Japan and an official observer in the Russo-Japanese War. Still not promoted, President Roosevelt then used a Presidential prerogative and promoted him to Brigadier General. This move vaulted Pershing over 835 officers with more seniority and caused no end of heartburn. Pershing wasn't the only officer so promoted. And, this presidential prerogative was limited to just that: Captain to Brigadier.

The American Army, while it had a different background and experience than the European armies, was similarly stuck in the past on many issues. I also think that what he observed in the Russo-Japanese War informed Pershing's approach to France when the AEF arrived.

Pershing was not going to hand over American units to the British and French. They wanted AEF units as replacements, to re-man the trenches, and be commanded by British and French officers. Nope, no way, nu-uh. How bad had it gotten? So bad that there had been mutinies by French units. This was the subject of Stanley Kubrik's movie "Paths of Glory" in 1957. French units had had enough; by 1917, many would not go on frontal assaults. If the Germans attacked, the Poiloi would defend. If trench raids and such were needed, OK, but a full-scale, over-the-top assault? Not happening.

The second thing to know about Pershing — while insisting that American troops have American commanders — was that their sections of trench and sectors wouldn't do frontal assaults. What he had in mind was a combination of the German trench commandos and American skills: American troops were to swarm the front, moving from one shell hole or another cover to the next, taking time to aim and fire on known or suspected German positions.

Instead of a Maxim crew aiming at and mowing down rows of walking troops, they faced individuals running, dodging and diving for cover. When not running, they were shooting at any machine gun position or German soldier they could see. It's one thing to shoot 100 men walking in a line and another thing to shoot 100 individuals when half of them are lying in one or another shell hole, trying to shoot you back.

Now, the French had not been entirely stuck in the past. They quickly developed the *Chauchat* (pronounced *show-sha*), a light machine gun, or LMG (think BAR with a really odd magazine) and fielded Maxim-hunting teams armed with the Chauchat. The machine gunner had the gun, and his three team members had rifles and spare magazines. They all had pistols, and they worked as a team to find and shoot Maxim teams. They, too, had been working on the idea of trench raid teams. The Chauchat comes in for much derision, especially in the .30-06 chambering. If you read up on it, you'll hear of its general unreliability, rough recoil, short service life, and in the

.30-06, unreliable functioning. It was developed as a crash program during the war: to make a light machine gun that could be carried over no man's land by one soldier and fire the existing cartridge. To make things worse, it had to be made without elbowing into the production output of the existing rifles and machine guns. So, it is a tube with a Browning long-recoil system, and stock, magazine, pistol grip, and bipod hung off of that.

It worked well enough to serve the last two years of The Great War and was retained afterward. It wasn't until the 1930s that the French finally had a replacement for it.

The French had also begun work on a self-loading rifle, even before The Great War, but one problem after another had plagued them, including the same level of secrecy they had used for the 75.

37MM LOVE TAP

What made life hard for the Maxim gunners was the 37mm M1916, the Bunker Buster. In essence, this was a scaled-down 75mm cannon, small enough to be transportable by a team (it could be hauled on a wheeled carriage, but it was usually man-packed into combat) and dealt with Maxim positions.

Now, a rifle company, swarming across the terrain, jumping from shell hole to cover, providing covering fire for each other, can get the job done. But it still means putting accurate rifle fire not just on the bunker but through the firing slit and hitting the gun or gunner. Not easy. But, if the rifle company has a 37mm team or two, and they can get set up to quickly come up out of their shell hole and hammer a bunker, well, life is a lot better — for the doughboys, at least. A 37mm shell, basically a one-pound steel hull packed with explosives, has an effect even if it "just" hits the bunker and doesn't go through the firing slit.

Combat has always been brutal. But trench warfare added extra hazards and problems, details unknown before WWI, and the troops on the ground had to solve the problems or pay the price. They did so with rifles, for the most part.

So, let's cover the rifles designed and used before, during and by the end of The Great War. Then we'll look at the developments in other countries before we get to the Garand.

BOLT-ACTION RIFLES

There were six main rifles in use during World War I and the years leading up to the Garand's introduction: the SMLE from Britain, the Berthier from France, the

The idea of a pocket artillery piece moving to the front was appealing. While setting it up in camp, on level ground, was one thing, hauling this 37mm M1916 through no man's land to whack a maxim position? The work of heroes.

Mauser in Germany and the Mosin-Nagant of Russia. The American was the Springfield '03. The sixth one was a British design but made in America. Let's get to that one first, the M1917.

M1917

After the Boer War, the British determined that bolt manipulation was critical, as essential as marksmanship. That's how the British standard of 10 aimed shots a minute came about. If you expected to stay in the British army, you had to be able to do that at an absolute minimum. Skilled shooters could easily do more — high teens or low 20s. The record is 38 aimed shots in one minute, with an SMLE. The 10-shot magazine to start, and five-shot stripper clips loaded with a second or two of effort, helped a lot.

However, they wanted range and a flat trajectory. So they designed a new rifle and a new cartridge. The new cartridge was hotter than the .303, with a flatter trajectory. Think 7mm Magnum, and you're on the right path. The .276 Enfield, with a .282-inch-diameter bullet of 165 grains at just under 2,800 fps, was on the path to adopting the .276 Enfield cartridge and the M1913 rifle when war broke out, and that was that. When they could not make rifles fast enough, they shipped samples and blueprints to America and asked U.S. arms makers if they could make it, but in .303. Sure thing, champ.

When we entered the war, the same makers changed it to .30-06 and produced even more — so many that by the war's end, the U.S. Army had more M1917s in inventory than '03 Springfields. In a curious circling of history, when my father was drafted in WWII and went off for Basic Training, the first rifle he was issued was an M1917 in .30-06. Even though the default issue rifle between the wars had been the Springfield, the government had kept the warehouses full of M1917s and used them for training in the Second World War.

Speaking of the Springfield, we'll cover it last because some of its aspects established requirements that the Garand had to satisfy.

Once the British had enough M1914s, and when America entered World War I, the rifle got rebuilt as a .30-06 and called the M1917 Enfield. Sweeney's father drilled with one of these in 1943 before being issued a Garand.

Seen in the Warsaw Uprising, the 98K Mauser was the basic rifle Germany depended on in two wars. While reliable to a fault, there were better tools for the job after about 1915.

SMLE

The Lee-Enfield, the British rifle, has a 10-shot magazine meant to be removed only for maintenance. It is very fast to manipulate but has some quirks and shortcomings. First, the bolt is cocked by closing it: you force the bolt forward to chamber a round and cock the striker. This feature is neither good nor bad but does require getting used to it.

The big shortcoming is that the bolt's locking lugs are at the rear, so the cartridge is not as well-supported as bolts with locking lugs at the front. Combined with the "just enough" proportions of the receiver, the cartridge case stretches more in an SMLE than in other designs. Since the British had no interest in reloading fired brass, this was not a problem. However, the action could not be adapted to any other cartridge. For military use, that's not a problem, but that dead end means no commercial opportunities, not so with the Mauser.

The British fought WWI with the MkI SMLE, a fast-working bolt-action rifle with a 10-round magazine. It stood up to the rigors of trench warfare.

1898 MAUSER

When the German army wanted a modern rifle, they put the word out. But rather than adopt the best, they took the features they wanted and made their design. Yes, a rifle designed by a committee. The 1888 Commission Rifle was a combination of all the good ideas of the moment, and none had any staying power. Peter Paul Mauser was so incensed that he designed a rifle still made today, the 1898 Mauser.

The 98 has locking lugs on the bolt's front, making it kind to brass. The receiver is strong by its design and doesn't require exotic alloys for strength. As a result, it can be built and chambered in any rifle cartridge you can fit into the receiver. For example, you can have a standard-sized 98 Mauser safely barreled for .458 Winchester Magnum, a much larger cartridge than the 7.92 Mauser it was designed for. However, under no circumstances would I ever fire an SMLE sporting a barrel in .458 Win. Mag.

The French were first with the Berthier M1907, but decisions they made early on locked them into an increasingly clumsy rifle, one that could not be improved, only replaced.

Nearly indestructible, the Mosin served Russia from the Tsars through to the atomic age. Not always well, but it served.

While a 98 Mauser can run quickly, it isn't as fast as an SMLE. And the five-round magazine puts you at a disadvantage from the start compared to an SMLE.

BERTHIER

The original rifle for the groundbreaking 8x50R cartridge was the Lebel. This gun used a tube magazine under the barrel, and while faster than a lot of designs around in the 1880s, by early 20th-century standards, it was painfully slow to reload.

So, as well as changing the bullet from a heavy roundnose to a somewhat lighter pointed bullet, the French adopted the Berthier rifle. It is a case study of getting locked into an original advancement and not upgrading or changing with the times. The 8x50R has a tapered case with a rim. When changing from a tube magazine, they should have redesigned the case, but they didn't. So, the Berthier had to deal with a tapered, rimmed cartridge. The British did it, but the French approach wasn't as elegant. The French went with a Mannlicher or en-bloc clip design, a sheet-metal clip holding cartridges in a line or column. The clip is also the feed lip portion of the mechanism. To load, you open the bolt and stuff a clip and cartridges into the receiver. (In an SMLE, Mauser, Springfield

The en-bloc clip Garand used holds eight rounds of .30-06. For hunting, you'll need to find a five-shot clip, and those competing in Camp Perry back in the day found a two-round clip useful.

The U.S. was not alone in trying to develop a working self-loading rifle, but we were the only ones willing to spend the time and money to see it through. This is a 6.5mm Brondbys from Norway. Note the length of the receiver, twice the length of the Garand. The rest of the rifle is as awkward as the receiver, and this was where most designers were in the 1930s. Garand was decades ahead; all the more luck for us.

or others, you strip the rounds out of the clip and into the rifle. In the Mannlicher and Berthier, it all goes in: rounds and clip.) Pushing the bolt forward strips a round out of the clip and into the chamber. When the last round is stripped into the chamber, the now-empty clip falls out of the bottom of the receiver.

That action required an opening in the receiver's bottom, and trench warfare proved it to be an entry point for mud, lots of it. The real problem was the rim. It meant that the clip held three rounds. Yes, three. After it became apparent that the capacity, and the opening, were wrong for the trenches, the French updated the Berthier 09 to the 09/15, a five-shot with no opening in the bottom of the receiver.

Even when trying to develop a self-loading rifle, the French stuck with the 8x50R cartridge through The Great War.

"THE U.S. ARMY WANTED IT ALL: BETTER PERFORMANCE, A STRONGER ACTION, STRIPPER CLIP USE AND YET KEEP THE SLICK AND FAST FEEL OF THE KRAG. SO, IT DESIGNED THE SPRINGFIELD '03."

MOSIN-NAGANT

The Russian Mosin-Nagant rifle was designed and adopted early in the smokeless rifle period. It had all the shortcomings of early adoption and was never updated significantly until the AK-47 replaced it. So, from 1891 through WWII, it was the Russian rifle. It used a full-length, full-power .30-caliber cartridge with a substantial rim. The feed mechanism was similar to the others, but instead of trying to stagger the timed cases, the designers stacked them, making the rifle tall for the five rounds it held. The receiver was split in the rear, with the bolt handle passing through the opening.

What endeared it to the Russian military was its simplicity and durability. The parts are large enough that they cannot be easily broken. Not to be unkind, but when issuing millions of rifles to illiterate peasants, simplicity and durability must be factors.

1903 SPRINGFIELD

When smokeless powder was developed, the American military used the "Trapdoor" Springfield, a single-shot blackpowder cartridge rifle, in .45 (the cartridge was known as the .45-70 or .45 Gov't) and the action hinged open like a trap door, hence the name. The first repeating rifle, and smokeless one, adopted by the U.S. was the

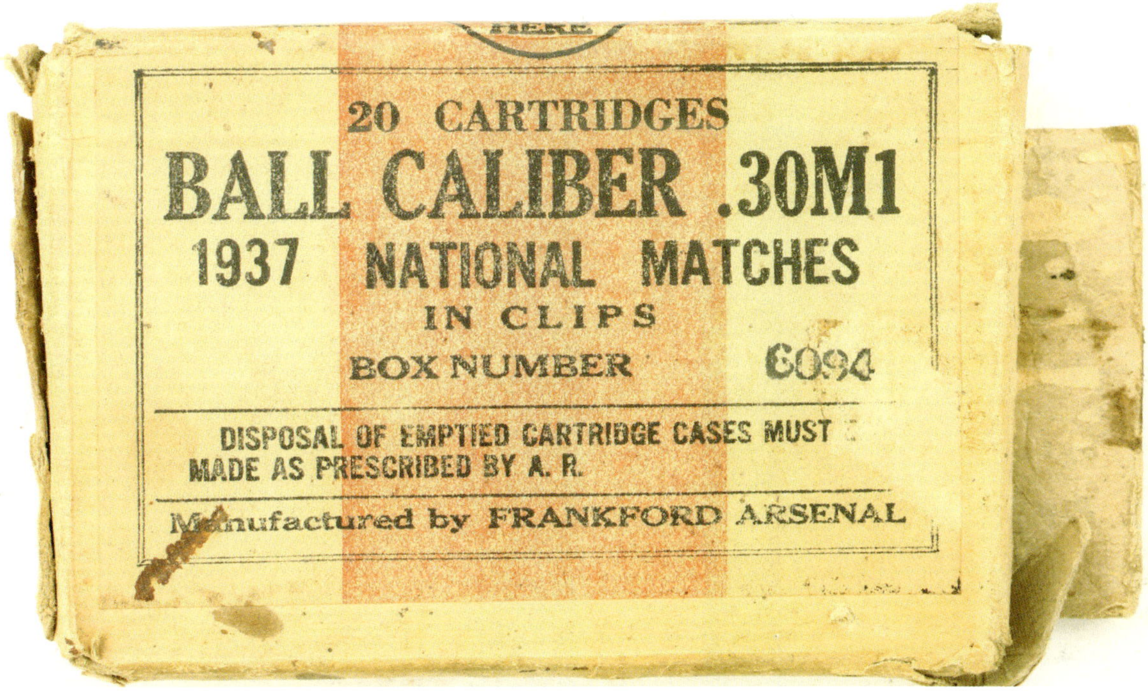

The .30-06 cartridge M1 was the gilding metal bullet version of the M1906, whose cupro-nickel jackets created much more metal fouling in the bore.

Krag. A variant of the Krag-Jorgensen, it was chambered in .30-40 Krag, a cartridge somewhat more potent than the .30-30, which was designed and adopted commercially a few years later in the Winchester 1894.

The .30-40 Krag fired a .308-inch bullet of 220 grains at a modest (although quite startling) 1,950 fps. This was a round-nosed full metal jacket bullet, and the Army experience of the Spanish use of Mauser rifles (1896 Mausers, predecessors to the 1898 Mauser) led the U.S. Army to adopt a new loading for the .30-40, a 200-grain bullet at 2,200 fps. However, the Krag had only one locking lug on the bolt (every other rifle previously adopted had two), and reports of cracked locking lugs almost immediately returned. So the ammunition was recalled, broken down (the bullets pulled) and reloaded back to original specs.

The Krag had other problems. While the magazine could handle pointed bullets readily (unlike the original French rifle, the Lebel), it could not be fitted to use stripper clips. Loading was clumsy in combat conditions, as the magazine had to be hinged open (on the side of the receiver) and then individual cartridges placed in before closing the magazine.

The U.S. Army wanted it all: better performance, a stronger action, stripper clip use and yet keep the slick and fast feel of the Krag. So, it designed the Springfield '03.

(Below) The 1903 Springfield was the primary rifle of WWI for the U.S., despite more 1917s having been made. Photo: Curiosandrelics

27
26
25
24
23
22
21
20
19
18
17
16
15
10
9
8
7
6
5
4
3

(Left) To use it at a distance, you had to stand up the "ladder" and slide the aiming notch up to the distance you estimated. Off by a hundred yards on your setting? A clean miss, and maybe not even noticed by your target.

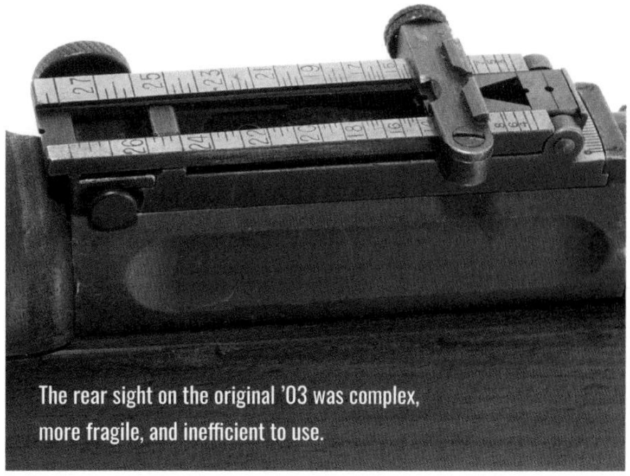

The rear sight on the original '03 was complex, more fragile, and inefficient to use.

The 1903 Springfield was a Mauser rifle for all intents and purposes. So much so that the U.S. government had to pay royalties to Mauser up until we declared war on Germany for the use of the stripper clip patents. It had a two-lug bolt, with the lugs at the front, a five-shot magazine, an elaborate rear sight, adjustable to 2,200 yards, and was chambered in the new cartridge, the .30-03 (.30 caliber, adopted in 1903). Previous cartridge designations had been a combination of the bullet diameter and the powder charge weight. So, the .45-70 was a .45-inch bullet and 70 grains of powder. The .30-40 Krag, while smokeless, had denominated what the powder charge would have been in blackpowder, so a .308-inch bullet and 40 grains equivalent, while being a much smaller charge of smokeless.

The new rifle cartridge was more powerful. The maximum pressure of the .30-40 Krag had been 40,000 PSI. The new .30-03 had a maximum pressure of 50,000 PSI. That pressure made all previous rifle designs unsuited for use. It fired the same 220-grain JRN as the Krag, but now it was at 2,300 fps instead of the 1,900 fps of the Krag.

The bullet jacket was an alloy known as cupro-nickel, and while it protected the lead core from the rifling, it produced extensive fouling in the bore, which had to be cleaned out. The priming compound was corrosive, a detail that took quite some time to discover (for a long time, it was thought to be due to the acids used to pro-

The original French light machine gun or LMG issued to doughboys was the 8mm Chauchat. This meant they had to be supplied with two types of rifle ammo they had to keep straight. Top, the .30-06 Chauchat, using a different magazine with American ammunition. This gun was hastily put into production, and there was one minor problem, which was readily solved with some gunsmithing, but never corrected at the factory.

duce smokeless powder being "driven into the steel" on firing). Lastly, the powders used were hot, abrasive, and quickly wore the rifling. It was not unheard of to arrive at the National Championships (aka Camp Perry, beginning in 1906) with a new rifle and, by the end of the full set or practice, sighting, competition in the various matches, and much ammunition fired, to need a new barrel by the time the matches were over. A few thousand rounds would use up a barrel, especially in rapid-fire.

The .30-03 did not last long. The adoption of lighter weight spitzer, or pointed bullets, to increase velocity, flatten trajectory and improve range estimation meant the .30-03 had to be updated. This came with a new designation, the .30-06. (Now you know how the name came about.) However, this change had its problems.

The rear sight on the original '03 was complex, more fragile, and inefficient to use.

The new M1906 cartridge used a pointed, flat-based bullet of 150 grains in weight. The muzzle velocity was now 2,700 fps. But the shorter bullet, with its point, was not a good fit with the long neck of the .30-03 case. The case mouth was not tight to the bullet but projected past the curve of the bullet, called the ogive. This gap was a problem. The case neck had to be shortened to make the .30-03 into the .30-06. The .30-06 chamber had to be changed. Rather than make new barrels for the existing rifles, the Ordnance Department took each rifle and removed the barrel. It then lathe cut the rear of the barrel shorter by the amount needed, cleaned up the chamber with a chamber reamer, and re-screwed the barrel back into the receiver.

If you delve deep into the specifications of the '03 Springfield rifle, you'll find peculiar barrel lengths — not 24 inches, but a bit less due to the shortening to make them '06 compatible.

Since it was set up for a 220-grain bullet, the rifling twist was also unchanged, which has lasted until today. (Proper or sufficient twist rate is determined by bullet length, not weight.) The standard twist for a 220-grain bullet is 1:10, a turn in 10 inches, which is more (faster) than is needed for a 150-grain bullet, but again, they weren't going to make new barrels. There is one more technical detail, but it doesn't bear on the Garand. The Springfield's designers did not like the Mauser's flat rear face and instead made the rear of the Springfield barrel a cone. This design required cutting a slot in the cone to provide room for the extractor. And it created more work for future gunsmiths who wanted to replace worn '03 barrels.

The Chauchat may have gotten a bad rep after the war (and after the Second World War, for sure), but it served for a couple of decades after being hurriedly rushed to the trenches. Here is one on maneuvers in 1934, still being used.

Getting hired by the Armory due to his light machine gun design (not adopted), John Garand went on to develop the iconic M1 Garand. It took over 15 years, however.

The Garand did, however, inherit all the changes the .30-03-to-.30-06 change produced. The barrel specifications remained 1:10 twist, with the exact chamber dimensions and pressure, bullet weight and shape, right through the shift from the M1906 cartridge to the M1 cartridge and then the M2 and M2 AP cartridges.

CHAUCHAT

A quick look at the Chauchat, a light machine gun that comes in for some criticism. Quickly developed and fielded, it was meant to fill a gap and do so without taking up resources otherwise used in the war effort. The first model was chambered in 8mm Lebel and used a curious half-moon magazine. The French trained with and fielded Maxim hunter-killer teams based around a Chauchat gunner and three riflemen. When the U.S. entered the war, they were first issued Chauchats in 8mm Lebel, but juggling two different rifle cartridges, supply, issue and use, was not, shall we say, optimal.

A crash program was developed to build Chauchats in .30-06 with a different magazine so that the supply system could get same-cartridge light machine guns into the hands of doughboys. But one minor glitch was overlooked in the switch, and the .30-06 LMGs had a bad rep as unreliable. Testing afterward with the small mod proved them as reliable, or even more so than the 8mm version.

Even crash programs have to have all the bugs worked out.

And despite the very common "this was an awful weapon" comments you'll read about the Chauchat, they not only stayed in inventory after The Great War but were worked on and improved. I've been in the vaults of the Belgian Army Museum and saw a rack of Chauchat that the Belgian army, after the war, rebuilt to take the Belgian 7.65 Mauser cartridge. New barrels and new magazines were tested, approved, and issued. So much for "not good enough."

1920S SELF-LOADING RIFLES

Once cartridges became the norm, everyone wanted a self-loading rifle because it was better for many uses and needs. The first successful one was the Remington Model 8, designed by Browning and adopted in 1906. The Model 8 was not chambered in .30-06. It uses a system known as long-recoil. The bolt and barrel are locked together at the moment of firing and recoil the entire length of the receiver (just a bit more than the cartridge length), and then the bolt is temporarily held in place. The bolt and barrel unlock, and the barrel moves forward to the starting point, driven by its spring, separate from the bolt spring.

Those familiar with Browning designs will recognize this as the same system in the Auto 5 shotgun. With the Remington 8 being available in 1906, you'd think that the various military organizations would be falling all over themselves to adopt it or something like it. You'd be wrong. It had several shortcomings and one great big fault, as far as they were concerned.

One shortcoming was the cartridge offerings. The Rem 8 was offered in four cartridges: .25 Remington, .30 Remington, .32 Remington and .35 Remington. The first three were rimless variants of the Winchester cartridges found in the Winchester lever-action 1894 rifle. When smokeless powder was invented, the switch from black-powder was rapid in the commercial field. It took less than a decade for a slew of rifles and cartridges to be designed, offered, and adopted. The exemplar here is the .30-30, which remains popular today. The .35 Remington was a cartridge designed by John Browning specifically for his Remington Model 8 to offer a .35 cartridge for those who felt the .30 was "too small" and yet still fit within the Remington 8 action. Notably, the .35 Remington is still popular today, although not like the .30-30.

His background as a machinist and toolmaker meant Garand could also design the proper fixtures to manufacture his rifle, which proved helpful later.

The Army did test the Remington Model 8. It fitted some .25 Rem 8s in .25 Remington with aperture sights and tested accuracy, rate of fire, and use in maneuvers, trenches, and structures. The rifles proved quite useful, but there were shortcomings. Why .25 and not .30? No idea, even though the .30 Remington was nowhere near the .30-06 in power. But let's do some thought experimenting, shall we?

Say you have a .30-caliber self-loading rifle with a five-shot magazine. Why would it not be adopted? One reason is that the .30-30 and the clone .30 Remington were not 1,000-yard-plus cartridges. Compared to the .30-03, with a 220-grain bullet (soon to be the '06, with a 150 gr.) at 2,200-2,300 fps, the .30 Remington produced a 180-grain bullet at some 1,700 fps. They were both round-nosed, while the Remington was a soft-point and the '03 an FMJ.

Let's consider things that might have been. If we reduce the case taper of the .30 Remington, shorten the neck a bit, and swap the 180 soft-point for a 125-grain pointed FMJ, we would have a cartridge that produces about 2,300 fps. Sound familiar? Or maybe we go down to the 6.5mm diameter and produce a 115-grain pointed boattail at 2,500 fps. Now we're cooking with gas, right? The Remington 8 is fed from a single-stack magazine, and you can reload the rifle with five-round stripper clips, taking a few seconds to do so. It would have been a trivial task for John Browning to have made the magazine a ten-shot. (I suspect that if you gave him a weekend to work on it, he could have re-designed it to hold 20 rounds, even with a detachable magazine.) In all fairness, in 1906, no one could have predicted that the Remington Model 8, with the mods so described, would have been an absolute ruler of trench warfare, raids, and trench-clearing.

But the unforgivable fault of the Model 8 was the barrel return spring. In the Auto 5 shotgun, that spring is a coil type wrapped around the magazine tube. In the Remington Model 8 it's wrapped around the barrel. A sheet metal cover then encloses the spring. In combat, denting the cover could bind the spring and make it inoperative. Suppose you mounted a bayonet to the Model 8 (an absolute military necessity in that era). In that case, you almost ensure that the tube will be dented, bent, warped, or otherwise a problem. And putting the barrel return spring around a tube or rod underneath the barrel negated one of the aspects that hunters found compelling: takedown. The Remington 8 could be readily disassembled into two major components and stored and transported in a compact case not much larger than an attaché case, which hunters loved. However, the military had no use for it. If there had been a return spring on the tube in the handguard, the barrel now would not have needed the tube/shroud and could have had a bayonet lug on it.

Regardless, the Remington 8 was a no-go for military adoption.

However, if someone had been forward-thinking, I'd bet it would have been a simple task for Browning to have solved all the problems with the Remington 8. If he followed the usual pattern of problem-solving in other applications, he'd have probably found three or four ways to solve each of the various issues the military had with it, and at least one of them would have been in the "How'd he think of that?" category.

It is an interesting thing to consider, a Model 8 or derivative for combat. A .30 Remington with a 125-grain spitzer at 2,300 fps in 1910 would still be in service today. We'd have probably pushed it up to 2,500 fps by now, but with such a cartridge, there would have been no M1 Garand, M1 Carbine, M14, or AR-15. Who knows what succession of designs and models we'd have had? There might have been a BAR, but it would have been a lot lighter and handier, and it might still be in service today. Hmm, a pistol (1911) and a light machine gun (BAR) in service, side-by-side, for more than a century, to this day? That would be something.

STANDARD

There was a self-loading .30-06 to be found before The Great War. But the Standard was even more than that, being both a self-loading and a pump action at the user's discretion. Those who know of the SPAS12 from the 1980s, yes, there was a dual-action firearm before that shotgun. For all we know, the SPAS designer knew of the Standard.

The Standard had several failings. First, it had no way to mount a bayonet. That could have been overcome if it had been reliable in function, which it was not. And, it wasn't very durable, at least not by military standards.

AUTOMAT

Now, this wasn't a pre-war design, at least, not much pre-war. The Automat was a Russian short-recoil design, using the 6.5 Japanese cartridge with a detachable magazine and select-fire. It's considered the first assault rifle. However, as soon as the

The Remington Model 8, despite being a handy and compact rifle, had faults that the military of the time could not overlook. If it had looked past the faults and seen the potential, things could have been different. But then, things could always have been different.

The Automat M1916 Federov was a Russian short-recoil design, using the 6.5 Japanese cartridge with a detachable magazine and select-fire.

war began, the Tsarist military wouldn't adopt anything new (not that there was much chance they'd have adopted something new before the war, either), and that was that. The Automat, while an interesting step forward, is a museum piece (literally) as it wasn't made in any volume, and samples are now found only in museums.

While the Automat is probably the first weapon designed to be an assault rifle, the M1 Carbine is the first one to be adopted and fielded. But that's another book.

THE GREAT WAR

The war started with combatants using bolt-action rifles in open country, tactically a war of maneuver. Once trench warfare became the norm, a 1,000-yard rifle wasn't much use. And, the rifles had another problem: sights. All the rifles in use had their sights designed and constructed based on open terrain. So, the basic setting, the battle zero, assumed a standing opponent. The idea was to aim for the belt buckle, and the rise and fall of trajectory would get you a disabling hit on the enemy soldier out to 300, 350, and 400 yards without changing sights. Past that, it was standard procedure to adjust the sight for the distance, as described earlier.

That meant that at 100 yards, the bullet would be striking 7 inches or more above the point of aim. It had to rise and then fall and still be on target at 300+ yards. Well, if the only target available to you at 100 yards was the enemy soldier's helmet sticking just a bit too much over the edge of the trench, your bullet was going to miss him, going high. Given stress, fatigue, hazy conditions, and the short time the helmet would be visible (if it was to be seen for too long, it was probably a decoy, and firing on it would get you shot at in short order) the hit percentages had to be pretty low.

The Pedersen Device replaced the '03's bolt. The Pedersen bolt was blowback, and the front of the device (left end of the upper device) was shaped like a .30-06 to fill the chamber.

Each doughboy was supposed to be saddled with this and more extra gear. The pouch holds a batch of 40-round magazines, one of which you can see at the top. Then there is the Pedersen Device and its metal holder to be attached to the belt. Extra ammo, a pouch for the '03 bolt when removed, any doughboy with less than a 36-inch waist would run out of belt room.

Rifles at this time had standardized in length, with barrels of 24 inches. Previous generations had 30-inch barrels, with the Cavalry using carbines of 20 inches or so. Bayonets were over a foot long, so a rifle with the bayonet mounted was a lengthy package. A rifle with a bayonet was unwieldy when sneaking across no man's land on a trench raid, trying to stay low and quiet. It soon became standard for trench raids to be conducted with pistols, grenades, knives and daggers, entrenching tools and clubs. When the Americans arrived, they added shotguns to the mix, drawing howls of outrage from the Germans. By the war's end, the Germans had developed the first submachine guns because a 9mm sub gun in the trenches trumped any rifle and bayonet.

The American inventors also came up with a "solution" to the volume of fire problem, which they called the Pedersen Device — a replacement bolt for the Springfield '03 rifle. You took the regular bolt out and inserted the Pedersen Device in its place. It was a blowback bolt and a chamber adapter filling the .30-06 chamber. The Pedersen Device (and we have to keep calling it the Device because there would be a later Pedersen rifle) used a special pistol-sized cartridge, feeding from a 40-round magazine. Of course, no one asked the doughboys about the need for all this extra gear: the Pedersen conversion, the extra magazines, the special Springfield marked the Mark 1 (non-Mark 1 Springfields could not use the Pedersen Device), and pouches for all these plus a pouch to store the regular bolt when you took it out.

And the cartridge? A straight-walled pistol-length case with a .308-inch bullet weighing 77 grains, more or less, going 1,100 fps, again more or less. Those steeped in cartridge history will recognize it as the French 7.65 Longue, the pistol cartridge adopted between the wars. Why this? Simple. In a bit of misdirection, the War Department gave the Pedersen Device the name "U.S. Auto-

The Springfield MKI, the particular rifle that could use the Pedersen Device. Without the ejection port on the left side, there was no place for the empties to get tossed out of the rifle on the '03. When the Pedersen Device was not adopted, all the special MKI rifles became oddities in arms rooms worldwide. They still worked just fine as '03 rifles, however.

matic Pistol, Caliber .30, Model of 1918." The French must have figured that if it was good enough for the Americans, why not?

The war ended before the Pedersen Device would be fielded. At the time of the American entry into The Great War, April of 1917, the expectation was that the war would continue into 1919 and even 1920, even with American assistance. Some planners were working out the production scheduling, shipping, and other logistics for "The Great 1919 Offensive" and others on "The Great 1920 Offensive," so the war's end came as a surprise. Once the Americans got used to working in the Western Front and made advances, it was the start of rolling back the German lines in "The Hundred Days," the three months and some that it took for the Germans to surrender.

With the war's sudden end, contracts were canceled, production was wrapped up, and the Pedersen Devices were stuffed into storage. Some 65,000 had been made, along with 1.6 million magazines and 65 million cartridges. A decade later, tired of the cost of storage, most were destroyed, with perhaps a hundred surviving. Collectors' items of the first order, they are.

Post-war, the "previous war" syndrome was in full effect, and everyone assumed trench warfare would be the new norm. Yes, those tank things were mighty useful, but it would be trenches and assault teams again in the next war.

In a photo from 1923, the Springfield Arsenal experimental shop is hard at work. This was where prototype parts were fabricated and experimental rifles assembled.

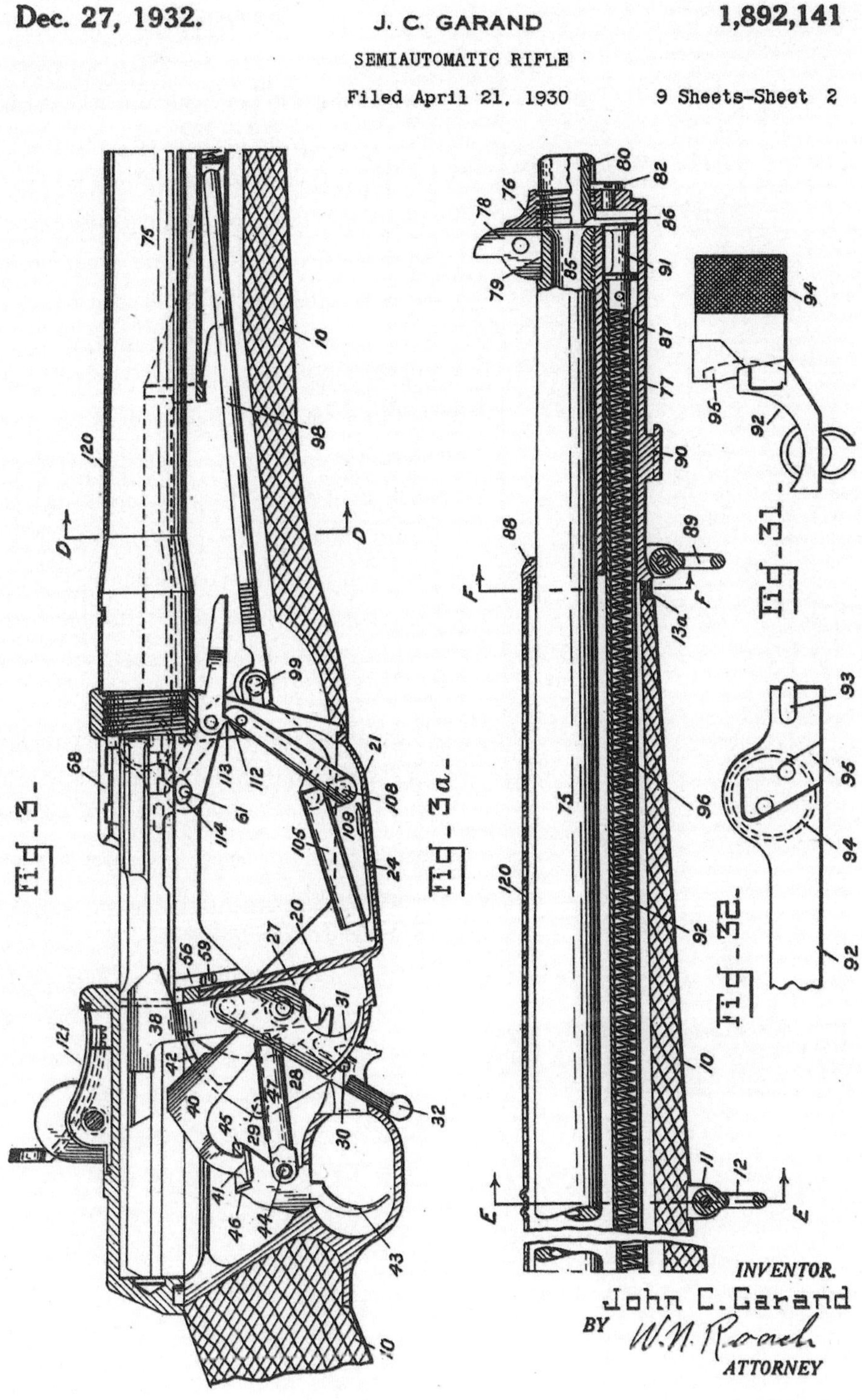

The almost-final design, dating from 1932, of the rifle Garand was working on. This is the 10-shot in .276, with the gas-trap gas system.

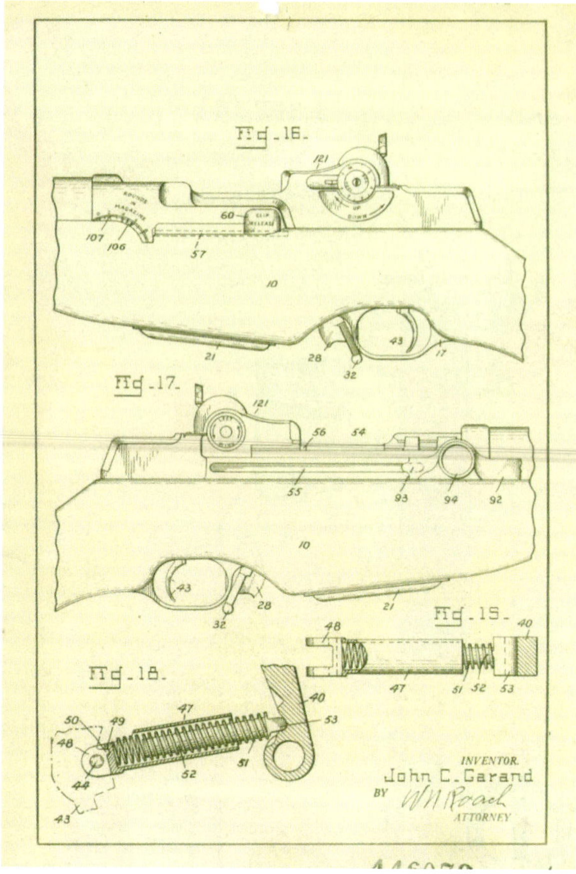

You can see that Garand wasn't missing a step in his design. Not only does it feature a range-adjustable sight, but there's a "round capacity" indicator to let the soldier know how many of the ten shots he has left.

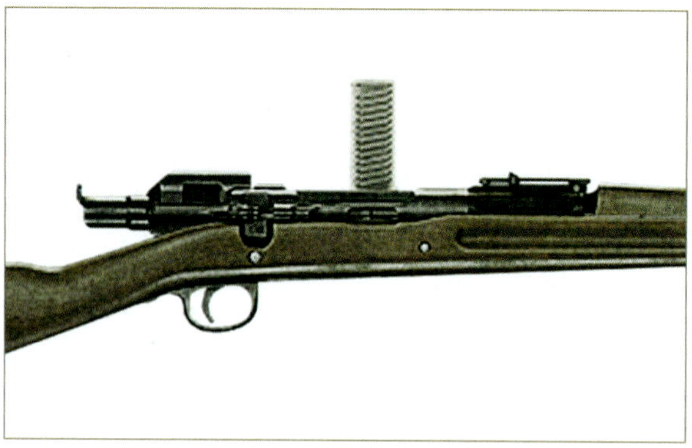

The Pedersen Device was a replacement bolt assembly and magazine that turned a .30-06 bolt action into a self-loading .32 magnum pistol.

I have heard people criticize the various armies about what they did post-war, after each war, as if what was going to happen in the future was a known quantity. Maybe it is, maybe it isn't. But you also have to consider what each army had to work with. Let's take Germany as an example and then compare and contrast others.

The German army was big on *blitzkrieg*, the swift maneuver and advancement on the enemy flank. It planned on swapping out the heavy Maxim guns for the lighter, air-cooled MG34. All well and good, but they did not have, despite being one of the most industrialized countries in Europe, a large enough industrial base to pull it off in the time they had. Tanks, yes, and Stukas and MG34s, but also an entire army equipped with bolt-action rifles, and a lot of their artillery and supply train still pulled by horses. France had a forward-looking army but could not decide on a given plan or equipment. They were still in the process of switching over in 1940 when the Germans invaded. They had good tanks and lots of them, but the top brass was still stuck in 1918.

Japan had the problem of good luck in previous wars (the naval actions against the Russians were little more than moving gunnery practice) and no real opposition to teach it how to manage a neer-peer opponent. Add in a small industrial base, and Japan was overwhelmed by volume and quality in WWII.

The American experience was different. Even before the war, we had the industrial base to overmatch any two opponents. Once we got up and running, we outdid the rest of the world. But the political will wasn't there, and it was not a minor miracle that we fielded a self-loading rifle in time for the war. Bolt-action rifles were the standard all armies were held to until the mid-1930s.

Those holdouts — and they were many — made the adoption of self-loading rifles, something everyone wanted, much more difficult. The main stumbling block was the requirement to maintain the existing full-power cartridge. Insistence on that meant all the Great Powers kept their existing cartridges and tried to build new rifles around them, except for the French. The French realized the futility of a self-loading rifle that used a rimmed cartridge and developed new rimless cartridges. They also understood the futility of having more than one rifle cartridge in inventory (at the start of WWII, the Japanese had something like seven different ones), making the task more difficult. They had first to develop a cartridge that would serve as a rifle, light machine gun (think BAR) and belt-fed machine gun cartridge, then design the firearms for each category.

In Germany, even into the early years of WWII, Hitler stopped the R&D into anything that didn't use the 9mm Parabellum or the 7.92 Mauser cartridge, which he used in WWI. Curiously, however, while he prevented advancements in rifle designs, his attitude didn't hinder the adoption of the MG34 and then the MG42. One can only conclude that the caliber was what mattered. One can only wonder: If in 1933, Germany had gone into R&D on a self-loading rifle in 7.92x57 with the same effort they put into the MG34, what might have resulted?

In the rest of the world, the attitude of "Good enough then, good enough now" was much the same between the wars. Plus, there weren't many countries willing to invest the time and money needed to develop a self-loading rifle that was up to the rigors of combat. Tired of war and wanting to invest in modernity or go back to the way things were, only the U.S. was willing (and then, just barely) to make an effort. •

On the Eastern Front, this MG34, wielded by a "Viking" SS unit member, was the cutting-edge machine gun of the 1930s and a big step up in mobility over the Maxim.

CHAPTER 2

HOW THE GARAND WORKS

In the second decade of the 21st century, a well-versed rifle shooter will likely have extensive experience with an AR-15, at least some with the AK, and bolt-action shooting, because that's the step up in precision and range. That won't help you here. So get ready for a ride.

On the one hand, Garand operation is simple. On the other, there are details that you cannot grasp, simply shifting from other rifles to it. An example would be switching from an AR-15 to an AK-47. To shove a magazine in place in the AR, make sure it is correctly oriented ("shiny end up, pointy end forward") and push straight up. On the AK, you hook the front lip into the mag well and pivot the magazine upward until it locks. The two differ, but the similarities make it easy to learn one if you're familiar with the other.

The Garand? No such thing.

Let's start with firing. When you press the trigger, the hammer hits the firing pin and the cartridge fires. The bullet, propelled by the expanding powder, travels down the bore until it reaches the gas port. When the bullet base passes the gas port, gas flows into and through the port. (Gases do that, they do not have to be directed, they will expand into any available area.) The gas enters the area in the gas cylinder ahead of the operating rod, and the pressure pushes the rod to the rear.

The rod has an angled camming slot that lifts the bolt lug on that side, rotating the bolt, and once rotated, presses the bolt to the rear. When the bolt-op rod combo reaches the rear of the receiver, the op rod spring pushes it forward, stripping a round out of the clip and into the chamber. The op rod cam slot rotates the bolt closed, and the rifle is ready to repeat the cycle.

That's the simple part.

Let's look at the gas port and op rod. The gas port is a half-inch from the end of the bore. When a gas-operated system cycles, there is a period known as the dwell time. That is the time from when the bullet passes the gas port (letting gas flow into the system) and leaves the muzzle to when the gas pressure vents to the atmosphere and pressure drops quickly to zero. (Not zero in a true sense, to atmospheric pressure. The relative difference matters; once it drops to atmospheric, it is essentially at zero.)

On the AR-15 and AK-47, the dwell time is when the bullet travels four to six inches down the bore. (The AK is a bit more complicated, as the gas system is designed to

To get the triggerguard unlocked to disassemble, use a cleaning rod section as a handle.

Note how the cleaning rod goes to begin disassembly.

Hinge the triggerguard down.

Then slide the trigger assembly straight down and out of the receiver. There are receiver slots in which the trigger housing ribs ride.

Hinge the receiver up out of the stock (or the stock down from the receiver).

The stock is hooked into the rear handguard band.

The buttplate started as stamped steel plates with a door (for cleaning gear) and a pressed checkering pattern. Decades of drill and dirt have made the non-slip pattern more random.

The receiver action assembled and upside-down.

To begin, pull the rod back, compressing the action spring (it is strong, you will have to work at it) and unhook it from the follower arm.

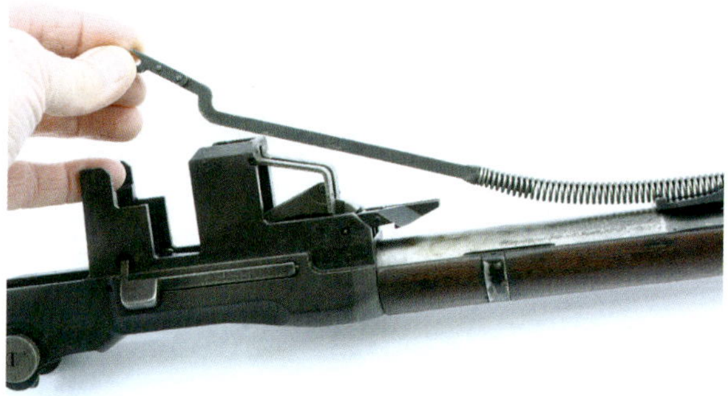

Once unhooked, pull the follower rod and spring entirely out of the op rod.

The follower arm and clip latch activator are held in by a pin, and that pin is sided. This is the large end, and it comes out from this side.

The pin partway out.

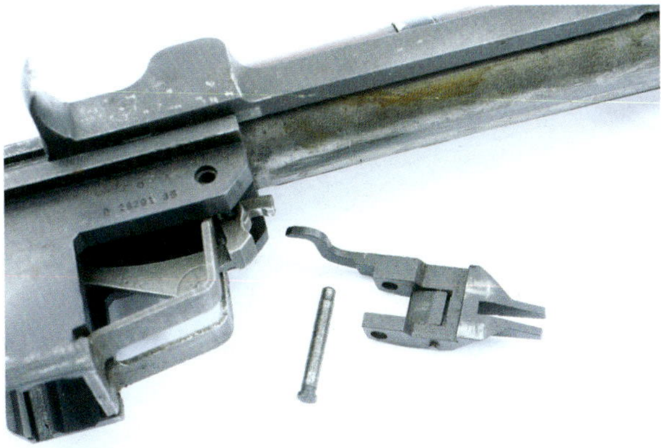

You can remove the clip latch lever with the pin out.

With the clip latch lever out, pivot the bullet guide upward. The press fit in the receiver legs secures it at the rear. With the bullet guide out, you can remove the follower arm.

The follower arm, the lever that changes the action spring force direction from parallel to the bore (horizontal) to a perpendicular (vertical) force to provide lift to the cartridge stack.

The follower rides in slots broached in the receiver legs.

Once free of the receiver, set the follower aside. Don't treat it harshly. It's essential to the proper feeding of your Garand.

The follower guide slides side to side on the follower and accommodates clips loaded either top-left or top-right.

Note the clearance cuts in the op rod guide slot at the rear of the receiver. These allow you to remove the op rod from the receiver once you remove all the other parts.

Pull the op rod to the side and tilt it, and it will come free once aligned.

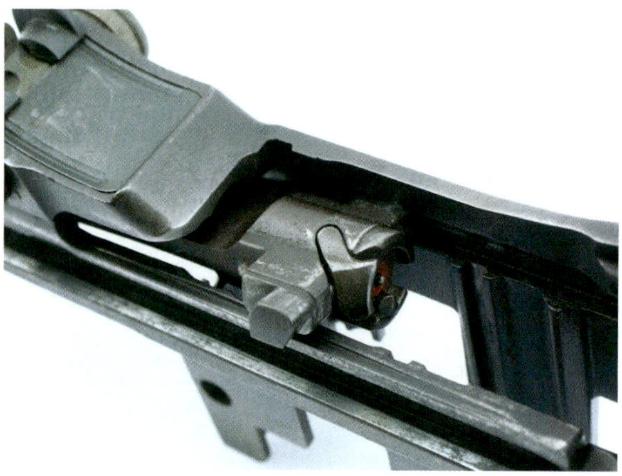

Now comes the hard part. The bolt has to be fiddled with until you learn the exact angle it will come free of the receiver. Don't force anything; you need to learn the touch.

Lift, tilt, wiggle, and pull forward, and you'll find the spot.

The bridge inside the receiver isn't there to keep the sides from being squeezed. The firing pin safety keeps the firing pin back from the primer until the bolt is fully closed.

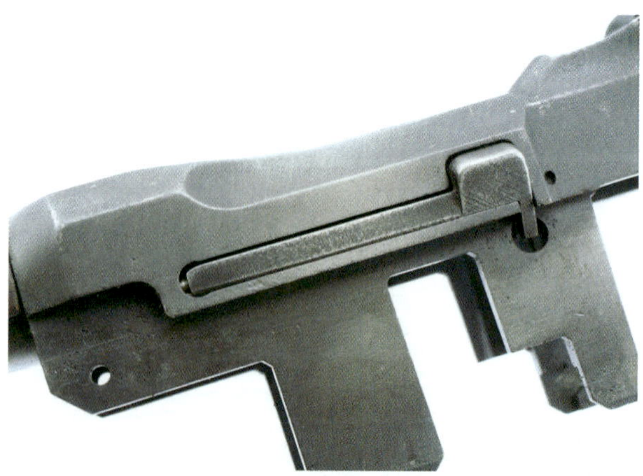

On the left side is the clip latch. If you want to unload, pull the bolt back and hold it, and then press the upper edge of the square back. The clip and the remaining rounds will spring free and fall to the ground.

This Springfield was rebuilt at one point, but the rear sight kept the locking bar assembly. Good enough was good enough.

vent excess gas early in the dwell time.) In the Garand, the dwell time is the period during which the bullet travels that half-inch. So, in the AR and less so in the AK, the gas system receives a more-or-less gentle push. (SBRs make this problematic, and much more like the Garand.) In the Garand, it is more like a tap. Complicating this is the pressure involved. Since the gas port is almost at the muzzle, the gas pressure is at its almost lowest before venting. So, in numbers, the AR has a gas port pressure that starts at around 17,000 PSI and pushes for a lengthy period (lengthy in a gas-flow and operational cycles timeframe) which can if appropriately tuned, make for a very easy-to-manage felt recoil.

The Garand has, at best, 12,000 PSI to work with, and the time is very short.

This is why, as we'll go into great detail later, the Garand is very powder-burn-rate sensitive, and you have at most four or five rifle powders to choose from when reloading. (By comparison, in loading the .223 for an AR-15, I have used powders from fastest to slowest of 40+ powder names on the burn-rate chart. And a bolt action could use even more.)

Also, when it comes to operating rods, the Garand has one of the longest. It also has one of the shortest receivers for a self-loading rifle.

The Garand op rod is essentially unsupported, despite its length. On the front end, it rides in the gas cylinder's bore, but that support is for a few inches and is not held in place. It simply rides in the bore. At the other end, the op rod engages the right-hand bolt lug, and a small tab rides in a slot in the receiver. One of the tricks of owning and running a Garand is learning the "jiggle and twist" of sneaking the op rod tab out of its slot at the one spot on the receiver where it's designed to come out when disassembling.

The only real constraint on the op rod location comes from the recoil spring and feed system arm. The long spring and the feed system arm act as the axis of alignment of the op rod.

GAS FEED SYSTEM

This brings us to the Garand's feed system: the en-bloc clip. Remember our discussion of the various feed systems of repeating rifles? We had the single feed like the Krag, the internal magazine like the Mauser and Springfield, and the Mannlicher clip. OK, try to imagine a self-loading rifle with each of these. The single loader would be an immediate non-starter. What kind of magazine could you have, opening a port and dropping in loose rounds, like the Krag? A clumsy one. A self-loading rifle with an internal magazine could be loaded with stripper clips. Rifle historians know that the M14 was designed so you could use it to load magazines by locking a magazine in place, locking the bolt back, and using the stripper clip guide to load mags. But that was a backup system, as the bandoliers came with stripper "spoons" to guide the stripper clips when loading magazines that weren't in the rifle at the time of loading.

The SAFN 49, made by FN post-war, was designed to be loaded that way. The 20-round magazine was not meant to be removed but loaded and topped off from stripper clips, while the magazine remained in the rifle, just like the SMLE mag.

That brings us to Mannlicher clips, which is what the Garand uses. Now, John Garand improved on the Mannlicher approach while taking advantage of its positives. Positives? Yes, like weight and cost. His improvements were making the clip out of heavy-gauge spring steel, which

You won't often need to take the gas cylinder apart for cleaning, but if you do, unscrew the gas screw. A proper wrench helps; while a large screwdriver works, you risk marring the gas screw.

The gas screw should unscrew with finger pressure once unlocked.

Once the gas screw is out, you can unscrew the gas cylinder lock.

This is as far as you need to go. Give a good scrubbing of the gas cylinder interior, and put it back together. If you take it apart more, you risk loosening the fit of the gas cylinder to the barrel, which could decrease accuracy.

was extremely durable. It can readily be re-used, something not all Mannlicher clips are happy about. And he designed the system to automatically eject the empty clip when the last round was fired. This eliminated the bottom opening, an entry point for mud, dirt, and debris. By automatically ejecting the clip, the shooter knows when the rifle is empty and doesn't have to remove the empty one. Sometimes, in a Mannlicher-clip rifle, the empty clip doesn't fall out depending on manufacturing tolerances, fouling or dirt. You have to push it out when you insert the next clip. That is not the case with the Garand.

Someone in the back of the room asks, "Why not a de-

tachable magazine? Wouldn't that have been easier still?" Yes, but remember, this was back in the 1910s, 1920s, and 1930s. Compared to where it would be by the end of WWII, the technology of stamped-steel construction was still in the R&D phase. Yes, box magazines were being made, the 1911 pistol was an exemplar, and the BAR was certainly not an unreliable performer. However, the military views things differently than we do.

Ping! When the last round is fired from the Garand, the empty case and clip are ejected. Yes, the ejecting clip will go "ping." No, that wasn't a problem in combat. Photo: CMP Archives

A pistol would be issued in small numbers, the BAR, not many more. For example, let's take our rifle company: 150 to 180 officers and men. We've got a Captain, three Lieutenants, a dozen or so Sergeants, and then the riflemen. A 1911A1 pistol and three magazines, one set each for the officers and NCOs, comes to 16 pistols and 48 magazines. The riflemen, if they're going to head out with 120 rounds of ammunition on their persons (a typical number, we are, after all, talking of the .30-06, there's no need for 200-300 rounds per man), means five magazines each. A rifle company thus requires 750 to 900 magazines to start. As soon as they get into the fight, magazines will get lost, damaged, and have to be replaced. The BAR? There would be one per squad, so if we assume 12-man squads, then we have 12 to 15 squads, or a dozen BARs, with five magazines each would be 60 magazines. Fifteen squads would be 75 magazines. If we jump that up to seven mags per BAR (one in the BAR and six spares), we're still talking only 105 magazines, max.

The experts in stamped-steel technology could be found in the auto industry at the time, but the firearms field was so insular that I would bet no one before late 1942 was talking to the auto companies about how to make stamped steel anything. They certainly wouldn't have been doing it in the 1920s.

No, to the militaries of the world, and weapons designers, box magazines were too expensive to issue en masse and too likely to be lost in action, requiring a resupply. And even if the expense could be borne, they were so new, and the powers that be were not all that certain they wanted every soldier to have 20 rounds he could fire them off in short order. The common opinion was that they'd needlessly shoot up all their ammo and not have it when needed.

YES, THE EJECTING CLIP WILL GO "PING." NO, IT WASN'T A PROBLEM IN COMBAT, "SIGNALING TO THE ENEMY THAT THE GI'S RIFLE WAS EMPTY." WHEN I FIRST READ THAT, I ASKED MY DAD. HE CHUCKLED AND SAID SOMETHING TO THE EFFECT THAT IT WAS A "PROBLEM PEOPLE NOT HAVING BEEN IN COMBAT THOUGHT WAS A PROBLEM.

(That was why late 19th-century bolt-action rifles often had magazine cut-offs, to make them single-shot rifles until the magazine capacity was needed and ordered.)

Thus, in the 1920s, there would not be a U.S. Army-issued service rifle that used a box magazine, period, end of story, even though John Garand first tried making a rifle using BAR mags. Find some other way.

Now for some details.

GARAND MANUAL OF ARMS

First, let's load up a Garand clip. The easiest way is to start with seven rounds. Place the clip with its back flat on the table. (You'll get good enough soon to do this by hand, but let's do it the easy way first.) Take seven rounds and drop them down, base first, into the clip, and arrange them in a staggered array, alternating right and left. Push the array away from you to one end so the topmost round on the end toward you is on the clip's left side. Now, press the eighth round in from the side through the opening facing you so it snaps in place. Ensure it has its base flat against the back of the clip, and you are done.

Repeat on all your clips.

To load the rifle, first, hold it properly. Let's learn the hand-roll Garand load. Your left hand (the Garand is a markedly right-handed rifle, but it can be operated left-handed) should be snugged up between the stock and sling, tight to the sling swivel. If you do not have a sling installed, then tight to the sling swivel. To engage the safety, press it to the rear into the trigger housing, where you can feel it. Now pull the bolt back until it locks in place. Hold the clip in your right hand, with your thumb along the top of the cartridges. Press the clip straight down into the receiver, and while you do that, let your right hand's fingers slide outside the receiver and alongside the stock. Pivot your thumb down, pressing the clip down into the receiver until it clicks, now locked in place. If you do not press it down far enough into the receiver, it will not lock into place, it will be lifted as a unit by the cartridge lifter, and the bolt will not go forward. Try again until you learn the feel. Keep your hand where it is, but press back on the op rod hook with the edge of your hand until you feel the click of the op rod unlatching.

Here's the fun part: rotate your hand, so your fingers point toward the muzzle, sweep your hand up and away from the receiver, and allow the bolt to go forward with its full power. You now have a round chambered.

Why do it this way? Because if you do not use your hand to hold the op rod back, it will close the action while your thumb is still pressing the clip down into the receiver. Your thumb will get wedged between the bolt, going forward, and the receiver, which is going nowhere. This is referred to as "Garand thumb."

You will also notice that there is no way to load the Garand and not have a round in the chamber. On many other rifles, you can load the magazine and leave the chamber empty, which was considered safer than having a chambered round. (I don't care if there is a round in the chamber or not, if you point the muzzle at me, known as "sweeping" or "flagging," we are going to have words.)

Now, to fire. The next unmodern thing you must learn and overcome is trigger finger placement. If you have learned on an AR-15, and you have learned recently, you will have had it drilled into you to "keep your finger outside the triggerguard." A good habit, but with the Garand, you have to place your trigger finger inside the triggerguard to work the safety and push it to the Fire position. Yes, even before you shoot, you must have your finger inside the triggerguard.

Each press of the trigger gets you one shot, and when the last one is fired, the empty case and the now-empty clip will both be ejected. Yes, the ejecting clip will go "ping." No, it wasn't a problem in combat, "signaling to the enemy that the GI's rifle was empty." When I first read that, I asked my dad. He chuckled and said something to the effect that it was a "problem people not having been in combat thought was a problem." Think about it: your rifle is not the only one going off in combat. There are other rifles, machine guns, submachine guns, grenades, and all manner of shouting, machines, and other noise. Who is going to notice a little "ping"?

GARAND DISASSEMBLY

Taking the Garand apart is nothing like the AR-15. Nothing you have learned there will help you here. So, go slowly until you get a feel for things, and always wear safety glasses — a good idea any time, but essential here, as some parts are under impressive spring pressure. Also, proper cleaning and lubrication of the Garand differ from the AR in some essentials.

Open the action and ensure it is empty and there is no round in the chamber. Close the bolt. Push the safety back until it clicks into the Safe position. Note: You cannot disassemble the Garand with the hammer in the forward or fired/down position. You must work the bolt to cock the hammer or use the triggerguard (a much more difficult operation) to cock the hammer before proceeding.

Pull back on the op rod with your right hand and hold it back. If your thumb is long enough, stick it into the action, and press the cartridge lifter down until it unlocks the bolt, which you are holding back. Ease the bolt forward. If it stops open, you haven't pressed the lifter down far enough. Hold the bolt back and press the lifter down farther. Once the bolt is forward and closed, turn the Garand over in your hands.

The triggerguard will be either a forging, with a circle through the rear part of the guard, or a heavy-gauge spring-steel stamping. It is clipped into the plate the trigger passes through. Holding the Garand in your left hand (if you are right-handed) at the rear handguard, grab the back end of the triggerguard and hinge it down from the retaining plate. It is meant to stay there until you take it apart, so it will not come easily. In fact, in some rifles, it can be a two-handed task to unclip it.

If that's the case, here's the trick: you will need a section

The barrel markings on this rifle indicate that while the receiver was made in late 1944, the barrel was a Springfield February 1965 production, rebuilt sometime after that.

of a steel cleaning rod. Aluminum won't do. If you have an early triggerguard, stick the cleaning rod crossways through the hole in the triggerguard, and use that as your handle to lift it open. If you have a later stamped triggerguard, poke the cleaning rod into the hole, and use the rod as a lever to hinge the triggerguard open. If your rifle needs this much leverage, you might want to retire this cleaning rod section as your new "Garand Disassembly Tool No. 1" because you might put a slight bend in the rod. That would be bad for your bore.

Hinge the triggerguard all the way open. Pull the assembly straight down and from the action. The trigger assembly has a pair of ribs machined into it that ride in slots machined in the receiver. There is no pivoting, twisting, turning, or other motion involved. It slides straight down.

Let's look at the trigger assembly before we go any further. First, you can see why the safety requires some force to move from one position to another: it engages the hammer. When you press the safety tab back into the triggerguard, it engages the hammer on a lug on the hammer's left side and cams it out of engagement with the sear. Unlike the AR-15, which blocks the trigger movement, the Garand safety disengages the hammer from the sear and holds the hammer in place. Pressing the trigger doesn't do anything because the hammer is locked out of the system.

When you push the safety forward to the Fire position, you are camming the hammer back into engagement with the sear. The hammer is driven by a stout spring, and your leverage with the safety is not all that great, which is why it takes some force to move it. This is a safety feature Garand built into his design. The safety tab is not easily pressed from Fire to Safe so that a soldier wouldn't find his rifle unready to fire at a critical moment. And when placed on Safe, it is doubly safe because of the force needed to press it to Fire. Moreover, since the tab is inside the triggerguard, it's shielded from inadvertent bumping.

You might ask, "How do I take the rest of this apart for a proper cleaning?" The quick answer is … you don't. The hammer is driven by a heavy spring, part of a highly durable assembly. The hammer guide rod, that piece that bears against the hammer, is a rod that extends down the center of the coil spring that drives it. The spring is enclosed in a cup, which rides on a pivot pin at the rear. That pivot pin also is the trigger pivot pin. To disassemble (and I'm not suggesting you do this now, perhaps not ever), you must restrain the hammer while you dry fire it to ease it forward. You then use a drift pin to punch the pivot pin out (it goes one way, out to the right) and control the hammer spring assembly as it tries to shoot out of the housing. With the spring tension off, you can pull or push the hammer pivot pin out (again, out to the right) and

If anyone needs to check, the receiver has the correct drawing number and heat-treat lot for a late 1944 production. So, not a re-weld, not that there are any signs it might have been.

remove the safety from its pivot boss and the clip ejector/safety detent spring.

As an aside, while photographing the disassembly of the Garand for this book, I took the trigger assembly apart. Getting it back together took 20 minutes of struggle and cursing and involved a padded vise mounted on the bench, slave pins, and a sturdy screwdriver to push things my fingers were too fat to push. With modern aerosol degreasers/cleaners, and penetrating lubricants, there's no need to subject yourself to that. And 20 minutes? I knew how to do it, having done it many times. It was more a matter of recalling muscle memory — if you've never done it, be prepared for more time than that and parts hurling themselves across the room. (Again, wear safety glasses!)

OK, set the trigger assembly aside, and return to disassembling the Garand.

Cup the receiver in the palm of your left hand at the rear sight while you pivot the stock down and away from the receiver. The front end of the stock will be hooked into a lip in the steel band at the front of the two handguards. The stock is one piece of walnut, birch or some other hard, sturdy wood. Set the stock aside.

Place the receiver assembly upside down on a padded surface. Look at the front of the receiver parts, and you'll see a bent steel plate with a slot in it, looking like the oil pan protector of an off-road truck. The steel rod protruding into the plate is the recoil spring guide rod, also the actuating rod for the cartridge lifter. The recoil spring is long and strong. To remove it, grasp the guide rod and press it toward the muzzle. But first, pay attention to the cartridge lifter or follower inside the bent plate, visible from the side. On many rifles, due to fit, grease, or just plain cussedness of mechanical devices, when you try to press the recoil spring guide rod toward the muzzle, it won't let go of the follower arm, and the follower moves up and down with it. Use a fingertip to hold the follower arm in place while you move the recoil spring. Once free, ease the spring away from the muzzle (it will be glad to help you in that direction) and pull it free of the op rod.

Now you'll need a small drift punch, but only for pressing. On the front end of the receiver, you'll see a pin. This pin holds the bullet guide (the bent plate) and the follower arm in the assembly. Push the pin out, then pry the bullet guide out (a tight fit in the receiver, at the front end) and the follower arm. The guide rod passes through the operating rod catch's front forks, which can also be lifted out.

Lift the follower out, and you are done with the rifle in this position. Turn the barreled receiver over so the op rod side is up. Look at the rear of the receiver, just under and forward of the rear sight adjustment knob. There is a square-ish notch machined into the guide slot of the op rod. Slide the op rod back to this notch, and lift the rear of the op rod toward the rear sight. It will come free of the guide slot, and you can then weasel it the rest of the way out. Yes, you are flexing the op rod when you do this, but it was designed to work this way.

Now we get to the fiddly, everything-looked-easy-until-now part: getting the bolt out. Ease the bolt forward and tilt the lug that engages the op rod up. You'll have to find the bolt position that allows the lugs and guide ribs to clear and the tail of the firing pin to pass around the safety rib in the receiver. There is no forcing this. Just wiggle it around until you find the orientation that works and get a feel for it. After a few iterations, it will get easier, but at first, you'll be glad no one is watching you.

You now have the various cycling parts of your Garand spread out on the workbench. Let's take a look at some of the more important ones. We'll start with the operating rod because it is a source of mystery and a vital part of the function. Then we'll delve into the gas system.

The op rod was, for the time, one of the most difficult items to manufacture. It's a long hollow rod with a cap of an absolutely precise diameter mounted in its center, and the rod has a bend, plus the extension has more bends. Garand wanted this because he felt the full stroke of a gas system was necessary for proper and reliable function. And it had to be this long because the military experts wanted as little movement of the parts as possible before the bullet left the muzzle. He managed that but, in so doing, crafted a marvel of a gas-operated lever. How much does the op rod move before the bullet exits the muzzle? The government was intensely curious about this, and the subject was tested repeatedly. We're talking single-digit amounts of hundredths of an inch, is how much.

The bends were necessary to get the rod's front-end piston to reach up and over to engage the locking lug on the right side of the bolt and work the mechanism.

The op rod tube is just that, a tube with a piston head silver-soldered on the front and the operating handle welded to the tube. The operating handle could be a forging, but the tube was fabricated as a tube. The welding was critical, but once the method was worked out, they were made by the millions. However, as we've mentioned elsewhere, the initial ones were made with a right angle in the joint or a stress riser, and they can, and did, crack under hard use. The correction was to machine the assembly with a round relief cut, and when Korean War production began, they were made that way from the start. Those wishing to build a period-correct WWII USGI Garand will search out unmodified, original right-angle op rods. The rest of us are happy with the relief-cut ones.

If you want to know whether an op rod was originally made with the relief cut, look at the drawing number. The clue here is drawing D35382 with no revision number and all the drawing numbers with a prefix of 65 or 77. These drawing numbers and revisions had the relief cut from the beginning. Any other drawing number is a pre-relief cut op rod. If it has the relief cut, it has been modified and will serve you well. If it hasn't been relieved, then a WWII retro builder wants it.

A primo op rod has the drawing number 7790722-RA (Remington Arms) or 7790722-SA (Springfield Armory), widely known as the National Match op rod. There was a subtle change to the tube's curve to fit it closer around the barrel. This design was initially intended for and used in building Type 2 National Match rifles at Springfield. As discussed later in the ammunition section, the supply of original op rods was used up in various rebuilds and repairs, so this design was used for many general rebuilds in the 1960s. They even went to Korea and returned as parts or assembled into rifles. It is still the same op rod if it has the correct drawing number but not the "NM" stamp.

A special gauge is used to check the dimensions of operating rods, which was (it may still be) seen at Camp Perry. It simply had all the dimensions located in space, in the gauge, to check an op rod against. Far from being a simple Go/No-Go gauge, it had to be incredibly expensive to produce.

If you want to amuse yourself, the end of the op rod is the gas piston. It is meant to have a close but not binding fit inside the gas cylinder, and the gas piston must measure at least .526 inch and no more than .526 inch. There is also a specification for roundness, but that is beyond any of our capabilities to measure as it is in the ten-thousandths range and not something you can find with even the best digital calipers or micrometers. If your piston measures .525 inch, then it is probably marginal. If it's less than that, it's a wonder your Garand works. If it doesn't work, and this is the problem, the fix is one of two things: either replace the op rod (they are running $120 to $175 right now, more in the future) or find someone who can braze a replacement piston onto your existing rod. You're probably thinking, "Cool, that's got to cost less." Nope. The CMP does a complete rebuild of your op rod for $175. That rebuild, however, includes more than just brazing a new piston onto your rod, so you might well consider it.

Next up, the bolt. The bolt is a solid piece of steel, with the extractor, extractor spring, and extractor plunger assembled and the firing pin passing down the center. You'll notice the lack of two parts you may think necessary: a firing pin retaining pin and a firing pin spring. The extractor is held in a recess machined in the right locking lug. To remove it, you need a disassembly tool. This process needn't be done very often, if at all. The M1 Carbine's extractor spring and plunger, which are similar in design, are not so strong, and you can (with a bit of risk and much struggle) retract the plunger and lift the extractor out. Not so on the Garand. Don't try it. You'll likely mar your rifle with a slipped screwdriver and maybe even injure yourself.

The firing pin does not need a retaining pin because the extractor's pivot shaft does that job. Like the cotter pin on your AR-15, the pivot shaft of the extractor passes through a recess machined on the firing pin and holds the firing pin in place. The bar in the receiver prevents the Garand's firing pin from striking the primer early. (The bar is evident once the parts are out and you turn the barreled receiver over.) Notice the small notch in that crossbar? That's the clearance slot for the firing pin tail. Look at the rear of the bolt, and see the tail protruding down? There's your combo.

When the bolt moves forward, it is tilted, not level, and runs along the receiver's rails. The tilted bolt also means the firing pin tail tilts, and as the bolt closes and rotates, the firing pin tail bears against the crossbar and is prevented from moving forward. Once the bolt has finished closing, the tail aligns with the clearance slot, but since the bolt isn't moving, the firing pin can't strike the primer. But, when the hammer strikes it, the firing pin has clearance and strikes the primer, setting things (literally) in motion.

One of the reasons you want to avoid the various craptastic Garand clones, rebuilds, re-welds and such (Fed Ord, we're looking at you, even though you are long gone) is that the dimensions of this crossbar and the clearance slot machined into it are critical. The crossbar has a slight angled edge to the clearance slot. If this is in the wrong place or at the wrong angle (and it isn't easy to see or measure), your Garand could "slam-fire," that is, discharge just from the bolt closing, as the momentum of the firing pin isn't arrested by the crossbar, and boom, broken rifle. The dimensions of the firing pin are just as important, but being a simple rod with a small tail, controlling the firing pin dimensions was a trivial task for the various makers. But the crossbar, that was tricky.

Let's turn our attention to the cartridge lifter or follower. This part drives the op rod spring and follower rod assembly, lifting the cartridge stack through the clip and presenting them to the bolt for feeding. The follower is a small part, but it's critical to proper feeding. It is, however, quite durable, as I do not recall ever seeing one that needed replacing except for inadvertent damage. You'll notice that the follower has an even smaller component built into it that slides from side to side. This part allows the Garand to use clips loaded either left-top or right-top. Whichever way the bottom-most round is, the slider gets shoved to one side or the other accommodating the clip. As you press the clip down, the slider shifts over. The loaded clip compresses the follower arm assembly into the op rod spring until the clip latch can click over the little nub on the clip.

With the clip in place, the follower can lift the stack and bolt since it was released when the latch clicked onto the nub, driving the top round home. As you fire each round, the bolt unlocks, is driven back, ejects the empty, and drives the next cartridge into the chamber. The follower lifts the stack until the last round is chambered, at which point its job is done. When the last round is fired, the clip latch gets tripped, the clip is unlocked, and when the bolt runs to the rear, the clip is also ejected by the clip ejector spring (cleverly named, eh?) and locks the bolt to the rear. The follower doesn't do anything but lift cartridges.

If you have problems with clips ejecting early, it's likely the nubs on the clip and not the rifle parts causing it. Try a different clip, and your problem will probably be solved.

While we're on the subject of clips and locking and unlocking, you might ask how to get rounds out without cycling each one into and out of the chamber? Simple: pull the charging handle back and hold it to the rear. On the left side of the receiver, you'll see a long, flat bar with a square end. That bar is the clip latch. With the charging handle held back, press the square portion of the clip latch into the receiver, and the clip will be unlatched, ejecting it and the remaining rounds. That's how GIs "topped off" their Garands: by ejecting the remaining few rounds and inserting a fresh clip.

OK, one last look at parts in the receiver area, and we'll consider the trigger assembly. You could spend your entire Garand-shooting career and never take the trigger assembly apart. It doesn't need it, as the parts are exposed when removed from the rifle and easily reached for cleaning. The assembly comes out of the Garand complete, and you can handle it, clean it, lubricate it and reassemble the rifle with it, all without having to take any of it apart or even have the parts in it move.

For all of its apparent complexity, the trigger assembly comprises only eleven parts. That most of these parts do multiple things is a marvel. The trigger design is two-stage, with a built-in lever that permits a first-stage initial pull and a second-stage sear release. The hooks on the top end of the hammer allow the two stages and act as the disconnector to prevent full-auto, or runaway, fire.

When the safety is applied, the cam surface on its edge contacts a boss on the hammer and cams it out of contact with the trigger. You can do this with the trigger assembly out of the rifle and observe the function of the various parts, so spend some time doing so. When the safety is pressed forward, it moves off that boss and returns the hammer hooks to contact with the trigger sear surface. If the safety doesn't move far enough forward, it won't release. It won't make the rifle safe without camming the hammer.

Do not dry fire the trigger housing when it is out of the rifle unless you are restraining the hammer. Letting the hammer fly is an excellent way to damage the trigger housing body. If you want to dry fire it to check the trigger pull or disassemble, put your thumb in front of the hammer and press back on it. Be careful. If you let the hammer fly and your thumb is in the way, it will hurt or even draw blood.

GARAND MALFUNCTIONS & TROUBLESHOOTING

There's good news and bad news regarding troubleshooting and fixing a Garand. The good news is that everything was worked out long ago and can be, in most instances, easily determined and corrected. The bad news is that almost all the people who worked it out back then are gone, most newer firearms experts are not up to speed on the Garand, and when you do know a solution, finding parts, tools and experts to do the work might not be easy or inexpensive.

Every other person you meet at a gun shop is an expert in the AR-15 (some of them are useful), and finding parts and services is as easy as falling off a log. Not so much with the Garand, but they can be found. To start, let's go through the malfunctions the various services and shooters in the past encountered and their fixes. To make it easier, we'll go through them in the sequence of operation: Loading, feeding, chambering, locking, firing, extracting, ejecting, cocking, and add in the Garand-unique one: ejecting the clip.

LOADING MALFUNCTIONS

Loading, here, is defined as inserting the loaded clip into the receiver and locking it in place.

Clip inserts with difficulty — Your clip is worn or bent, replace it.

This is becoming more common, as the original-production clips are now, in some instances, heavily used.

Bullet guide and follower arm binding — This is an "oops, I dropped it" problem most of the time. The bullet guide, the bent flat plate, must be flat. The follower arm, the connector between the op rod and the follower, cannot rub against the bullet guide. The problem here is often not these but the follower rod assembly. The assembly has a fork, and if one side of the fork is bent, missing or chipped, it can fail to lift the follower straight up.

The clip ejector spring is broken — Replace it. A rare item, as the clip ejector spring is a stout length of spring wire. But, if it is messed with when out of the trigger assembly, it can get bent or broken.

Clip latch failure — Here, the clip latch is worn, or the clip latch spring is worn, tired, broken, or missing. Replace the clip latch or its spring, whichever is causing the problem.

Bolt won't release when loaded — Here, the clip is inserted and clicks, locked into place, and the bolt is supposed to go forward, sometimes with a gentle bump. Check lubrication. If the op rod bearing cam is not properly lubed, the op rod will bind while cycling and not be happy about chambering a round. Make sure it has a sufficient amount of the proper grease.

Op rod failure — If the op rod has the bearing radius worn from too much use (or too little lubrication), then your only option is to replace or rebuild it.

The firing pin's tail interacts with the receiver bridge to create a safe bolt closing.

The firing pin tail is also where the hammer strikes.

The extractor is held into the right-hand bolt lug, which is enlarged for this purpose.

On the underside of the bolt, note the end of the extractor pivot pin, which also holds the firing pin and ejector in place.

The firing pin can protrude through the breechface only after fully closing the bolt. That is, if the receiver hasn't been welded back together from pieces. Then, all bets are off.

If the op rod has burrs, debris, or excessive tool marks, it won't go forward without a bump. A replacement rod can have a short radius (someone rebuilt it who wasn't quite up to the task), and it will have to take a trip to the CMP.

FEEDING AND CHAMBERING MALFUNCTIONS

Feeding is defined here as moving out of the clip, and chambering is when the round fully enters the chamber but does not include locking, where the bolt rotates closed.

Failure to feed — This malfunction is almost always from a lack of lubricant. AR-15 owners who have bought into the "gotta run it dry" school of thought (incorrect) will not put enough oil and grease into their Garand. It can also be caused by rusted clips or dirty ammo.

Failure to chamber — Usually another lack of lube-created problem. Also, a dirty chamber or ammunition will cause a failure to chamber and deformed cartridge cases.

Use calipers to measure the firing pin protrusion as you press the tail fully forward. Use the clearance gap on the bolt face to get the calipers onto the bolt face.

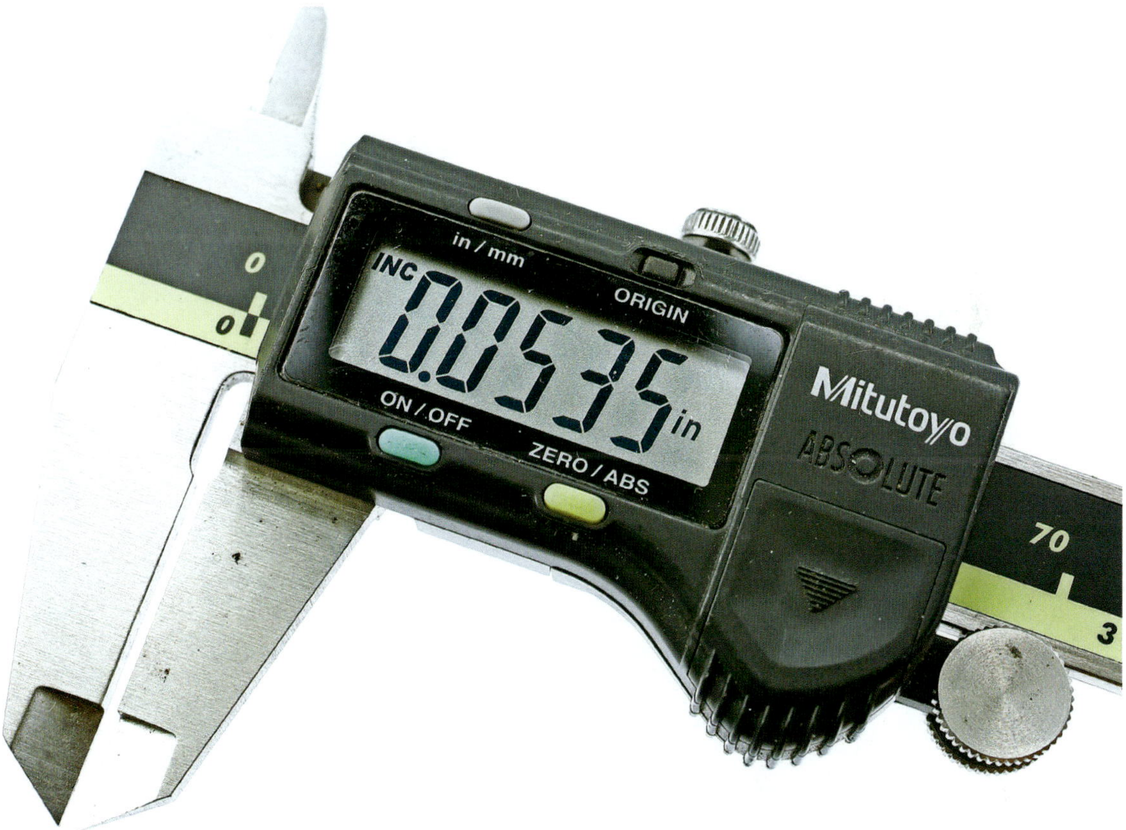

The author's firing pin protrusion measures .0535 inch, nicely within the allowable parameters.

The trigger assembly, with the hammer cocked.

Ease the hammer forward as you press the trigger if (and you need not) you disassemble the trigger housing.

If you want to, this is where you start. The trigger/hammer pin is headed, and this is the large end.

The spring pressure makes it even more difficult once you get it started. (This should be a clue to stop and press it back into place.)

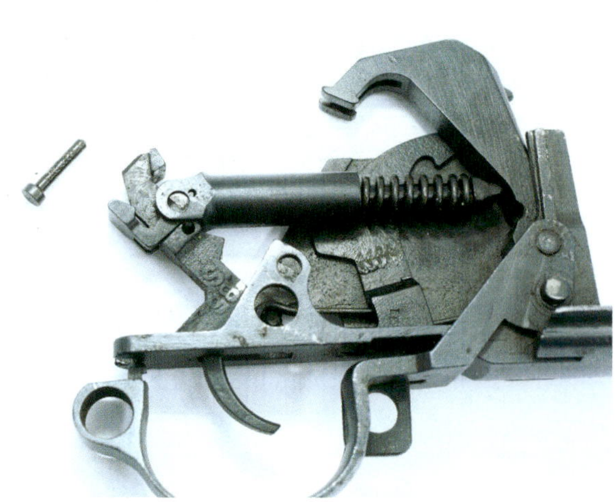

Now you're into it. The spring will push the parts out of alignment. This is where reassembly becomes tricky.

The hammer pin is headed, and this side comes out first.

The safety pivots on a boss, which rides in a hole drilled through the trigger housing plate.

The trigger housing, stripped down to the clip spring. Unless it breaks, there is no need ever to remove this from its place.

The hammer hooks and the trigger hooks as they relate to each other. If your trigger pull is not what you want it to be, do not do anything. Do not stone, polish, "clean up," or otherwise mess with it. Send it to someone who does it for a living and has the correct fixtures. Doing this wrong can mean an inoperative rifle and an expensive parts replacement.

The cam slot in the op rod. This is where you want to apply Lubriplate, Slide Glide, or some other quality grease.

The Lubriplate company still exists and uses the same formula. This is a box of original individual vials of Lubriplate for use by GIs.

The rear of the op rod has lugs that engage the guide slot of the receiver. If these get too worn, they must be rebuilt by welding, machined to spec, and then re-Parkerized.

This op rod was WWII production that was rebuilt by machining the joint to remove the stress riser. You can tell (by the number, for one) by the machine cut being up into the arm of the rod, not just on the joint.

The Garand's gas port is under the gas cylinder. The diameter is ground to a precise dimension, and the port is drilled to an exact size. Don't mess with either. Make sure they're clean, and the port is unobstructed if you ever disassemble to this point.

FAILURE TO LOCK MALFUNCTIONS

Locking is when the bolt rotates into place, and the bolt lugs move firmly and evenly to the bottom of their machined recesses. More lube issues can also be caused by debris in the locking lug recesses, a binding extractor, or an extractor spring frozen in place by corrosion.

Binding op rod — In rare instances, if the op rod has been bent or otherwise damaged, it can bind on the stock or barrel. This is not easy to track down and will require a new op rod or the old one rebuilt.

Insufficient headspace — This is rarer than the binding op rod for a couple of simple reasons: all the bolts you will ever encounter for the Garand will have been made by a real-deal mil-spec manufacturer, so the odds that a bolt has locking lugs-to-bolt-face size to make the chamber too small are minuscule. If your barrel is mil-spec or Criterion, the chamber is the correct size. If you run into this, you will find it is a problem caused by one of two origins. Most likely, your GI parts have been assembled into a non-GI receiver, and the location of the locking lugs (or the receiver face or receiver threads) is wrong. Or, someone spectacularly unskilled replaced the original barrel, and they did something heinous to the parts to "make them fit."

Insufficient headspace is not a home-gunsmithing operation to fix in the Garand. You need a specialist. If the receiver is USGI and has not been re-welded, then the CMP can solve your problem once it figures out the cause. But it might not be pretty or inexpensive.

The right-hand bolt lug has a big slot milled in it for the extractor. That slot also has a hole drilled for the extractor pivot pin, and the extractor holds in the firing pin.

FIRING MALFUNCTIONS

Firing is when you press the trigger, and the rifle discharges.

Hammer falls, but no shot fired — Check the safety. It can still catch and stop the hammer if you have not pressed it fully forward. Dead primers mean your ammo is too old, or your reloading skills need to be improved. If, on extracting the dud round, you find a full impact, then one of those is the problem. If you find a very light strike, you have a binding or defective firing pin.

Firing pin binds — This could be petrified oil in the firing pin channel. The firing pin could be burred, worn, or short. The use of WD-40, in particular, causes problems with firearms. It is meant as a water-displacing oil, not a long-term lubricant. When I was gunsmithing, I saw a regular stream of firearms with binding parts due to the combination of WD40 evaporation, dust, and heat.

If you have light firing pin hits, disassemble your Garand and inspect the firing pin protrusion first. Press the firing pin tail into the bolt, and measure the amount the tip pokes out of the breech face. This check will require calipers. The minimum amount of protrusion you can accept is .044 inch. The maximum is .059 inch. If it's within those limits, you're good. Don't worry if the tip is shiny (it should be round and smooth) because the parkerizing it received back in 1944 has long since worn off. It still works.

If the firing pin tail is burred, it can bind in the slot in the receiver or the bolt. When pressing with your finger to check protrusion, you might not notice it, so inspect the tail closely.

Trigger pressure does not release the hammer — This is often debris in the trigger assembly, binding the trigger or preventing the sear from moving far enough to release the hammer. The few times I had a problem like this come into the shop, the cause was the same; something used to clean the assembly (in one instance, a bristle brush, the other a shop cloth) had left behind pieces of the cleaning tool, and they were blocking the movement of the parts enough to prevent firing.

Slam fire — OK, this one is serious, and probably, if it has happened, has resulted in a damaged or inoperative rifle. The best correction is to make sure it never happens. There are two causes for a slam fire: ammo and receiver.

Disassembling the Garand bolt requires using either the SMP block or the M10 multi-tool. You will not do it with bare hands, a bench vise, and a screwdriver.

The op rod cam slot unlocks the bolt, drives it back when fired, pulls it forward, cams it down, and holds it in place when closing. It needs quality grease, not just some light oil.

The extractor assembled, including the extractor spring and plunger.

If your ammunition has what is known as a high primer, that is, the primer isn't seated to be below flush with the case head, the pressure and friction of the bolt closing can set it off before the bolt closes. The solution and prevention here are to ensure your primers are seated below flush. You can add an extra level of insurance and use only No. 34 mil-spec CCI primers meant for loading military rifles.

The other cause is the receiver, and here it is the small bridge inside the receiver meant to keep the firing pin from moving forward until the bolt is fully closed. If this bridge, and its ramp, have been altered, you have a rifle that probably cannot be fixed. Or, your receiver is not a USGI receiver, and the ramp has been poorly crafted. Assuming any parts on your Garand are still serviceable, the only real solution is to replace the receiver with a good one and install all the parts that will work into it. Then replace the damaged or substandard ones.

If it goes off when fully closed, the rifle cycles more or less normally. If it goes off before fully closing, you can have a broken bolt, peened locking lug recesses, and more.

The solution, or prevention, is to strip your rifle down and assemble it with just the receiver, barrel, bolt, and op rod. Then slowly operate the op rod, moving the bolt, observing the engagement of the firing pin tail to the bridge cam slot, and making sure it can't move forward (by pushing the firing pin with a fingertip) as you hand-cycle the bolt and op rod.

LOCK MALFUNCTIONS

Here, the bolt is rotated by movement of the op rod and lifts the bolt lugs out of the receiver recesses.

Failure to unlock — This is almost always a gas issue. For this, you'll have to be familiar with the bible of gunsmithing, the Brownells catalog. Your gas port could be clogged or corroded. Disassemble the gas cylinder and

The gas cylinder holding wrench is a simple piece of steel or, in this case, aluminum. It keeps you from applying your gas screw unscrewing force into the gas cylinder and potentially loosening it.

The gas screw is an X-slot part, and while you can get away with using a screwdriver, this wrench makes it easier, and you are less likely to mar your Garand.

Left or right? On most Garands, now, it doesn't matter. But for a long time, it did. If yours cares, then make sure you load clips correctly.

Blanks are not all the same. On the left is a grenade-launching blank. It's more powerful than the ceremonial blank in the middle. On the right is an old-style blank with a wooden bullet, which should be kept solely for collecting purposes and never used. (Even wooden bullets go someplace and can injure.)

The Greek M2 Ball that the CMP imported and sold for several years. It is all gone now (gone from the CMP, it is still in basements, garages and gun safes), and you'll have to find or load your own ammo these days.

check. You'll need two drill bits, a #47 and a #46. Use the #47 to clean (do not use a power drill, do this by hand) and then check with the #46. The #46 is too large and should not fit. The gas piston might be too small or the gas cylinder too large. If so, you need an expert's help to either replace the gas cylinder (if too large) or replace the piston with one larger to fit the cylinder properly. The gas piston must be no smaller than .525 inch. The gas cylinder can be a max of .531 inch on the inner diameter. (Some say .532 inch, but I'm not comfortable with that. Measuring the ID of the cylinder isn't an easy task.)

Your gas cylinder lock screw could be loose and leaking gas, but this is an easy check.

You could lack lubricant on the op rod cam slot, or your chamber or ammunition could be dirty or corroded. (You'd be surprised what people try to use for ammo.)

EXTRACTION MALFUNCTIONS

OK, your rifle is cycling the bolt to the rear. The empty brass is supposed to be extracted before being ejected. If it doesn't, the solution depends on the nature of the problem.

Brass remains in the chamber, but the rim isn't broken off — This is usually caused by an extractor that lacks tension or has a broken lip. The solution is simple: Unload, use a cleaning rod to punch the empty out, then disassemble your Garand. Remove the extractor, and replace it if chipped or worn. Replace the spring and plunger if the extractor is good.

The brass remains in the chamber, and the rim has the extractor portion broken off — This indicates that your chamber is dirty or pitted or your ammunition is dirty or corroded. Dirty or corroded ammo or a dirty chamber is an easy fix; clean things up. Use good ammunition. If the problem is a pitted chamber, the only solution (and I mean the only solution, do not think of "polishing" your chamber) is a new barrel.

EJECTION MALFUNCTIONS

In this step, the empty brass is hurled away. It is distinct from extraction in that ejection is powered by the spring-loaded ejector that runs in a tunnel in the bolt.

Failure to eject — This is almost always the ejector's fault. It's binding in the bolt, the spring is wedged (petrified oil or grease can do this), or the ejector is broken. The solution is to disassemble the bolt (the extractor shaft holds in the firing pin and the ejector), scrub, lube, and reassemble.

In rare instances, you can have a short stroke, which was quite the subject of AR-15 interest for many years. Short strokes are almost all the same as unlocking problems: improper gas flow.

Op rod disassembly — If the operating rod is seriously worn, it can "jump the tracks" and come out of the receiver when fired. This will sometimes cause failure to unlock, but usually, it's enough to unlock but not cycle far enough to eject. The only solution is to rebuild or replace the op rod. Putting a rebuilt op rod back into the rifle with a tired or broken spring will wear the op rod out of spec in short order.

This Springfield has the rear sight set to two index lines right of center. Is it zeroed? There's only one way to find out: get to the range with some ammo and a solid rest.

Spring length should be no less than 19 inches and no more than 20.25 inches. Replacing the original with a newly made spring is not a bad idea for many rifles.

COCKING MALFUNCTIONS

The bolt cycling back has multiple tasks to perform. In addition to extracting and ejecting the empty, it must also cock the hammer for the next round. If it fails to cock the hammer, this is usually a result of short stroking, so see above. To figure out if it is a short-stroke problem, ask yourself this question: does working (hand-cycling) the charging handle cause the bolt to cock the hammer, and does the hammer stay cocked. If so, then it is likely a short-stroke problem.

However, you may (in rare instances) find that you have a "dead trigger" when you try to fire a round. What has happened is that the hammer has failed to stay cocked and has ridden the bolt forward, now resting on the back of the bolt. If so, you'll feel that you have to cock the hammer when you go to retract the charging handle. Once you get the bolt open and feel the force needed, heave a sigh of relief. If you have a high, non-flush primer, a sensitive primer, or an excessively long firing pin, the hammer riding the bolt down could have caused it to fire when closing, probably prematurely. You would have had a two-shot burst or more if it had fully closed.

The trigger is driven by the same spring that runs the hammer, so it is not likely that the spring is the problem. You probably have some previous owner's attempt at "improving" the trigger pull by stoning, filing, or polishing the engagement surfaces — or shortening the hooks. The solution is a new trigger. Well, new-old-stock trigger that hasn't been used before. Or, you could send it to a specialist who can replace and tune the trigger. Yes, the Garand was made to have complete interchangeability, but these are 75-year-old rifles, and the parts may have literally been around the world.

I TEND TOWARD "JUST ENOUGH" LUBE IN MY GARANDS, UNLIKE MY AR-15S. IN THE AR, YOU MUST DEAL WITH HEAT AND GAS PRESSURE BLOWING OFF THE LUBE AND DRYING THE PARTS — BOLT, CARRIER, AND FIRING MECHANISM. IN THE GARAND, WHAT YOU HAVE IS PRESSURE RUBBING THE LUBE OFF.

EJECT CLIP MALFUNCTIONS

When the last round has been fired, the empty is extracted and ejected, and the now-empty clip is also ejected. Yes, the famous "ping" heard 'round the world.

Failure to eject the clip if the clip is unlatched but not ejected or ejects feebly — First, check all the usual sources, and ones we've discussed to this point: faulty ammo, lack of lubrication, carbon fouling. If any of these are present, they have likely caused other problems, so don't dive into "solving" the clip ejection failure until you've solved the other, more straightforward problems with a thorough cleaning, lube, and proper ammo.

If you've solved all those issues (or ruled them out), then inspect the clip ejector spring. Is it there? Is it intact? Is it free to move and not bind? Is it misassembled, frozen by rust, or some other problem? Next, look at the operating rod catch. This is the one with the curved arm. It may be binding (an internal toggle must be free to move), bent, or broken. Look at the clip latch (the external bar alongside the receiver). If this part is frozen by rust or debris or the spring is bound and can't move, it can interfere with the clip ejection.

Clip ejects prematurely — This is most often a clip problem. Small nubs hold in the clip on the rear; if worn, they won't hold. The clip latch gets a prominent mention here, as well. If the clip latch spring is weak, it lets go too soon. It won't retain the clip if the latch tip is worn, chipped, or missing.

You've undoubtedly heard about "bent op rods" from using the wrong ammo. The problem can be more subtle

While the Marine on the right is firing, the one on the left is loading in the usual Garand manner. Note that the one firing has a Japanese Nambu holster. A close examination of the photo also shows that the 1911 in his holster has something wrapped around the grips, perhaps an attempt at waterproofing his pistol.

and common because the follow rod is more likely to get bent with the wrong ammo. It is a smaller-diameter steel part than the op rod, and if it gets hammered back by a strong impulse, it can get bent, or its fork ends broken off. If that happens, it throws the timing off, and the clip quits its work too soon.

GAS CYLINDER

OK, now that we've seen all the ways the Garand can go wrong, and having told you many times to measure and clean things, let's get to the gas cylinder.

The gas cylinder is easy with all the other parts off of your Garand. You'll need a gas cylinder wrench or a big screwdriver that fits the opening. (Don't be shy about grinding a cheap big-box screwdriver to fit. Your Garand gas cylinder screw will thank you for it.) Unscrew the gas cylinder screw (aka gas plug) and remove it. This might take some wrestling, as the screw gets hammered by gas pressure every time you fire and can be carbon-locked. If it doesn't go at the first attempt, apply some penetrating oil to the edge of the screw where it bears against the gas cylinder lock, and let it penetrate.

The gas cylinder and its various parts are a snug fit to the barrel. If they move, the front sight on top of the cylinder can move, affecting accuracy. Also, if the front handguard presses on or binds against the barrel, it can harm accuracy. For these reasons, those interested in an easier takedown and maintaining proper fit and accuracy will have a special wrench that holds the gas cylinder lock while unscrewing the gas cylinder screw. If you're inter-

The gas cylinder, gas screw, and gas lock are ahead of the stock and handguards. Note the front sight, on its dovetail, clamped in place.

One of the bar sights, the original modification to keep the sight tight after adjusting.

ested in "minute of plinking" accuracy, you don't need to be that OCD, but you should exercise some care to avoid loosening the fit.

Once you break it loose, it simply unscrews and comes out as a single item.

GAS CYLINDER SCREW HISTORY

The first gas cylinder screws were threaded plugs to hold everything together and seal the front end of the gas cylinder. The first one, the simple plug, has a slot, not a cross, on the front face. Like the rest of the gas cylinder and lock, it's made of stainless steel. It was first given drawing number B147428, but you won't find that stamped anywhere. The part is too small to take a drawing number, and the Armory gave up on marking all the parts, even the smallest, early on.

These worked fine until the idea of rifle grenades became a thing. The grenade launcher fits over the Garand's muzzle and locks into the gas plug opening and the bayonet lug. The gas pressure of a grenade blank was over-driving the op rod and bolt, causing problems. So, the idea of a valve was implemented. This is the Type 2; its drawing number is B147851, again, not marked. The grenade launcher stud would open the valve, bleeding off excess gas. The second iteration of that design, the Type 3, also known as the one with the "poppet" valve, used a spring to return the valve to the closed position when the launcher was removed. Type 2 and 3 gas plugs have a cross opening on the front face, and Type 3 have a "P" stamped on their face with drawing number B7310079. If the drawings were numbered in the order they were adopted, there was much changing going on from the 1 to the 2, and then the 3.

Why the spring? In Type 2, if you used a grenade launcher and removed it, the valve would stay open until you fired the next round. With Type 3, it closed on its own. You keep it clean by pushing the valve down with a punch and dropping some oil into it to allow it to move if it needs to or when you go launching grenades. (Yes, a bit of tongue in cheek there.)

The gas screw is a detail that period builders need to know. Springfield Armory used Type 1 and Type 2 through most of the war, but by January 1944, all the gas screws it made and assembled on rifles were Type

3 — except for Winchester, which made the Type 1 to the end of the war, not switching over to Type 3 until 1945. All Korean-era Garands have Type 3 gas screws installed when manufactured.

Replacement gas cylinder screws, like the Schuster, are designed to let you shoot non-GI ammunition in your Garand with relative impunity. I've never used one for a simple reason: I have plenty of other rifles I can use that ammunition in, and when I shoot my Garands, I'm happy shooting GI or GI-spec ammo through them.

Next up, the gas cylinder lock. The gas screw was threaded into the gas cylinder lock and projected far enough into the assembly to engage the front edge of the gas cylinder. The gas cylinder lock is threaded on the barrel. The screw, poking through the lock into the cylinder, kept the lock from unscrewing. Once the screw is out, the lock should unscrew with finger pressure.

This leaves the gas cylinder, which also has the bayonet lug as an integral part, and the stacking swivel and front sight attached. "Stacking swivel?" you ask. Yes, out in the field, where there are no rifle racks, the military had to figure out a way to neatly arrange rifles when the troops were busy with non-rifle work. You know, digging ditches, latrines, trenches, unloading wagons or trucks, eating, showering, etc. (In combat, there is no putting down a rifle if it's your primary weapon. If you need to, you put it down to service the crew-served weapon you are working, but sometimes not even then. It stays slung on your person.)

The stacking swivel was a way of standing up three rifles in a tripod, hooked at the stacking swivels, and keeping them off the ground. For our purposes, it is about as useless an item as you can imagine, but since it's part of the original design, you leave it on.

The front sight is fitted onto a dovetail on the gas cylinder and has a screw at the back to tighten it. The screw does not bear on the gas cylinder; when you tighten it, it pinches the front sight base down tightly onto the

The clip latch on the left side of the receiver. This allows you to unload the Garand without running each round through the chamber. To unload, put the safety on Safe, pull the charging handle back, and press the clip latch. The clip and all remaining rounds will ping out of the receiver. Note that this clip latch is a Beretta part, as denoted by the "PB" stamp.

The Garand's gas cylinder (and the other gas parts) is made of stainless steel. This means it can become shiny with use and wear. Sometime in the past, someone tried to paint it to keep this one black.

Using a grenade launcher on a Garand was hard on the rifle. The Type 2 and later Type 3 gas screw eased that gas spike, but in WWII, most rifle grenades were launched from Springfield '03s.

Feb. 20, 1945. J. C. GARAND 2,369,669

GAS REGULATOR FOR FIREARMS

Filed Aug. 3, 1942

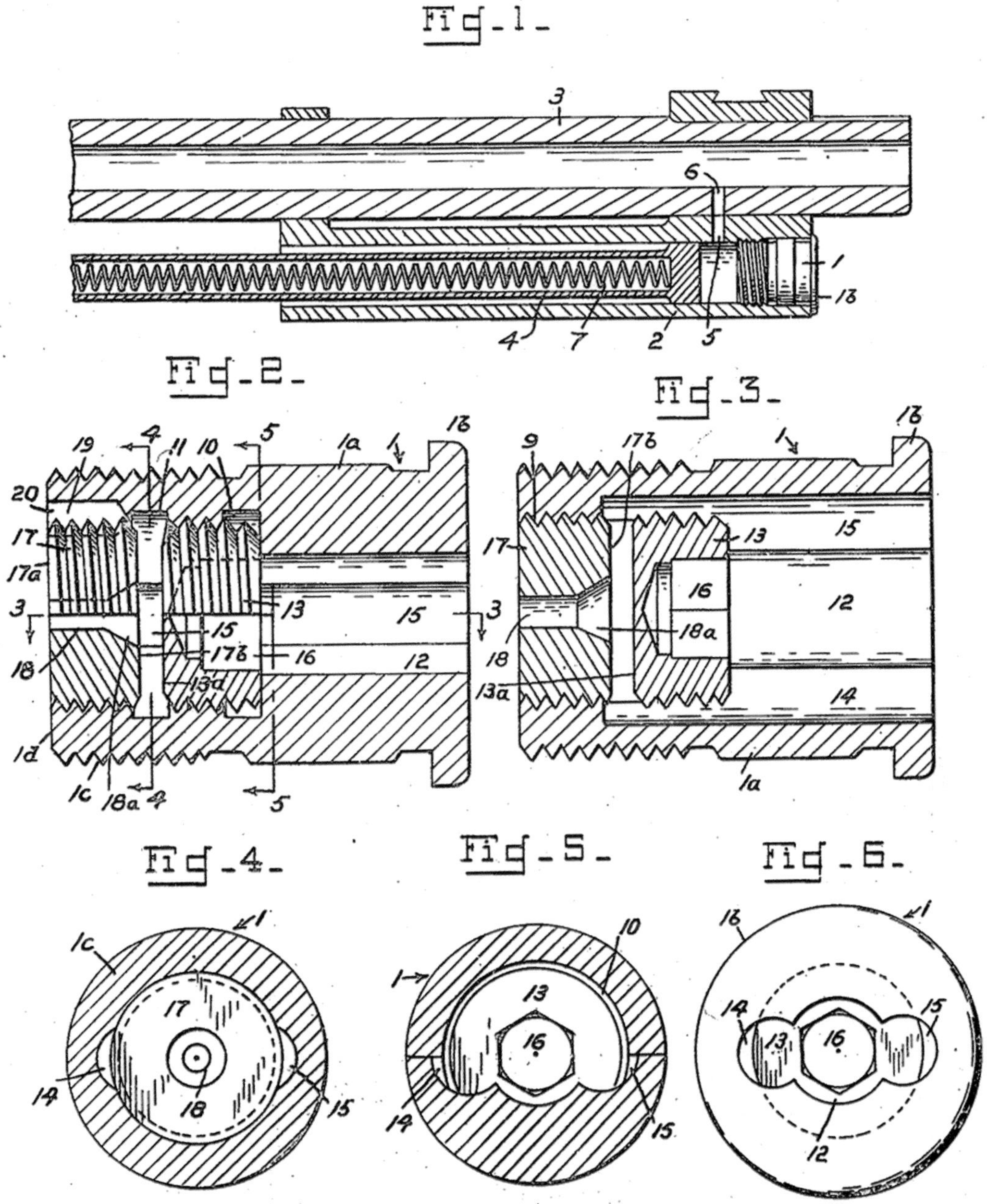

Inventor

John C. Garand

By G. J. Kessenich & J. H. Church

Attorneys

dovetail. I do not recall ever seeing a loose front sight on a Garand, so as simple as the system seems to be, it does the job.

GAS CYLINDER

Before we remove the gas cylinder, note that you can clean it without removing it. It is stainless steel and won't need much cleaning anyway, but it does not have to come off unless you feel the need. Doing so will wear the fit and introduce slight accuracy loss.

Again, the gas cylinder is stainless steel along with its parts, unlike the rest of the Garand, which is made of carbon steel, also known as ordnance steel. This protected the gas cylinder since it would receive a blast of salt-laden hot gas on every shot fired. The bore could be cleaned with a bore solvent, dissolving the residue. The piston on the head of the op rod could be scoured since it was fully exposed once out of the rifle. But the gas cylinder was too large to provide a bore-brush-like brush, and patches would not have scrubbed the interior clean. So, stainless it was. This was possible because stainless alloys had been developed in the earlier decades of the 20th century and thus were available. Since the gas cylinder didn't receive any impact, it didn't have to be as hard as other parts of the Garand, like the bolt or receiver. But it did have to stand up to the harsh conditions the gas system doled out.

This did lead to problems. Stainless is shiny. That's why they call it "stainless." But a shiny part on a rifle used in combat is not a desirable thing. So the manufacturers applied a darkening finish to the gas cylinder, a process called DuLite. That finish, however, didn't last in use. Unlike Parkerizing — the durable phosphorous finish applied to the other parts — the blackening of the gas cylinder would rub off in use and cleaning. GIs would use whatever they had to knock back the shine. Later, they might even be given a coating of black paint.

What to do if yours is shiny? Leave it alone. That is part of being 75 years old, and having gone around the world, maybe a couple of times. If you really must have it looking "like new," not shiny, then Garand specialists can apply the old finish or something close to it. Me, I'd leave it be.

Removing the gas cylinder, if you want to, may require some effort. The barrel has three shallow, sharp-edged slots milled along its axis on the exterior. The gas cylinder has tabs that match these slots, called splines. It is supposed to be a snug fit, but someone may have peened it to fit tighter. To remove it, you would usually slide it forward, off of the barrel. If it is carbon-locked or has been peened, you may need to gently tap it with a plastic-faced mallet to encourage it off. Once off, you can give it a good scrubbing with a bore brush once you

Photo: CMP Archives

find one close enough to the gas cylinder's inner diameter. What would that be? A Go gauge is a nominal .528 inch, and a No-Go is .532 inch. An Internet search will come up with a 28-gauge bore brush, which should clean a .550-inch bore, meaning it will be a tight fit, but it will scrub the interior.

Peened? How?

The gas cylinder tabs slide in the slots on the barrel. If they're too loose, the gas cylinder will wobble. A few thousandths of an inch wobble is not likely to cause a malfunction, but it will cause a loss of accuracy. A quick calculation using the law of equal triangles tells us that a thousandth of an inch of movement of the front sight (attached to the gas cylinder) translates to a shift of a tenth of an inch. No big deal, you say? Tell that to someone who lost a match because their "X" count at 600 yards wasn't high enough. At 600 yards, that thousandth translates to three-quarters of an inch, and the X ring on the 600-yard target is six inches across. No one in competition would want to give up three-quarters of an inch before they even started.

That's why yours might be tight.

To peen it, take a flat-faced punch and a hammer and strike (gently, it is difficult to undo too much) the edge of the slot to knock some steel into the slot and tighten the fit. Should you? I'm not sure it matters unless you depend on your X-count to win, so I'd leave well enough alone.

FURTHER DISASSEMBLY

Do you need to remove more parts? Heck, did you even need to take the gas cylinder off? This is when you can remove the handguards, but unless you have to deal with rust under them or repair or refinish the wood, there's no need. But here you go.

The front handguard slides off of the barrel. The rear handguard has a pin holding it in place, driven through the lower band and along a groove machined in the barrel. Drive out this pin. It may be solid, or it may be a roll pin, and it may be peened on one side. If peened, drive from the non-peened end. A solid or roll pin may require a special drift punch to fit. Use the proper one, as knarfing the pin and the band can take time and money to fix. Once the pin is out, tap the band toward the muzzle to move it off its boss on the barrel. The rear handguard is also clipped to the barrel. A spring steel clip bent to fit over the handguard slides in two barrel grooves. The clip should never be removed. Removing the rear handguard is not easy, as the fit can be tight, and the wood is thin. If you crack it, it will be challenging to repair or replace.

REASSEMBLY AND LUBRICATION

If you carefully read the malfunctions section, you will repeatedly find that the cause is a lack of lubrication or uncleaned fouling. You did all this disassembly to remove the gunk, fouling, dirt, debris and perhaps even some rust. Now you must put it back together and adequately lubricate it.

Remember that if the Parkerizing has been rubbed bright and you can see steel underneath, that is a point or area that needs oil to reduce friction and protect the surface from corrosion. All surfaces should be wiped down with an oily cloth. If you used a degreaser to scour something clean, the entire surface of whatever you cleaned must be re-oiled.

PARKERIZING

Parkerizing is a proprietary process involving a hot soup of acid, dissolved zinc, manganese phosphate, and various chemicals to allow the process to happen. The steel is coated with a thin, hard, sponge-like zinc or manganese phosphate layer. (It can only be applied to ferrous alloys, not stainless or other metals.) While Parkerizing offers abrasion and some corrosion resistance, it adds corrosion resistance when the sponge-like structure is filled with oil or grease.

When you use a chemical degreaser on your Parkerized part, you have removed that protection and changed the appearance. The various hues of green you see are the oxidized oils in the Parkerized layer. You must re-oil the Parkerized surface to produce the expected corrosion resistance and lube the bright spots.

ASSEMBLY AND LUBE

If you took the handguards off, put them back. Wipe the bright ring around the barrel at the gas port clean. Place a drop of oil on it and spread it around the barrel band. Slide the gas cylinder on and ensure it snugs in place and aligns with the handguards.

Place a drop of oil on the gas cylinder lock threads of the barrel, and screw the lock into place. Put oil on the gas cap screw, and screw it into place.

Put a drop of oil down the bolt's firing pin hole and into the extractor gap to lube the extractor plunger and spring. Turn the bolt over and squeeze a drop of oil into the firing pin channel. Now it's time to learn the Garand bolt mamba. The Garand bolt's firing pin tail must pass through the bridge slot while the tilted bolt fits into the receiver opening; it then gets laid down on top of the receiver rails, where it rides when cycling. You'll feel the firing pin pass by the bridge, and then you can push back and lay the bolt down onto its rails. This process cannot be described in terms such as "at this angle, go this distance, then," but must be learned by feel. There's no way around it other than simply doing it enough times to learn the feel when the angles are correct. If you have to force it, you are doing it wrong.

With the bolt in place, take up the op rod without the recoil spring. You need to do more than just oil at this point.

One detail 1930s-era firearm designers were concerned with was lubrication in adverse conditions. In particular, rain. Rain washes off lubricant, and there was even a test to see how resistant grease (yes, we will be using grease) was to rain. The test, like all government standards, has a title. This one is MIL-G-46003, Water Spray Test. It involved the greased rifle being exposed to a "rainfall" of 24 inches per hour, plus or minus three inches, for five minutes at a time, bolt open or closed and loaded. And it was test fired or inspected every five minutes during the testing. The test involved just over an hour and a half of heavy rain and 500 rounds of firing, which I'd not want to be exposed to. (Neither the rain nor the need to fire 500 rounds of .30-06 in 90 minutes.) But then again, recall WWII: GIs in the jungle of Guadalcanal, New Guinea, Burma, or other places might be out in the rain that heavy for longer than an hour and a half. And they'd have to fight while it was raining.

Not that the testers were thinking of precisely those places, but some may have been stationed in the Philippines, and it also rains hard there.

So, it required good, water-resistant grease. The result was Lubriplate 130A, which you can buy now at Brownells, but when I was running a Garand, it was a standard automotive store item. It was so good that the auto companies used it and, as a result, the last tube I bought cost me a couple of bucks. If you aren't planning on spending your time shooting in a tropical downpour, you can use pretty much any brand-name medium-weight grease. Check the label. You are looking for something that stands up to pressure. You needn't worry so much about the heat, but the cam slot on the op rod is subjected to a great deal of pressure as it works.

One modern grease I have found very useful is offered by an old shooting competitor and friend, Brian Enos. His Slide-Glide works just fine, but I have to admit I haven't subjected it to a heavy rain test —just the lots of shooting test.

You want the cam slot on the op rod to have an even layer of grease. Don't pack it with grease; the excess will splatter you as it flies out during cycling. Use just enough to cover the engagement surfaces with a light, even layer. Then, a light layer along the slot in which the op rod rides. Apply this with a Q-tip, and you don't need much.

Once greased, run the front end of the op rod into the gas cylinder at a shallow angle, and line it up with the clearance notch on the right rail of the receiver. Ease the bolt back until its right-hand lug is aligned with the cam slot, and then press the op rod over onto the lug and down into the slot. This, too, is a "Do it until you learn the feel" operation. With the bolt caught by the op rod and the rod and bolt running smoothly in the receiver, turn the Garand over and rest it on its sights.

Next up, the operating rod catch, which triggers the clip ejection. With the muzzle to the right and the Garand resting on its sight, the catch's dogleg will be nearer to you. Weasel it down into the receiver, and hook the dogleg over (under, from your perspective) the clip latch tab. The bullet guide is next, and it is a press fit. Its front end must go under (from your perspective) the catch, as the catch rests in the receiver. Tilt it back and press it into the receiver leg. It is a press fit, so you will have to push on it.

With the bolt forward, slide the follower down into the receiver, with the follower slide (the part that moves side-to-side) down toward the bolt. Take the follower arm and get ready for some fiddling and juggling. The follower arm has a long leg with a crossbar, which goes into the grooves in the follower. This must happen while the angled part, with its two legs, is up toward you. Meanwhile, the short end, with the two holes in it, is toward the muzzle and down, away from you. And this must happen while you turn it sideways and poke it through the slot in the bullet guide. This will sound familiar, but once you learn the feel for it ... yes, you'll do it easily in the future.

Now, all these parts are just sitting there. Take the follower arm pin and push it through the receiver legs, the catch, and the follower arm. It may be easier to line things up if you take the spring tension off the catch by depressing the clip latch on the outside of the receiver. I've not had a problem since about five minutes after the first time I reassembled a Garand, but people learn differently. The pin goes in from the right side, the side presently away from you, in the receiver.

OK, time to lube all these parts. Put oil on all the contact points of the parts you just installed. Yes, you could do that before you assemble, but that makes assembly more difficult. I prefer to use a fine point or needle-like spout and put a drop where needed after the receiver parts have been assembled.

Last up, the op rod spring and follower arm.

If this is a new rifle, measure the free length of the spring. The starting point is 20.25 inches and gets shorter as it wears or tires. Once it hits 19 inches, it is done. Replacements, either original (or better) newly made, should be measured before installing, just to be sure. Check the installation of the follower rod into the spring. The follower rod should be stuffed into the spring right up to the rod's shoulder, which is the stopping point. The spring is wound to be smaller on one end than the other, and the smaller end is meant to be tight enough not to come off the follower rod unless you pull it off.

Once everything is correct, lightly oil the spring on its entire length. This raises the question: Do you ever need to clean the hollow op rod? In everyday use, no. You might want to if you have fallen into the water or your Garand has been buried in the dirt or sand. If you decide to try cleaning it, be warned: if you get anything stuck in there or what you are using comes off the cleaning rod, it will be hell to get it out.

You're in for another "getting a feel for things" session here. If the op rod is not in the fully forward position, then slide it there. Slide the open end of the spring into the opening in the op rod, and push it completely in. Use the follower rod to compress the spring, then push it into the receiver through the bullet guide slot. The follower rod must be oriented so the arm with the hooks is farther from the barrel than the section inserted into the spring. Hook the fork end of the follower rod over the two studs on the follower arm. Note that the arm rides too low to make this easy, so poke a fingertip in from the side through the gap in the bullet guide, and lift the follower arm enough to let the follower rod hooks connect. Then ease it all to rest.

OK, the receiver group is assembled. Holding the receiver group in one hand, pick up the stock and hook the stock's front end inside the lower band's lip. Pivot the stock up to the receiver and press the receiver legs down into the milled gap in the stock. If the fit is proper, it will take a bit of pushing. Some might be so loose that it just falls together.

For the trigger group, be sure the triggerguard is fully hinged open. Use oil on all the bearing points and bright spots here as well. On the sides of the trigger housing, you will see vertical ribs behind the bottom plate. These ribs slide into the slots milled in the receiver legs. Press the trigger group fully into the stock until the trigger group plate is flush with the stock. Close the triggerguard. The triggerguard has a set of hooks that cam over the bottoms of the receiver legs, clamping the assembly together. The stock is clamped between the receiver and trigger housing, and this design needs no screws.

GREASE-US MAXIMUS

If you delve into the literature, you'll find many who advocate lots and lots of grease in many locations. OK, I can understand that. If you're attempting to duplicate the lubrication that a GI in a tropical environment or in Europe where he won't be able to do much in the way of maintenance (rifle or personal) in the next week or two needs, yes, grease up everything that moves.

You'll also splatter yourself with lots of the stuff (heated) when you shoot.

Conversely, you'll hear AK adherents who brag about their rifle working even if it isn't lubricated. I'm not a Neanderthal (with apologies to Neanderthals), so I use modern lubricants. And that's the clue, modern lubricants. Modern lubricants can do as much as you need for a day's shooting, then cleaning and back in the rack. Any brand name CLP, synthetic, or anything made for automotive use will serve you well.

I tend toward "just enough" lube in my Garands, unlike my AR-15s. In the AR, you must deal with heat and gas pressure blowing off the lube and drying the parts — bolt, carrier, and firing mechanism. In the Garand, what you have is pressure rubbing the lube off. Well, CLP won't be rubbed off by the movement of Garand parts.

Now, if you want to track down a tub or tube of Lubriplate 130A, and slop the grease into your Garand according to the boot camp instructions of 1944, go for it. Your rifle will not suffer, and you will have one that works just fine. You'll also find your shooting glasses and clothes splattered with grease, which might not be so satisfying.

As I've said many times before: This is America. You get to choose.

FUNCTION CHECK

OK, you've put your Garand back together but want to ensure it works properly. Short of firing it, of course, which is likely something that will get you in trouble if not done at the range or gun club.

You can check with your bare hands, but a clip and eight dummy rounds provide a much better test.

Ease the bolt back far enough to ensure no round is in the chamber. (I know, you just put it back together, the chances of a round in the chamber are below minuscule, but it is a Very Good Habit to cultivate.) Ease the bolt closed, which is the first test. The bolt should close fully and smoothly and not need assistance.

Press the Safety back to Safe. With the muzzle in a safe direction, press the trigger. Apply about 10 pounds of pressure. You don't need more, but you want to ensure the Safety holds more than just the normal trigger pressure needed to fire. If the hammer falls, your safety is not in spec, and you'll need to do some trigger housing surgery to find out why.

Push the safety to Fire. The hammer must stay cocked. Again, if the hammer falls, your safety is out-of-spec (or perhaps, your hammer, a less expensive part to replace, if more difficult to source) and must be repaired or replaced.

The next step requires both hands and some care, so a cleaning cradle might be a good idea. Press the trigger to dry fire your Garand. Hold the trigger back, and pull the charging handle back. While still holding the trigger back, use your left hand to press the follower down into the receiver until the charging handle unlatches. (You'll have to also use your left hand to retrain the bolt and charging handle, or else it will try to chamber some part of your hand. That usually hurts.)

Ease the bolt forward, and then let up on the trigger. The hammer should hold.

Press the safety to Safe.

I don't mean to alarm you, as most Garands will easily pass this test. But if yours doesn't, you want to know before you load it up at the range.

RANGE TIME, ZERO THE SIGHTS

The Garand has the best adjustable sight system ever developed on a battle rifle in any period. Nothing comes close. And, you will likely have to put in a minimal amount of effort to get yours spot-on. But when you go to the range, you'll want to know how this is done.

Let's start up front with the front sight. The front sight is riding in a dovetail cross slot, and the locking screw pinches it tight to the dovetail. The front sight should be centered on the gas cylinder base it rides on. That's how it was designed and, in all likelihood, where it is now. If it is off-center, be suspicious. Look at the rear sight. You'll see a row of vertical lines forged into the receiver. These are your centerline indexes. The rear sight should be at or near the center-most of these lines.

The starting point is "mechanical zero." Begin at the 25-yard line. Here, the front sight is centered on the base, and the rear sight is on the center index mark. Crank the rear sight down until it stops, then come up eight clicks. Shoot a group, three to five rounds. If the group is on-center on the 25-yard target (don't worry about vertical yet), you're on your way. Set a target at 50 or 100 yards, and fire another group. You will likely find that your 100-yard group is still several inches left or right. Again, using the law of equal triangles, a quarter-inch offset at 25 yards translates to a full inch at 100. If your group center estimation is off half an inch at 25, you'll be two inches off at 100.

Here's the tricky part: Loosen and adjust the front sight. I've seen the advice of using a China marker, pencil, or other methods to indicate location, then loosening and adjusting the front sight by eye. I have a different approach: dial calipers. Find a hard, flat, even surface you can use as an index. This can be as simple as laying your Garand (unloaded) on a flat bench. Measure the distance from the surface to the side of the front sight. OK, time for a bit of arithmetic. The sight radius of the M1 Garand is 28 inches. One-hundred yards is also 3,600 inches, so with a little division, we come up with a change of .007 inch in the front sight, which will effect a shift of one full inch at 100 yards.

To move your group, shift the front sight in the opposite direction you want the group to go. If you want to move your group to the left, shift the front sight to the right, and vice-versa. Each inch requires .007 inch of shift, so write down the sight's location, loosen, move, tighten, re-measure, and repeat until it is where you want it. Then shoot another group. You may have to do this a few times, but tighten the sight-locking screw and leave it once it is done. Pro tip: Use a dab of paint on the screw head (something unobtrusive) to keep it locked in place. Even so, I haven't seen sights come loose once properly tightened.

Once zeroed for windage, it's time to do elevation. There, your choices are many. Adjust the rear sight using

Photo: CMP Archives

clicks if you want a 100-yard zero for plinking and having fun. Each click is 1 MOA, meaning that at 100 yards, a click is roughly an inch, while at 200 yards, a click is two inches, etc.

Get your windage nailed down and adjust the elevation by however many clicks it takes to be spot-on at 100. Once that's done, loosen the rear sight adjustment knob (or locking bar), and once the adjustment knob moves without changing the sight setting (that is, it doesn't "click" when you rotate the knob), adjust it to the "1" setting and lock it down. You are now zeroed, and you have a reference point.

For just having fun shooting, you are set. If you should go to a competition and need to adjust for distance, the distance markings on the sight itself will get you very close, assuming you're using ammunition with the same trajectory as the sight was designed for. You'll be afforded a "sighter" shot or two in competitions to ensure you are at your actual distance value.

The rule of thumb for adjustments for added range, called "come-ups," once you have a solid windage and 100-yard elevation are:

- 200 yards, add two clicks to the 100
- 300 yards, add five clicks to the 100 (so, plus three from the 200)
- 600 yards, add 11 clicks to the 100

Now, every rifle is different from the initial zero. You may find that eight clicks up on one Garand puts you almost off the paper at 25, and with another, zero clicks up is dead-on at 100. Go with what your particular rifle wants and needs when starting. Then, it will be a lot more consistent. For example, almost regardless of what hoops you had to go through to get your 100-yard zero, you will find that one or two clicks will get you on-center when going to 200 yards.

Jumping to 600 is much more uncertain because it depends more on the particular bullet (its BC is the big thing here) and the velocity you are pushing it. You could have two identical rifles and find that one only needs nine clicks to get to a 600-yard zero, but the other takes 12. Or, your buddy runs a higher-BC bullet at a higher velocity than you do, and he only needs nine clicks up, while you need 12.

That's why you practice and keep a shooting log, to know what you need at what distance.

CLEANING THE GARAND

Once you are done shooting and back home, it is time to do your cleaning. Yes, you can be a slacker and do it "next time," but inevitably, "next time" gets shifted into "never," and then one day, you realize you haven't done it since "I can't remember" and now it becomes a great big hassle and task.

The Garand cannot be cleaned like the AR or the AK. Since the rear of the receiver is solid, there's no shoving a cleaning rod down the bore. This means one of two things: a rod guide that fits over the muzzle or a pull cable system. Do yourself a favor and spring for an Otis cable system in .30 caliber.

With the assembled rifle in a cleaning cradle, lock the action open. (If you don't have a cleaning cradle, lock the action open and lay the rifle down on the left side, with the charging handle sticking up.) Install a patch on the end of the Otis cable, and poke the weighted end down the bore. Shove it until you can see it poking out of the muzzle. Pull the cable until the patch gets to the chamber. Then (and only then) apply bore solvent to the patch. You won't need much. Pull the cable out of the muzzle, pulling the patch the length of the bore.

Now scrub the chamber with a chamber brush meant for the Garand or M14/M1A. It won't take much, simply because you aren't a GI needing to maintain his rifle in the forests of Germany or the jungles of the Pacific. Take the patch holder off your cable and screw in a bore brush. Then pull it through the bore as you did the patch. Now, back to the patches and pull dry ones through until they're clean. Note the color of the first dry patch — it means powder residue (black) and jacket fouling (blue/green) are coming out. Repeat the patch, then brush, then the dry patch until the first dry patch after solvent and brush comes out with solvent and no black or blue/green. This means the fouling is cleaned out. Run another dry patch to sop up any remaining solvent.

Finish using one patch with lubrication oil, not grease, and you are done.

If you need to do the complete teardown and cleaning, follow the instructions from earlier in this chapter, and you can also do the bore cleaning once your rifle is disassembled.

CORROSIVE AMMO CLEANING

Cleaning the Garand after shooting corrosive ammo is more involved simply because it involves water. Yep, good ol' water. Once you get a feel for this task, the attraction of "inexpensive" surplus ammo that is corrosively primed may fade. You'll need paper or shop towels, a funnel, and a place to get wet or splashed.

Start by doing the cleaning job above. The next part is easier if you disassemble your Garand and work with just the barreled receiver. Take the gas screw out of the gas cylinder assembly, but leave the gas lock on. (It will keep the gas cylinder in place, which doesn't need removal.) Prep your water. You want water as hot as possible, and boiling works if you can work with it safely. Stand the barreled receiver up, muzzle down, in a place that drains (bathtub, laundry tub, gravel parking lot of the gun club, whatever works). Hold the funnel, so it is directly over the chamber, and pour the hot water down the bore.

You want hot water not because it dissolves the salts you are washing away better but because it will evaporate faster and be less able to hang around and cause problems. Pour fast enough that the entire bore interior is washed, and the stream doesn't just dribble down one side. You can, if you wish, even put a shop cloth on the bottom of the basin, tub, or whatever to slow water exit and fill the bore. Be careful. If you over-fill, the water will slosh out into the receiver, and you'll have to do some wiping and drying. Two pours of about a quart each will take care of things.

You might be thinking: "GIs didn't boil half a gallon of water per Garand to clean their rifles. If they were heating water, it was for making food or washing socks." You're right. But the bore-cleaning solvents they used were lanolin-based, and their main constituent was … water. So they cleaned their bores with a water solvent, which cleaned the powder residue and the primer salts, and did nothing for the jacket fouling. And they would run an oiled patch down the bore and call it good before the next day's action. Modern cleaning solutions do not have that much water and can't be counted on to wash the salts from corrosive ammo out — if they do, great. If they don't, you have a pitted or ruined barrel.

What solvent? What oil?

People ask, "What's the best? What do you use?" It has been a long time since the difference between the best and the worst was something to worry about. Back when I started, it was still possible to find solvents that didn't do squat. But those formulas, and those makers, are no longer around. Now, we have an embarrassment of riches regarding cleaning solvents. The difference between the best and the not-so-best is slight, and you should go with the brand you're familiar with or the formula that is easiest to use or doesn't cause problems at home. Problems? Yes, the odors of some chemicals might be a bit too much for the rest of your household, and if so, change to something else.

When I was a full-time gunsmith, I found that I was becoming allergic to the industrial-grade mineral spirits I had been using (by that time) for over a decade. When my wife remarked one day after I had come home, "You smell like a gunsmith," I switched. I found a grade of mineral spirits that wasn't reclaimed/recycled and was of higher purity, with much less odor. (The reclaimed/recycled stuff had kerosene and other components, which were the real culprits.) Life was better for both of us after I made the change.

Similarly, if the solvent you've been using is too "nose-full," use something else.

The simple answer to all this: I'm a gun writer. I get free stuff. I use whatever shows up. I have not done an article making/testing a comparison of the cleaning ability of various solvents, and until I do, I'll stick with … free. •

CHAPTER 3

ADOPTION AND TEETHING PROBLEMS

While previous rifles had progressed quickly through the approval and adoption system, the Garand's finalization and adoption took a long time. In 1892, the Krag's adoption took less than a year after a trial of various designs was held. The Army spent the next six years refining, updating, and modifying the Krag. It was "settled" in 1898, but the Spanish-American War (1898) had the American Krag facing the 1893 Spanish Mauser, to the detriment of the American troops. (Or so it was felt at the time.)

The Krag, despite being obsolete by the end of the 19th century, was still in use half a century later. Here, Spc. McCarthy, left, examines a Krag from a pile of weapons captured in Andernach, Germany, in March 1945.

The Krag's failing was twofold: it had only one locking lug and, as a result, was a bit weak. And it lacked stripper clips for fast reloading. From 1898 it was a mere five years to the adoption of the Springfield 1903. Those, and other shortcomings, were corrected, including the use of stripper clips. One problem: that technology was patent-protected by Mauser. Ironically, we paid royalties on stripper clips to Mauser until we entered the war in 1917.

So, the 18 years from the end of WWI to the official adoption of the Garand were different from what anyone expected.

Even by the day's standards, it was a long, hard grind for John Garand. Initially, he had a different idea about how his rifle would work. His initial design used a plunger in the bolt that bore on the primer. When the cartridge fired, the primer pushed the plunger or sleeve back partially out of the case. Yes, he intended to use what we would consider a "blown" primer as the unlocking initiation of his system. It sounds crazy, but it worked. It worked until the Army changed the M1906 cartridge, which it had adopted for rifle use. Machine guns were new, expensive, and consumed vast amounts of ammunition, and no military would adopt them in volume, right?

The idea of a billion rounds of machine gun ammo as a wartime supply in the warehouses would have been just crazy talk in 1905-06. And machine guns, blowing through hundreds of thousands of rounds in a day? No one could afford to run an army that way, right? Well, the U.S. did in WWI, and in so doing, found a few problems.

Machine guns were hard on ammo. The stresses of yanking each round out of the belt, shoving it into the chamber, and closing the bolt behind it, banged the cartridge around. And back in those days, machine gun belts were made of canvas, and the cartridge was pulled backward out of the belt before being shoved forward. If the gun got worn, the headspace could become so excessive that the primer could loosen and fall out during firing, tying up the weapon. So, the Army changed the cartridge design to crimp in the primers. This change made the design Garand had been working on a non-starter, so he had to start over.

Oh, and here's a tidbit you might not have run into: the initial models Garand worked on were made to use the BAR magazine. Yes, that's right, he started with a 20-round box magazine as his feeding source. He even made a prototype with a 40-round magazine. Now, imagine that the idea of an inexpensive, even disposable clip had not been so fixed in the minds of the military. In a different timeline, Garand makes a rifle that uses 20-round magazines of the same model as the BAR and a 40-round version. You know that the soldiers will use the 20s in Garands and 40s in the BAR, and the life (or the ending thereof) of enemy soldiers would have been affected much more quickly. Oh well.

The next wrench in the works was the insistence on the part of military organizations around the world that drilling a hole in the bore would destroy accuracy, cause male-pattern baldness in the officer corps (they probably wouldn't have cared if the troops went bald), and crop failure. And if the hole itself wasn't deleterious to accuracy, the fact that the cycling parts would start moving before the bullet left the bore would. The French knew better, but because they had been keeping their self-loading rifle R&D a secret from everyone (even most of their own army, let alone ostensible allies like the USA), no one else knew that they had tried it and found it not the failure it was alleged to be. A small port in the bore did nothing to harm accuracy.

The Springfield Armory experimental shop, Building 28, was where the test rifles, modifications, and other specialty or one-off work was done.

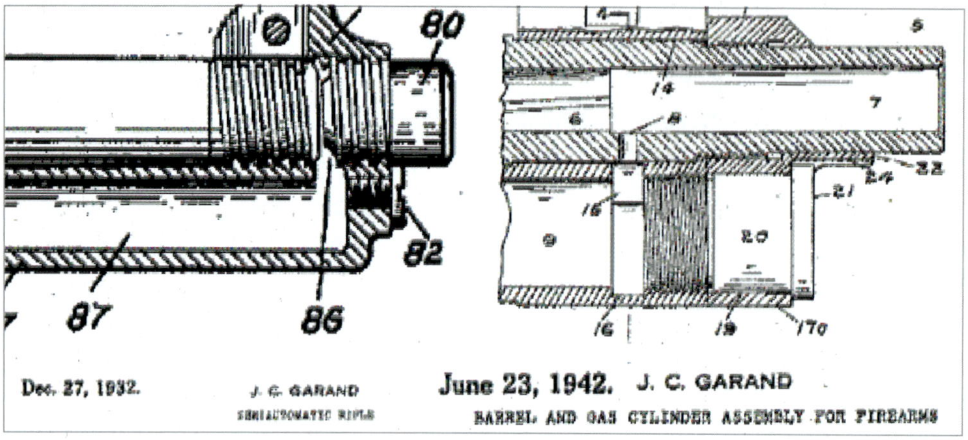

The earliest designs Garand worked on were subject to the "no holes in the barrel" requirements of the U.S. Army. This mandate meant a lot of engineering hanky-panky and an inefficient design.

... THE INITIAL MODELS GARAND WORKED ON WERE MADE TO USE THE BAR MAGAZINE. YES, THAT'S RIGHT, HE STARTED WITH A 20-ROUND BOX MAGAZINE AS HIS FEEDING SOURCE. HE EVEN MADE A PROTOTYPE WITH A 40-ROUND MAGAZINE.

One early exemplar of the "no gas port in the bore" design was the Danish Bang rifle. It used a cone-shaped gas capture cowling or a sleeve around the muzzle, and the cowling would be driven forward by the gases, which cycled the action. The problems were several. First, the amount of gas that could be captured and the gas pressure outside the muzzle made the system marginal in power. The interior of the cone, hit directly by the gases, needed studious cleaning, or it would rust and then not cycle reliably. Or, it would get carbon-fouled and not cycle properly. The Bang concept was widely copied, tested and finally dropped by most of the world's military ordnance departments.

Since Garand either didn't know what the French knew or had to do as the "experts" told him, he had to use a different approach, one that many other designs used, namely the "gas trap." How to describe a gas trap? Think of a muzzle brake without ports or openings to the outside. Instead, the port or opening leads to the rear, to the op rod. The gas pressure, trapped in the (you'll pardon me, I hope) gas trap, vents in the only direction possible while the bullet mostly plugs the exit: back to the op rod. The Bang design allowed the gas trap, the cone, to blow forward, and used a lever to transfer energy via a rearward impulse and push the op rod. Garand didn't like that. He designed his gas trap to be fixed and vent the gases back against the op rod. There were fewer parts in his design to be bent, rusted, misaligned or improperly assembled. But it was also an unsealed system, as gas blew past the bullet even as it was fed to the operating rod or "op rod."

What were the problems with this approach? One was that the gas port had a slightly lower gas pressure than the Garand's gas port. Second, since the bullet needs clearance in the exit hole, the gas can vent out of the gas port exit hole even before the bullet has left, bleeding the gas out of the system before the op rod can even get started. The gas trap has to be a tight fit to provide an operating margin for gas flow, but it has to

The Bang rifle influenced military adoption boards and designers in the 1920s. It took a long time to overcome the lust for its "advantages" and realize the downsides.

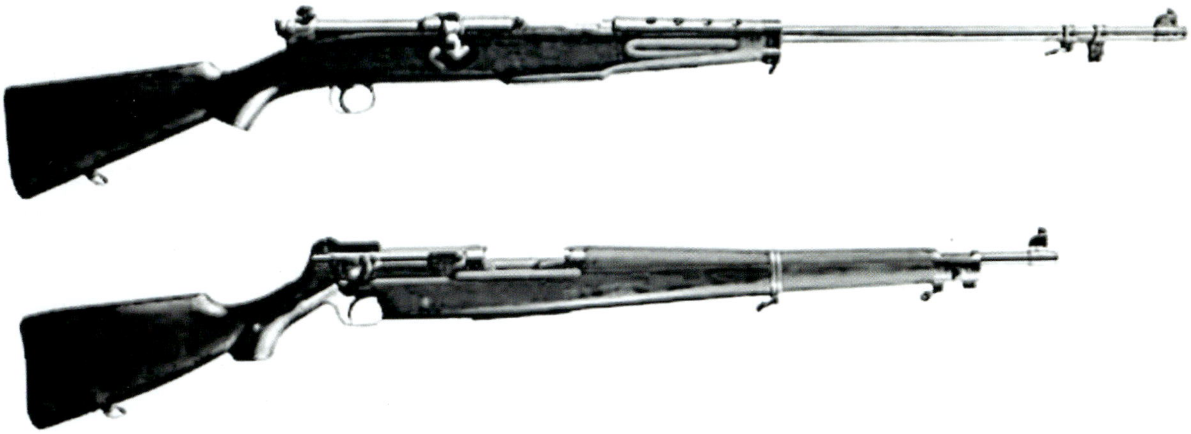

It was only a few years after The Great War was over, and already there was competition for the next service rifle. The then-Garand, on the bottom, is built using as many Springfield parts as possible. If the parts fit, why not?

be sturdy because if it gets bent, dented, or knocked out of alignment, it will contact the bullet and destroy its accuracy. That was a big deal since all military rifles at this time still had to have a bayonet attachment provided.

Last and certainly not least, since all ammunition at this time had corrosive primers, corrosion of the gas trap parts was a certainty without thorough cleaning. So, the gas trap parts had to be sturdy, tightly fitted, secure, and readily removed for cleaning.

THOMPSON AUTO RIFLE

You've heard of the Thompson submachine gun, the "Tommy Gun," right? Designed by Brigadier John T. Thompson, it is a .45-caliber submachine gun. You've probably heard it described as an "unlocked blowback" design. Well, the later one was. But the initial design used the "Blish lock" in the bolt — a bronze locking block fit into an angled slot in the bolt. When the pressure from the fired cartridge pressed the bolt back, the angled block resisted until the pressure increased and then released, unlocking the block and allowing the bolt to cycle.

You're thinking to yourself, "What? It does what? Why? How?" This was noticed in the use of artillery pieces. Artillery uses a threaded locking bolt, and in some of them (most, actually), the threads are "interrupted' in that half of them are machined away. There were multiple threads, but you could unlock the artillery piece and swing the breech open with half a rotation.

Someone observed — precisely who is lost to history — that if you loaded an artillery piece but only used the smallest powder charge it could handle, the bolt would sometimes partially unscrew itself. The pressure of the round firing would push the bolt, but the threads would slide along their faces, and the bolt would slightly, or even completely, open.

That was the operating principle of the original

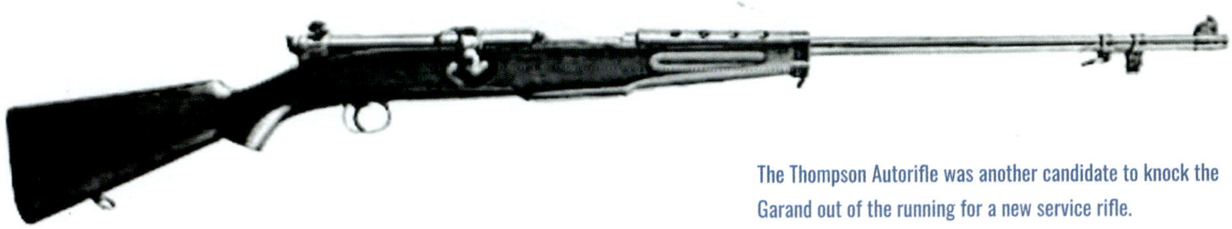

The Thompson Autorifle was another candidate to knock the Garand out of the running for a new service rifle.

Thompson. When it came time to produce in quantity (designed in WWI, it was a luxury, an expensive submachine gun between the wars), testing showed that you could dispense with the Blish lock, and the Thompson worked just fine as a blowback design.

OK, but in the early 1920s, Thompson was pushing a rifle in competition with the Garand-to-be. His idea was too good to pass up, so he made a rifle in .30-06 that used the same principle, but instead of a sliding block, he used interrupted threads. Yes, he was making a blowback .30-06, and if that idea doesn't scare you, you need help. This was one way around the problem of corrosive ammo and gas systems, albeit not a good one. The interrupted thread bolt was inefficient in function, and to make sure the bolt could extract each case, the plan was to fit the magazine with felt pads, which would be oiled. Each cartridge would be oiled on its way into the chamber and thus have less friction during extraction.

Since Thompson was a Brigadier General (retired), I'm sure the Ordnance people were polite, but it was a non-starter. The Thompson auto rifle went nowhere, but it does show the lengths inventors were willing to go to push the idea of a self-loading rifle.

PEDERSEN RIFLE

John Pedersen, a designer for Remington and the U.S. government, offered his rifle for consideration in the mid-1920s. It had a 24-inch barrel, the new standard for infantry rifles. Before WWI, infantry typically got rifles with 30-inch barrels, and cavalry got "carbines" with shorter barrels, some down to 20 inches or less. Even before The Great War, the standard had become 24 inches.

His rifle differed from others in that it used a different locking system: a toggle lock. Working just like your knee and the Luger pistol, the Pedersen bolt hinged to unlock. (The famous BAR also uses the same sort of locking system.) The design is solid, as, at the moment of ignition, the cartridge is supported by a solid bar of steel. The only weak points — and they are not very weak — are the pivot rod (think your knee joint) and the hinge (think your hip). But there can't be more than a few thousandths of an inch of play and flex in such a system. The locking surfaces are so large that wear is not an issue.

Pedersen also offered a new cartridge, the .276 Pedersen. He had done his homework on infantry tactics and felt that a smaller-diameter bullet with less mass would serve as well, and he offered his idea of a proper cartridge. It was a shorter-than-.30-06 case with much the same base diameter. (Well, a little smaller, but not enough to make it that much more compact in a receiver) and using a 7mm bullet of 125 grains at 2,700 fps. By today's standards, that's not much of a change, with a case too long for the bullet weight and velocity. But back then, it was quite radical.

In testing, which involved shooting pigs, it punched well above its weight. Despite the lighter weight and smaller diameter, the .276 produced more significant wounding than the .30-06. I can only guess this without a sample rifle to measure, but I suspect the twist rate of the Pedersen had something to do with that. With its 1:10 twist rate, the .30-06 was over-stabilized so the stable bullet would punch through the target. (Sound like the M855

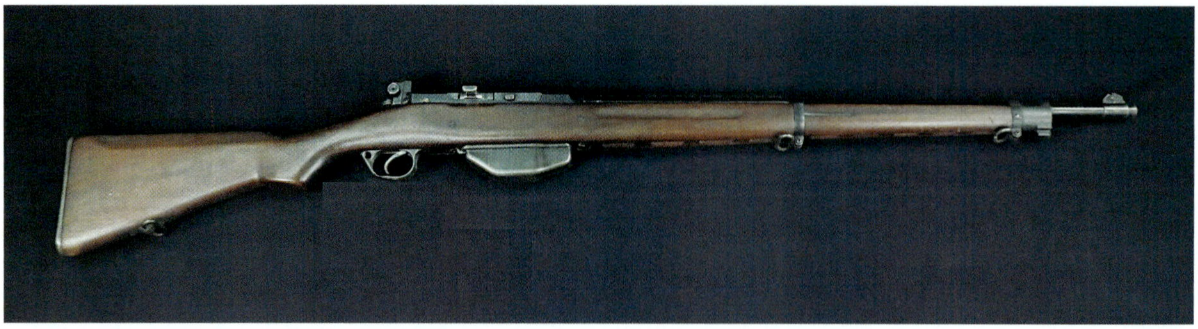

Pedersen's rifle had the advantage of being built for the new and impressive .276 Pedersen cartridge, which had the disadvantage of requiring a wax coating to function correctly.

out of an M16? Are you surprised?)

But like many around the world, the U.S. Army was still locked into the long-range marksmanship model and uninterested in anything that wouldn't deliver a killing blow at 1,000 yards. There was one other problem, and it was inherent in the Pedersen design but not in the Garand. Think of the bolt on the Pedersen, and imagine it moving. When the action unlocks and is cycled, the bolt moves straight back from the chamber. On the Garand, it rotates a small amount before moving back. That rotation is something firearms designers call "primary extraction." When the round fires, the case expands to fill the chamber. At 50,000 PSI and made of brass, it has no other choice. When the pressure drops, it springs back slightly but not entirely. That's why you have to resize your brass in the reloading process. Expanded, the brass clings to the chamber walls, and that friction relieves some of the thrust on the bolt from firing. The brass still clings to the chamber walls even after it has contracted, and the rotation of the bolt breaks it free. This is primary extraction, the case's breaking free (or at least some of it) from the chamber.

The Pedersen, lacking primary extraction, could

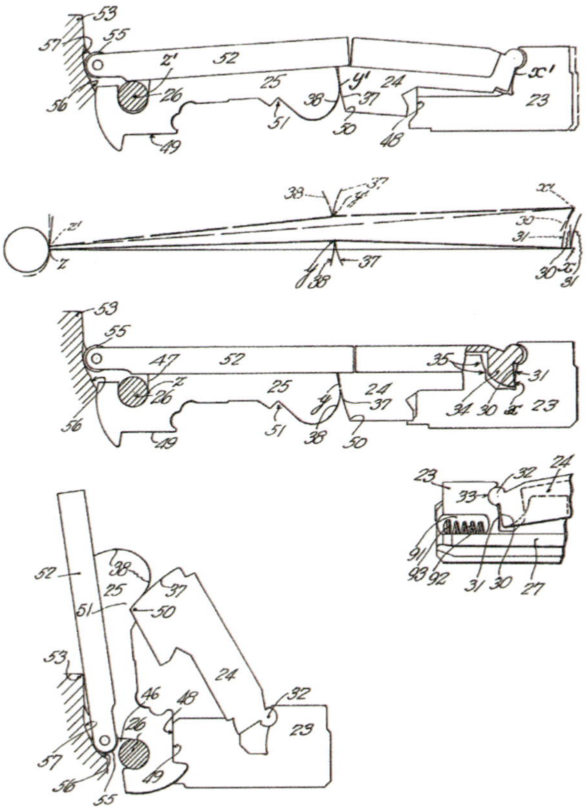

A page from the patent for Pedersen's toggle action for his rifle. He may have patented it, but the idea was not new, and the lack of primary extraction is what finally stopped his project.

Any rifle that would replace the Springfield would be tested against the Springfield. And, it had to deliver the goods to 1,000 yards and beyond, as the Springfield "could." (Not really, but that's another story.)

A soldier of the 2nd ID at Fort Sam Houston shooting one of the early gas trap rifles. Notice that he has a tight sling, which wasn't just a target-range affectation pre-war. It was how you shot a rifle. Also, notice how close his brim is to the action. The Pedersen would have tapped that brim for sure.

only sometimes pull fired cases free. If the system were adjusted to pull the cases out consistently, the recoil would increase (not good when you're touting your rifle as "lower recoil"), or the extractor would rip through the rim, leaving the case in the chamber.

To solve that problem, Pedersen produced his ammunition with a wax coating on the brass case. Yes, wax, and yes, the testers could see all the problems that wax-coating could create. I have two words for you: dust storm. Pedersen could not solve this problem and still keep his action design, and if he wanted to change to a rotating bolt, Garand was a good decade ahead of him there. And yes, wax as a different "solution" to the oiled-cartridge idea was better, but only slightly.

There was one more "fault" to be found with the Pedersen. The toggle travels upward, and when the rifle has fired, the last round locks it open, blocking your field of view and making it evident that you are out of ammo. So far, so good. However, the almost universal hat worn at this time was the campaign hat. You know, the wide, flat brim and peak-with-four-creases-in-it hat? As hats go, for use in all weather and outdoors, it was excellent. However, the Pedersen had the annoying habit of its toggle slapping against the hat's brim when fired. It seems like a minor thing today when the only hat is a baseball cap, but it was annoying enough for the testers to comment on it.

Despite top brass's insistence on full power, the Ordnance people were very interested in the .276 and hot on the idea, so Garand was forced to make his rifle in .276. However, at the last minute (so to speak), he also produced a test rifle in .30-06. That proved to be the last step to approval, as then Chief of Staff General Douglas MacArthur (yes, that MacArthur) laid down the law; there would be no ammunition change.

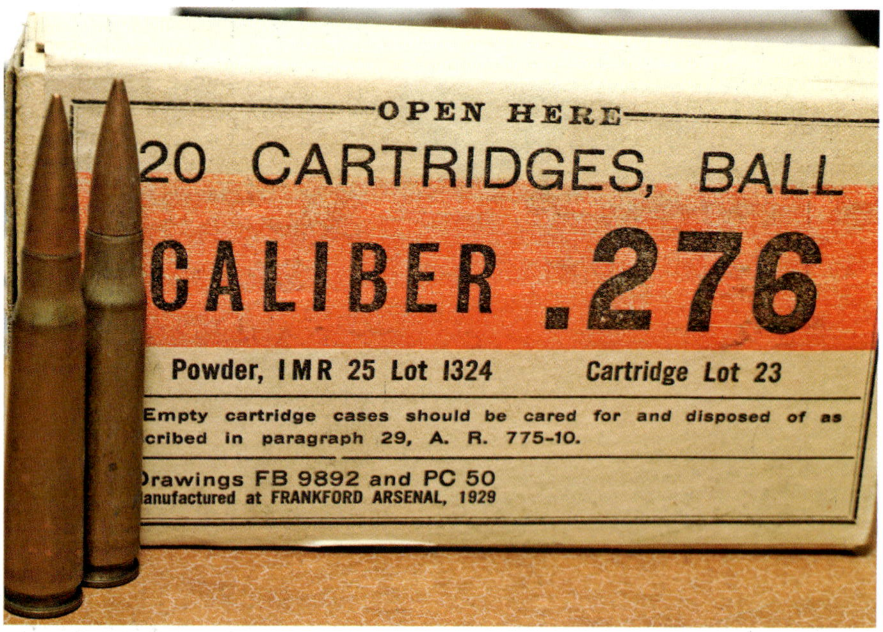

The .276 Pedersen cartridge was far enough along that it was manufactured in bulk at Frankford Arsenal and packaged in the same 20-round boxes of .30-06 of the time.

A brief aside here; it has been fashionable to decry this "short-sightedness." The .276 was superior (or so the argument goes), and since the rifle was new and all the existing ammunition was old, we could have made the Garand in .276 and rocked. Well, yes, except for all those pesky details.

Detail One: adopting a

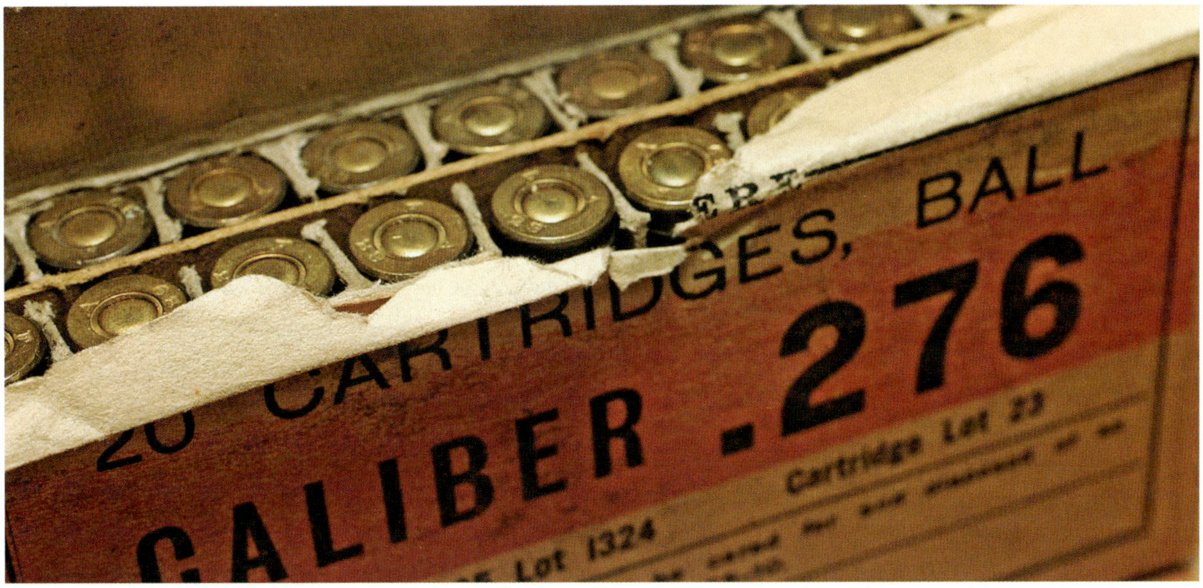

As was all military ammunition by 1929, the .276 was manufactured with crimped primers.

new cartridge takes time and money. The new round has to be tested, its weaknesses found and corrected, and all the old loads duplicated in the new one. That means ball, AP, tracer, match, blanks, and grenade-launching rounds must be developed, tested, adopted and produced. Then there is the existing stock of machine guns. No, they can't be left in .30-06. Trying to supply different ammunition for rifles and machine guns is madness. So, new barrels for the existing machine guns would have to be produced after the design is drawn up, made, tested, refined, and then production begins. That also means new ammunition belts for the machine guns, new cleaning rods, brushes, patches, etc.

In 1936, when the military adopted the Garand, the Army was on a tight budget. It was all it could do to adopt the new rifle, and only because some members of Congress insisted on adopting it. (Back then, Congressmen and Senators knew guns and how to shoot and concerned themselves with such matters.)

There wouldn't be enough money for the wholesale change a new cartridge would require. So, .30-06 it was going to be.

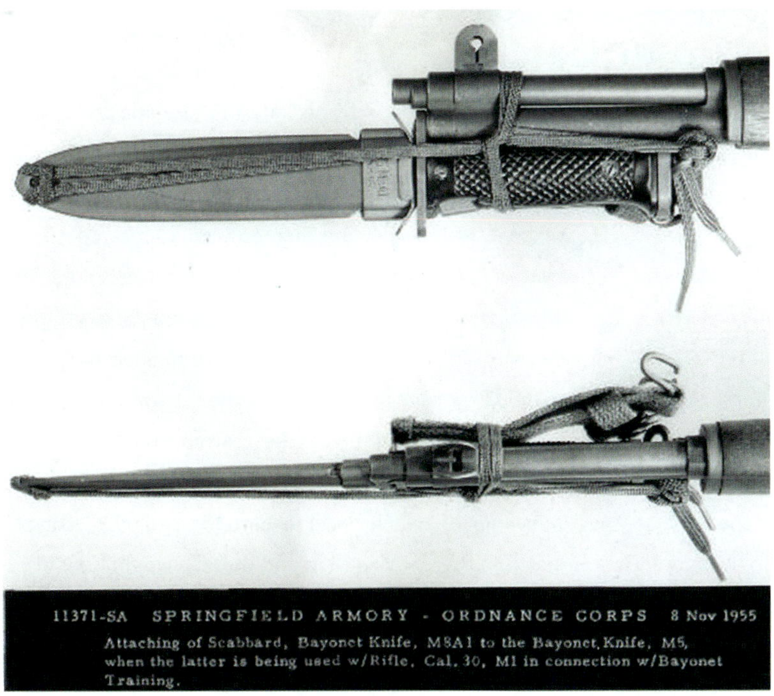

The bayonet is such an ingrained military requirement that Sweeney suspects that even after we have laser guns, they will have bayonet lugs. Here you can see how the bayonet attaches. The cord? That is usually for tying the scabbard to your leg to keep it from flopping around. Here it is used to keep the scabbard on during bayonet practice.

In the pre-war era, marksmanship was seriously taught, and even generals were expected to be able to shoot. Here, General Easley is testing the new service rifle. Easley was in combat in the Philippines and Okinawa, where he was killed by enemy action.

TESTING

Adoption is one thing. Acceptance is another. The Garand had to be accepted by the end-users, and in the 1930s, the (relatively small in numbers) military was a pretty salty and experienced lot with high expectations. The competition shooters expected the accuracy they could wring out of their hand-fitted Springfield bolt-action rifles. Consider: the competition shooters at the National Matches, aka Camp Perry, had years or even decades of scores to keep up. The Marines expected accurate rifle fire as a norm. And no one in either camp was going to warm up to a rifle that wasn't reliable. So, there was a lot of accuracy testing.

ADOPTION IS ONE THING. ACCEPTANCE IS ANOTHER. THE GARAND HAD TO BE ACCEPTED BY THE END-USERS, AND IN THE 1930S, THE (RELATIVELY SMALL IN NUMBERS) MILITARY WAS A PRETTY SALTY AND EXPERIENCED LOT WITH HIGH EXPECTATIONS.

One reliability test, in particular, I find illustrative. The Marines were used to going ashore and expected to do so in a hostile environment, as they would be assaulting beachheads. (This was even before they knew that the Pacific would be a big part of the coming war.) So, the unscientific but very reality-based testing they did was simple: tie a rope to a Garand, throw it down the beach, drag it to you, load it and shoot it. Toss it into the surf and do the same. Keep at it until the rifles being tested quit working or the testers tired of the exercise.

Today, this casual, unscientifically un-measurable test would be laughed out of use. But it worked then and proved that the Garand was up to the task.

TEETHING PROBLEMS

Once adopted and accepted, the Garand went into production. The initial work was done at Springfield Armory, the government arsenal. Springfield would work up the process, develop the tooling, fixtures and workflow, and expand the process or hand it off to some other manufacturer should a war break out. And, yes, Springfield was a government facility. The idea of a "defense contractor" had not been invented. The government made some things "in-house," like small arms. Well, at least, rifles, since Colt made the 1911. Other items, like aircraft, were made by airplane manufacturers, but they made the designs the government requested.

The Garand was made pretty much as John Garand had designed it, but not entirely, and we'll get to that. The gas trap Garands got issued and tested, and then problems appeared. (It's always a good idea to do field testing before making things by the bazillion.) The screw holding the gas trap assembly could loosen, and if the gas trap got misaligned, it would be struck by a bullet. Solution: Have soldiers check the screw's tightness. The gas trap would get coated with high-pressure and high-temperature carbon deposits on its interior, which could be hard to clean off. Getting a patch in there wasn't easy, and the rifle would have to be taken apart to get it clean, requiring more cleaning instructions and perhaps a special brush or brushes.

The first gas trap design used a single blade for a front sight, just like that on the Springfield. This sight was deemed too prone to damage, so the design was updated to a more substantial front blade, with wings on either side to protect it. The first design used straight upright wings, and with some testing, sometimes soldiers would use one of the wings to aim with, resulting in a wide miss. So, the final sight design was one with bent wings.

The last one, however, was unforgivable and had to be changed: the gas trap was not a solid attachment point for a bayonet. Bayonets were a near-religious detail in militaries then; if you could not attach a bayonet, it wasn't a real military rifle.

Handily enough, testing showed that a Garand with a gas port did not have accuracy problems, so the gas trap design was changed to a gas port. However, the old parts had to be used up, and it was not until 1940 (the Garand was adopted in 1936) that the last gas trap Garand was assembled. That's how hard-up for money the Army was in the late 1930s.

The new Garand had a longer barrel. The G-T Garands had 22-inch barrels, and the trap added length. The new ones with the gas port were 24 inches long in the barrel but the same overall length. So, the original gas trap Garands were not simply re-fitted with new parts. In 1940, the new gas system was adopted, and all subsequent Garands used the gas port. The original production of gas trap models stayed in inventory, but when they needed a new barrel, they had a gas port barrel installed and were sent back into service. How many gas trap Garands were made? Records indicate 48,199. But there have been reported gas trap Garands in the 50,000 serial number range. I can only assume that someone found some extra gas trap parts, enough to make a few more complete rifles, and did so to use up parts and meet the day's quota.

An unaltered gas trap Garand (a Springfield receiver, and a serial number under 48,119, unless documented) would be a collectible of the first order. I have seen auction prices as high as twenty-thousand dollars. (Oh, to win the lotto big time and own one.) Most of them were used until the bore was shot out and re-barreled with the new gas system. So, if you see a Garand with a Springfield receiver marking, and a serial number under 48,119, it was a gas trap but is no more and got rebuilt.

There was one other problem. This issue came up only when the top round in a fully loaded clip was on the right

The receiver starts as a forging, and its front is drilled, reamed, and threaded. At Springfield, the process changed, nicking one of the guide rails.

While all Garands are supposed to work with the top round on either side, it is customary to load "top round left" just in case.

side. (Being symmetric, it didn't matter "up" or "down" since left or right was the same regardless of which end of the clip was up.) With a clip loaded "top round on right," the Garand in testing would, in some instances, when the sixth round was fired, misfeed the seventh round and wedge the point of the cartridge against the receiver face, failing to send it into the chamber. This was a mysterious malfunction, and the only solution short of an arsenal fix (which no one could figure out) was to load clips with the top round on the left and only on the left.

The problem was so bad that it was a source of constant "what do we do to fix this?" questioning in Springfield, made all the more mysterious that the pre-production sample rifles did not do it. Things came to a head when the War Department determined that, to publicize the new rifle, 200 of them would be made available at the National Matches for competitors to try out. Under normal circumstances, this would be a PR coup, getting the new rifle into the hands of the country's best riflemen. But, if they had a host of malfunctions, that would kill the program.

The solution was two-fold. Specially modified cartridge lifters were fabricated to only accept clips loaded "top round left." The army staff handling the program at Camp Perry checked each clip to ensure they were only loaded "top round left."

The rifles worked fine, but the efforts did not go un-

(Below) One of the two rails that would get clipped in the Springfield tooling setup until that was corrected. The misfeed this can cause is why it is customary to load Garand clips with the top round on the left side.

Johnson kicked up such a fuss — and the minor glitches in rolling out the Garand didn't help — that legislators got involved. Here, (L-R) Senator Sheppard, Gen. Lynch, and Senator Chandler look over two Johnson rifles and two Springfields.

noticed, which would be a problem.

The problem ended when the program director and the Springfield Assistant Foreman were walking through the Springfield assembly line, inspecting everything being done. Looking at an in-process receiver, they happened to have on hand a receiver from one of the pre-production runs to compare it to and noticed that the clip guide ribs differed. In setting up the tooling to machine the receiver, the engineers and machinists at Springfield had arranged the reamer that bored the hole in the receiver for the barrel to pass into the receiver forging deeply enough that it nicked the rib. This extra distance made it easier and faster to ream the barrel-line receiver bore and to knock out the machining chips the cut produced. Initial testing revealed no problems, so off they went.

There's a reason Garand made the rib go all the way up. Correct that, and the problem will be solved. Why did this happen? Simple: money. In designing his rifle, Garand had also designed the tooling to make the parts.

(Below) Johnson was so sure his rifle was the best that he even made a light machine gun out of it to replace the BAR.

The Johnson had some admirable features, such as the 10-round magazine that could be topped off. But the recoil operation meant it could be picky in function, and adding a bayonet didn't always improve reliability.

With their own experience making rifles, the people at Springfield felt they could do as well and made changes without consulting Garand. And remember, this was when the Great Depression was still going on. There were even considerations in some quarters that perhaps, his job now done, there was no reason to keep a "superfluous" John Garand on as an employee of the government and that his salary of $3,500 could be put to "better" use. Now, he was well-paid. That's not a point of disagreement: $3,500 in 1939 is the equivalent of $67,700 in 2022 — not exactly rolling in dough, but comfortable. This idea was turned down, and I'd like to think that whoever suggested it was exiled to the worst post in the Army, but I'd bet not.

Staff Sergeant Spurrier, holder of the Medal of Honor, giving tips on cleaning and maintenance of the M1 Garand to soldiers in France in 1945.

In later decades, when a Garand came through for a rebuild, armorers would weld up the top of the ribs (it is not near enough to a locking surface to cause problems from the heat generated) and then clean the weld to correct the problem. But not all were so corrected,

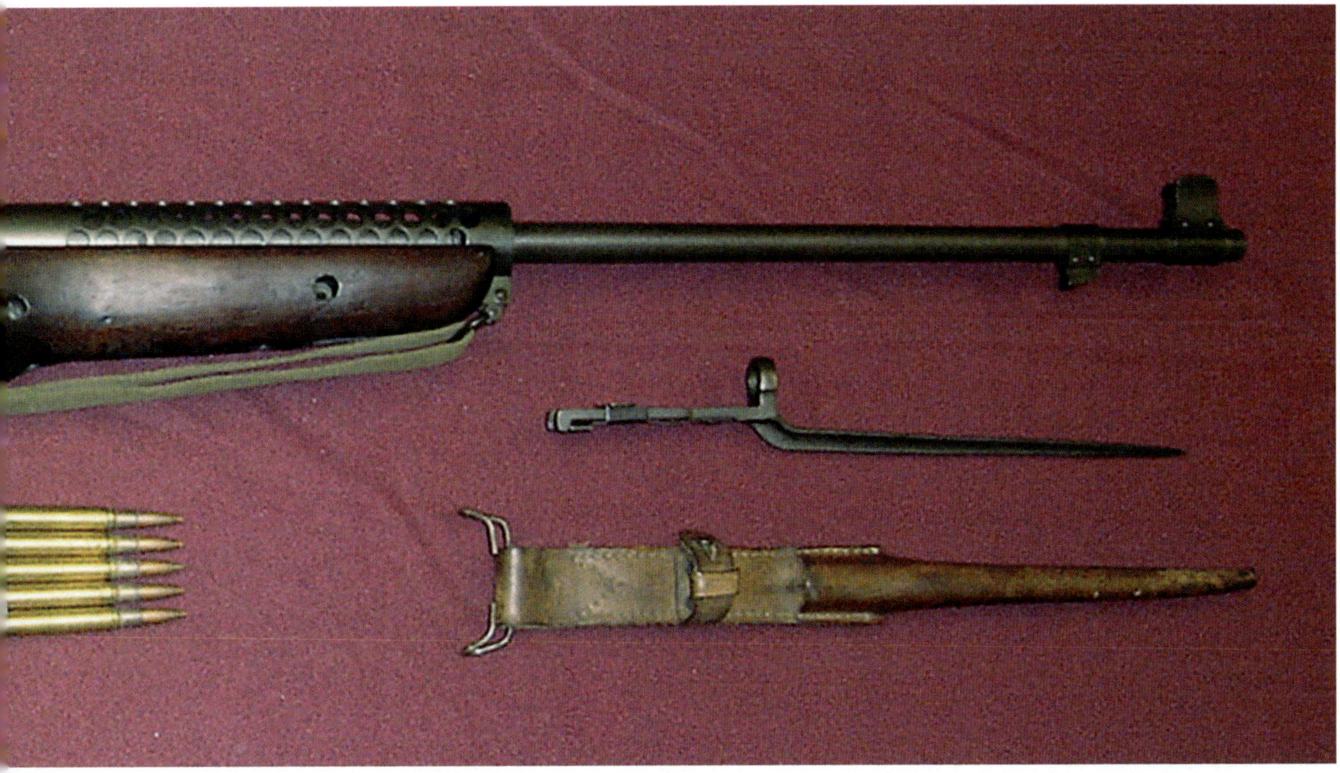

and you might find yours had that. No problem, load the top round on the left, and life is good. And, if yours is a "nicked-rib" Garand, and it hasn't been corrected, it is a collectible.

Don't get it changed.

The M1 Carbine was designed as a defense tool for those working with other weapons systems. While the observer is armed with a Garand, the radio operator has an M1 carbine, most likely, based on the magazine pouch on his belt.

COMPETITOR

The Garand, despite being adopted, still had at least one competitor. Melvin Johnson had an idea for a rifle, and he made it (well, he had them made, being a lawyer and not owning a production plant) and pushed it as a replacement for the "flawed" Garand. The flaw? The Garand used gas, and the Johnson was recoil-operated and thus did not have a gas system that could be fouled or rusted. Johnson's design also used a rotary magazine, which could be topped off using stripper clips. If you fired a few rounds with a Garand and wanted a fully loaded rifle, your only option was to eject the rounds in the rifle and insert a new 8-round clip. With the Johnson, you could quickly strip five more into its 10-round rotary magazine, or even one at a time, from loose rounds in your pocket.

The Johnson design also made it easy to remove the

barrel, and this was somewhat attractive to the new parachute units who could pack a Johnson with the barrel out as a smaller package and assemble it after landing.

As a recoil-operated rifle, the Johnson barrel moved back and forth on each shot. Remember my mentioning that the gas trap Garand had to be changed because of problems with a bayonet? Well, Johnson had similar issues. The bayonet's weight could cause cycling problems, so it was rejected as a replacement for the Garand. At the beginning of the war, when the demand for small arms was so great that there was a rifle shortage, the Marines bought a bunch of Johnson rifles and light machine guns. But as soon as they could replace them with Garands, they did so.

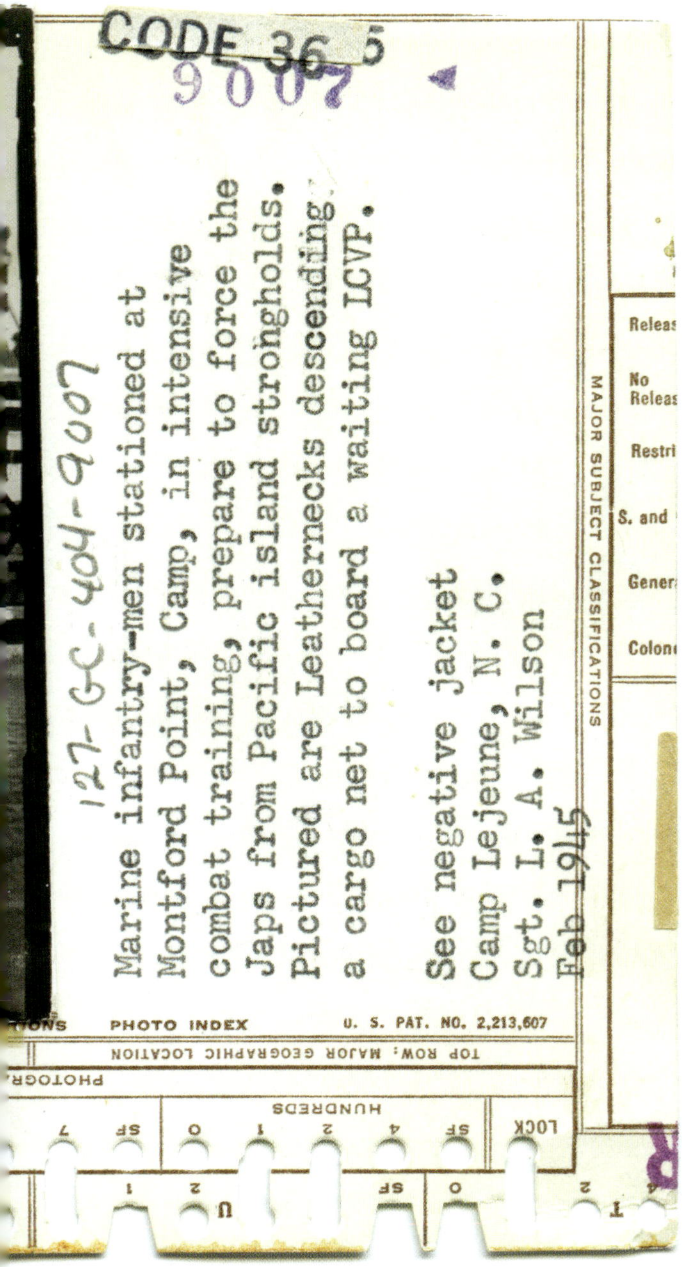

A card from the National Archives showing Marines at Montford Point training to get into and out of landing craft. A close inspection of the photo shows they are using Garands.

COMPATRIOT

The M1 carbine was meant to be an extra weapon, not to replace the Garand. Before the Garand, a "carbine" was typically a shorter version of the service rifle. Where the infantry would be issued a rifle with a 30-inch barrel (because they needed the length to engage in bayonet combat with opposing soldiers), the cavalry, artillery, etc. would be issued the same action, but with a 20-inch barrel. The effect of experience just before WWI led many armies to make all of them the same, so the service rifle used a 24-inch barrel, and the carbine disappeared except in some unique instances.

The Garand was not mechanically capable of being built with a shorter barrel, so there were no carbine variants. But when the U.S. Army did want a carbine, it was for a different reason: to replace the 1911A1 pistol with something more capable in a fight and not as heavy as the Thompson. The M1 Carbine used a different cartridge than the Garand and fired a 110-grain bullet at 2,000 fps, compared to the Garand and its 150-grain bullet at 2,700 fps. The M1 Carbine was to be issued to crew-served weapons teams, vehicle crews, mortar and artillery crews, and radio operators as what we would call a Personal Defense Weapon or PDW today. They'd have a means of defense against an enemy breakthrough but wouldn't be burdened by a heavy and bulky Garand.

However, the compact size and light weight meant the M1 Carbine was an attractive tool for those in the fight, and it ended up being used at the front, not just for rear-echelon troops. We made even more M1 Carbines in WWII than Garands, partly because they were simpler and more efficient to produce.

The carbine used a detachable box magazine holding 15 rounds, and you could quickly load it using stripper clips and a guide called a "spoon." The M1 Carbine was a complimentary weapon, not a competitive one to the Garand. •

CHAPTER 4

WARTIME PRODUCTION

When WWII broke out, the War Department thought it was ready for the coming conflict. The war had been going on for some time by the Day of Infamy. On December 7, 1941, the Japanese had already been meddling, big time, in China. In 1931, they staged the Mukden Incident as a pretext to invade Manchuria and form the puppet Manchukuo government. They kept the pressure on the Soviet Union for land acquisition on the borders of Manchuria. In 1935, Italy, under the resurgent Fascists, invaded Ethiopia. Wait, Ethiopia? When the European powers in the latter half of the 19th century took over control of Africa, two countries remained unclaimed: Ethiopia and Liberia. Italy tried to conquer Ethiopia in the 1890s, but the loss at the Battle of Adowa in 1896 ended that. So, it was part score-settling, part colony-grabbing, and "Look how great the Fascists in Italy are" war-making.

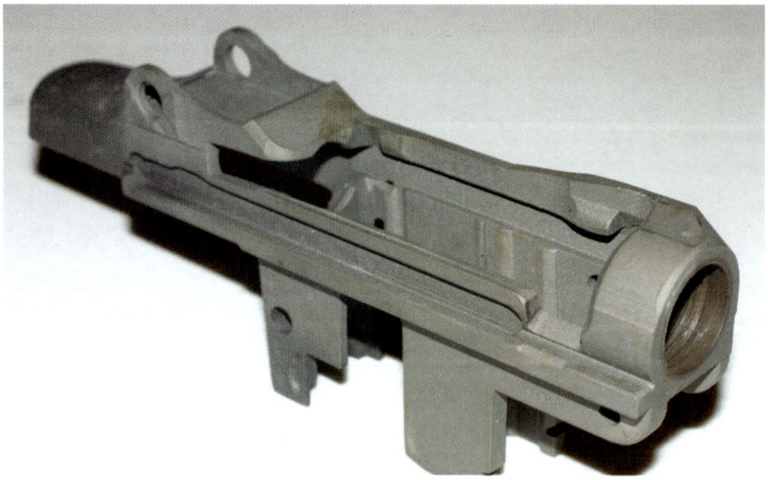

The Garand's receiver was the high-tech product of its age, starting as a forging and requiring many machine operations to get to this stage, ready for assembly.

The Spanish Civil War (1936-1939) was widely seen, then and since, as an "experimental" war where both sides tried out new equipment, tactics, and organizing systems. The Germans and the Soviets sent personnel to test and bring back the intel. Not content with Manchuria, the Japanese staged the Marco Polo Bridge Incident and started a full-scale invasion of China. In 1938, the west, trying to appease Hitler, stood by as he moved into the Sudetenland, part of Czechoslovakia. Further demands followed this incursion, and rounds of diplomatic negotiations ensued. All this came to naught when Germany invaded Poland on September 1, 1939. The Soviet Union signed a cease-fire with Japan and invaded Poland.

In April 1940, Germany invaded Denmark and Norway, ostensibly to protect its iron ore shipments from Sweden. Invading Denmark and Norway gave the Germans the desired territory and caused British Prime Minister Neville Chamberlain to resign, replaced by Winston Churchill. On the same day Chamberlain resigned, Germany invaded France. In June, Italy invaded France and also began attacking the British possession of Malta in the Mediterranean. Italy invaded Yugoslavia, and Greece got bogged down and called on Germany to pull their chestnuts out of the fire.

Then the real fireworks began. In June 1941, Germany invaded the Soviet Union. This was across a broad front and involved three army-sized thrusts; one north, one south, and one right down the middle. By the time of the Japanese attack on Pearl Harbor, the German army had advanced 500 miles into Russia and was on the outskirts of Leningrad in the north, Moscow in the middle, and east of Kharkov in the south.

Two soldiers fire into the entry of a Japanese bunker. Note that the far soldier has a Garand with the finish already worn off his gas cylinder, leaving it bright.

I mention all this because it is now a long time ago to many of my readers. Those holding this book might not have even had grandfathers, but great-grandfathers, who fought in that war. Memories fade, and history isn't taught. So a bit of context can be useful. And the terrain and towns the Germans encountered going East and backing up westward are the same areas that Russian and Ukraine are now fighting over.

The United States was new to modern warfare in the Fall of 1941, and some of the combatants already in the fray had had years of experience by then. How far behind the curve was the U.S.? That autumn, we had a combined

Along with training for the new rifle, soldiers needed instruction on how to use it in combat. The five shots and reload habit had to change, but also the idea of "keeping their heads down" because you had a self-loading rifle and plenty of ammo.

military of 334,000 soldiers, sailors, and Marines. When the Germans invaded Russia, they did so with 3 million men. We had 2,400 aircraft in the Army Air Corps, and the Navy had 2,500. That was greater than the German total of 3,100, but some of the German pilots had years of combat experience by late 1941. Ours had none. Further, we would be split between the European theater and the Pacific, although we didn't know that until December 7.

In all the materiel needed for war, we were behind. But we caught up in a volume that could not be matched. I realize it is a bit glib, but I have stated more than once, on the subject of aircraft, that we made bombers faster than the Germans could shoot them down. The Willow Run plant, outside of Detroit, manufactured ready-to-fly B-24 bombers at the rate of one per hour. That meant all instrumentation, engines, and ten .50-caliber machine guns per plane, rolling off the line every hour.

On the weekend of Pearl Harbor, we had just over 400,000 M1 Garand rifles in inventory. We also had the Springfield 1903 rifles and Enfields left over from The Great War, but we were not going to fight the next conflict with bolt-action rifles. In 1941, Springfield Armory produced about 30,000 rifles a month.

ON THE WEEKEND OF PEARL HARBOR, WE HAD JUST OVER 400,000 M1 GARAND RIFLES IN INVENTORY. WE ALSO HAD THE SPRINGFIELD 1903 RIFLES AND ENFIELDS LEFT OVER FROM THE GREAT WAR, BUT WE WERE NOT GOING TO FIGHT THE NEXT CONFLICT WITH BOLT-ACTION RIFLES. IN 1941, SPRINGFIELD ARMORY PRODUCED ABOUT 30,000 RIFLES A MONTH.

Winchester, which had been instructed to build the tooling and production line and learn how to produce Garands, began making rifles in December 1940 under the "Educational Contract," as specified by the Educational Order Act of 1938. Indeed, it was a far-sighted act of Congress that paid companies to tool up and learn how to make essential wartime items so that if and when the country needed them, they would not start from scratch when war broke out. Winchester made 500 Garands that first month and finished the contract by March. Even before it had finished that contract, the war clouds were forming, and Winchester received additional contracts. By December 1941, it had upped its production rate to 6,000 a month. Now, that seems like a lot, and it was, for a peacetime military of 300,000 men, give or take a few companies. But the coming war would require millions of men, and they all had to be armed.

Consider the scale of modern warfare. In Germany, the 98K Mauser rifle was still the mainstay of the *Wehrmacht*. At the height of the war, damaged, worn-out or otherwise unserviceable Mauser rifles were shipped back to Mauser by the train-car load. There, it refurbished several thousand rifles a day. A flight of 50 B17 bombers (not an overly large formation, by

A muzzle erosion gauge for field unit inspection. The factory would have had more sensitive measuring tools to ensure the barrels were produced correctly.

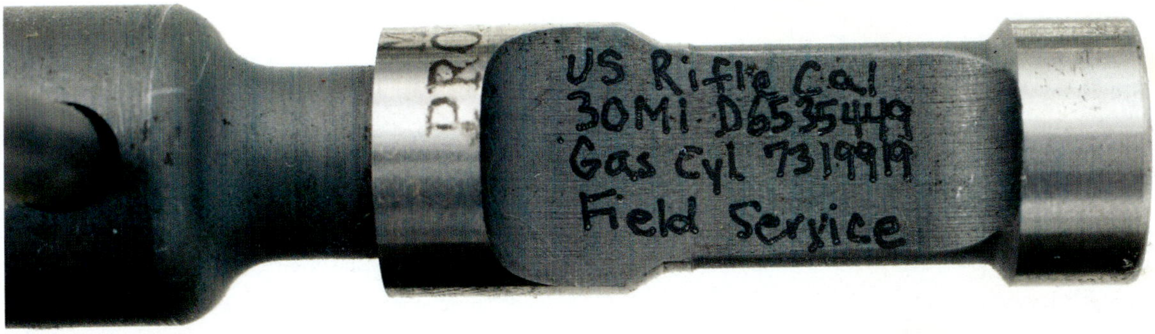

Like the muzzle erosion gauge, the gas cylinder gauge was a field tool. In the factory, a machinist doing QC work would use a precision micrometer or calipers and get an exact readout.

the way) taking off for a raid over Germany would have 500 M2 machine guns and 200,000 rounds of .50-cal. ammunition on board. (Now, if they were all B17Gs, like later in the war, that would be 650 M2s and 260,000 rounds of .50-cal. ammo.) And that was just for defense, as each of them would be hauling up to 8,000 pounds of bombs, depending on the distance to the target and type of ordnance. Let's call it a long-range raid and halve that. We now have, in addition to 50 B17Gs, 500 crewmen, 100 tons of bombs, machine guns, .50-cal. ammo, and gasoline. Fighting a modern war costs money.

How much did we need rifles? The tooling for Springfield '03 rifles was shipped from Rock Island to Remington, and it started producing. It didn't take long before Remington returned to the War Department with improvements; the result was the 03A3. This version used many stamped instead of forged parts and speeded up production. We still needed rifles, so Smith-Corona, the typewriter manufacturer, was also called on to make 03A3 rifles. Remington and Smith-Corona had separate serial number blocks, but like Garands, there were numerical overruns. All told, we produced over a million "obsolete"

A post-war inspection gauge gave a go/no-go or pass/fail check on various parts.

(Below) Winston Churchill inspects and tests an SMLE No 4. Despite being adopted in the late 1880s, the Lee-Enfield was still the issue weapon for Britain in WWII. And Churchill? He was a veteran of the Boer War and knew how to shoot.

bolt-action rifles for the war effort adding to the ones already in inventory.

Back to Garands. In Winchester's defense, it was also making other firearms and wrapping up the commercial, civilian production it had contracted. The company made the M1 Carbine under contract and the Model 1897 and Model 12 shotguns for guard duty and training aerial gunners. Winchester also produced vast quantities of ammunition for the war effort.

A war fought across the world required massive amounts of materiel and small arms beside the B17s. So Springfield scaled up, as did Winchester. At their peak production, spanning 1943, 1944 and the first half of 1945, Springfield Armory was manufacturing 90,000 Garands a month. In that same period, Winchester made 20,000 to 30,000 a month, in addition to all the other firearms.

One interesting detail about wartime production is that some changes were made, and others were not. One example would be the gas cylinder screw, the slotted screw that threads into the gas cylinder and holds the front end together. If you have an early Garand or one with early parts, yours might have a plain, slotted screw. That's a Type 1. Then came a Type 2, with an X slot on the front and a valve in the center. Type 3 has the simple valve replaced by a spring-loaded, or "poppet" valve, and its "X" face is marked with a "P" stamped on the screw head.

Type 2 and 3 were made for grenade launchers. The grenade launching system on the Garand involved a special launching extension clipped onto the muzzle, and the grenade was slipped onto the extension. You launched the grenade by using a blank, not a Ball round. The gas produced caused the op rod to be driven much harder, and the bolt could peen or crack the receiver. So, Type 2 and 3 screws used the valve (opened by installing the grenade launcher) to bleed off excess gas and prevent damaging the receiver or bolt. However, the two upgraded screws were not rushed into production. Winchester went through WWII without using anything but Type 1. Springfield Armory introduced the Type 2 after reaching serial number 1,470,000 and mixed the Type 1 and Type 2

The soldier on the left has a carbine, while the other two have Garands. And curiously, they both have rifle grenades mounted on their Garands while they break down a door.

Striking a balance of capacity, recoil, range, power and handiness, the Stg44/45 was the future in Germany in 1944.

The 03A3 Springfield that Remington brought about ditched the complex rear sight for a faster, more range-reasonable aperture on the rear receiver bridge.

Remington made as many parts as possible from heavy-gauge stampings to speed production. So gone was the milled and removable floorplate, replaced with a stamping, complete with all parts in one assembly.

in production, depending on what it had in stock.

If it was so important to make the new screws to reduce damage to bolts or receivers, why wasn't it used during the war? Simple: the Springfield was the primary grenade-launching rifle in WWII. Remember, it took blanks to drive the grenade. When set up for grenade launching, a Garand wasn't readily swapped back to Ball ammo use. But the Springfield could be set up and left that way and loaded only with blanks, as the squad needed. You could even have some poor Joe assigned to be the Grenadier and carry his Garand and the Springfield with grenade launcher mounted. Since the ammunition for each was in different clips (a five-round stripper for the Springfield, the 8-round en-bloc for the Garand), he could not inadvertently load

Not only did Remington build rifles, but the typewriter company Smith-Corona made 03A3s. Typewriters? Think of a printer without a computer attached; you had to press each key to drive the letters into the paper.

the wrong round into whatever rifle he was using.

After WWII, the Springfield '03 was retired, and only the Garand was in use, so it became essential to rebuild them with the Type 2 or Type 3 gas screws. So, if you're building a retro early-war Garand, you need to find a Type 1 gas screw. Such is life.

Winchester ended WWII with 520,492 M1 Garand rifles manufactured. Those rifles were spread across serial number groups, as the War Department wanted all Garands to have individual numbers. No way did the government want to have "Springfield number one million" and "Winchester number one million" in inventory.

OTHER EFFORTS

The advent of the self-loading rifle did not pass without notice. While the French were out of the running (occupied by Germany, and when they did fight, it would be with U.S.-supplied equipment), the Germans, Soviets and Japanese did not lack for trying. The Germans managed to field some useful self-loading rifles in volume enough to be useful. The G43, a box-fed rifle in 7.92x57, was also made with a mounting rail on the receiver and commonly issued with a magnifying scope. It would serve the purpose of a DMR (dedicated marksmen rifle) for the *Wehrmacht*. For sniping, the Germans stuck with the Mauser and the best optics they could provide, which were very good.

There had been other self-loading rifles. The Ljungman, a Finnish rifle developed from captured SVT-40 rifles, was a direct-impingement system (long before the M16) and worked well. It has a curious manual of arms, and the bolt snapping shut makes "Garand thumb" seem like a mosquito bite. You can lose a fingertip to one, so if someone shows you one, ask how it works before working the action.

The Soviets, having already had and mostly turned down the Avtomat (although I have read they issued them to assault units on the front with Finland), designed and issued the SVT-40. This was, miracle of miracles, a self-loading rifle, box-fed, that used the same rimmed

Germany tried to update from the 98 Mauser, but it wasn't politically easy. The G43 worked, but it wasn't as ergonomic as the Garand and was never available to them in sufficient quantities.

Modern warfare requires an immense volume of materiel. This is one of the D-Day beaches after the landings. Note how many men there were, what it took to transport them, and their supplies.

7.62x54R cartridge of the Mosin. (And the Russian Maxim, because adding a new cartridge was worse than designing a rifle that would feed a rimmed cartridge.)

I have shot both, and the results were not as good as the Garand. The G43, while robust and reliable, is not exactly an ergonomic masterpiece. The SVT40 sports a muzzle brake to tame the recoil of the 7.62 Mosin round, and it's perhaps the loudest shoulder-fired small arm I have ever fired. Why they needed it — since the SVT40 weighs almost as much as a Garand — I don't know.

These were all stopgaps, as those involved realized something else was needed. The cauldron for this was the Eastern Front, where those 3 million Germans fought more than that number of Soviets. What mattered to tip the scales was the volume of fire. When a Russian tank laden with a squad of infantry roared into a village, you wanted to have more firepower than a five-shot bolt-action rifle. German infantry tactics called for the base of power to be the machine gun, either MG34 or MG42, with the riflemen in support.

So you and your four comrades, with bolt-action rifles, had to deal with the dozen Bolshies who just fell, slid or jumped off of the tank. (Oh, someone has to deal with the tank, too.) Yes, someone with an MP40 would be useful, but the 9mm bullet would not penetrate as many chance obstacles as a rifle round. And even if you succeeded, there would be another tank and another …

(Left) The first direct-gas impingement service rifle to be issued, the Ljungman pre-dated the M16 by decades.

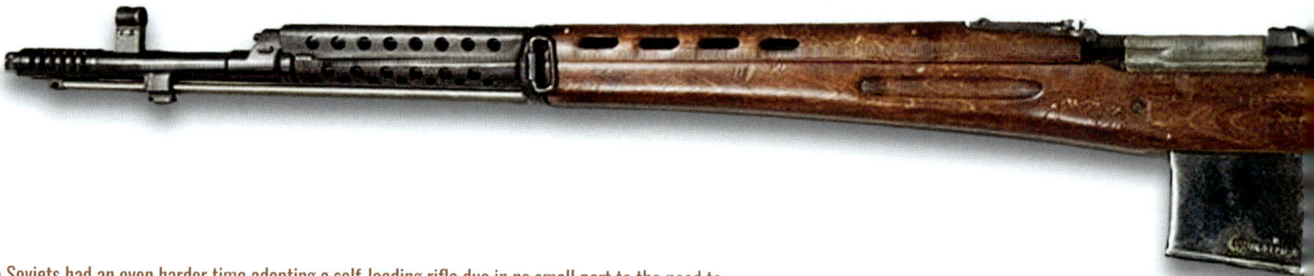

The Soviets had an even harder time adopting a self-loading rifle due in no small part to the need to use the rimmed Russian cartridge. Combine that with a muzzle brake, and these SVT-40s are *loud*.

This need caused the development of a rifle or carbine that filled the gap between bolt action and SMG. With better penetration than 9mm but less recoil than 7.92x57, the MP43 started things off. The bullet was the same diameter, 7.92, but the case was shorter, the bullet lighter, and it was self-loading and select-fire. The FMJ 125-grain bullet, at 2,250 fps, was better at chance obstacles, as controllable as an MP40, and held 30 rounds.

As much as fans of the AK-47 would like to claim otherwise, it indicated to the Soviets that they had to advance beyond the Mosin and the SVT40 and offer more. In its final form, the Stg44/45 also caused the post-war attempts to break out of the full-power rifle cartridge paradigm to fail.

We had our own STG, the M1 carbine. (I know this is a book on the Garand, but stick with me, it will all become clear.) We had the M1 Garand and the M1911A1 pistol and nothing in between. If your job was running a radio for the Lieutenant or Captain or stoking a mortar, a

(Below) The MP40, a 9mm submachine gun, offered high fire volume, but the 9mm didn't penetrate as much as rifle cartridges. It took something in between to replace the Mauser.

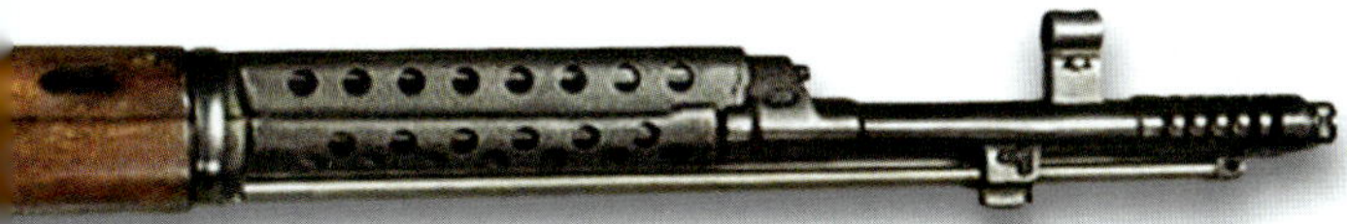

Garand was a real impediment. And a pistol wasn't much of a weapon if the fight came to you. So the Army asked for a weapon in between, specified a .308-inch bullet, gave an idea of the size and power, and asked for samples. It took an amazingly short time, but we had a light carbine that fired the .30 Carbine round and had a 15-round magazine in production almost before anyone could object. This gun was meant to be a behind-the-lines weapon for truck drivers, cooks, etc. It was so handy and put out such sufficient volume of fire that it was commonly found at the front, where it was put to good use. In the war, from what amounts to a standing start in production terms, we produced 6.5 million M1 carbines. But, the carbine was a lot simpler than the Garand to make.

My father wasn't a fan of the carbine, but then he had particular problems to solve that the carbine wasn't too good at. When he was in a line company, he had to deal with buildings, "French farmhouses" was the generic term he used for the villages and cities. He wanted to reach through walls, and the M2AP his Garand used worked

The future had arrived. This German *soldaten* or soldier uses an Stg45 with optics on top. A setup like this would not be common for another half-century after this photo was taken.

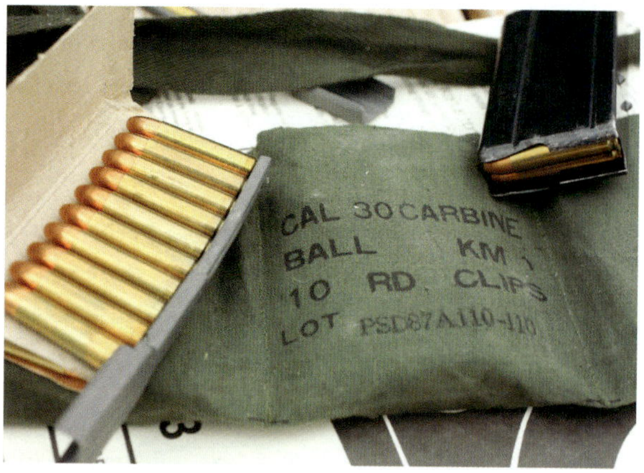

The M1 Carbine used box magazines, and to load them, ammunition came in bandoliers of stripper clips to load magazines quickly — even more reasons for GIs and Marines to love it.

The M1 Carbine also had a magazine pouch that fit on the stock, so a GI could have 45 rounds ready and on his weapon.

just fine. When he went to the Combat Scouts, he needed volume of fire and shock, so an M3A1 SMG and a satchel of grenades did the job. The M1 Carbine neither offered penetration on the first job nor volume on the second.

Oh, and the Japanese? They had so many problems of their own making that a self-loading rifle was way down on the list of must-have items. They finally tried their own, using captured Garands as samples. They made some changes. For one, they tried chambering their design in the 7.7 Japanese cartridge. That was a necessity because they were already trying to supply their army, navy and air force with seven different rifle-caliber cartridges for the rifles and light machine guns they had developed and built. The Japanese were worse than the Germans in this regard, with each branch fighting for materiel, coming up with their own designs, and trying to field their own equipment without consideration of interoperability.

The rifle they made reflected the limitations they faced. It fed from a 10-round box magazine but was loaded with stripper clips of five. I guess the plan was, like the SMLE, to have soldiers top off from strippers, not replace the empty box magazine with a loaded one. It had an open rear sight, not an aperture like the Garand, and the first run had reliability problems. Not surprising, as

The Japanese tried to copy the Garand, but they had everything against them: no industrial base up to the task, no suitable cartridge, and ... we were bombing them flat.

the 7.7x58 has a vestigial rim, which would make feeding from a box magazine problematic. (The British spent quite some time refining their system back in the 1880s and 1890s.) I suspect the variability of the ammo was part of that as well. When making ammo for bolt actions, you can live with a wider variance of pressures and powder choices than you can in a self-loader.

They made something like 250 of them at the war's end, and they never got issued. The surviving samples now reside in various museums as examples of how not to run things.

At the start of the war, the scramble for enough weapons of almost any kind led to the U.S. buying whatever could be found by whoever could make it. One example is the Reising submachine gun. Chambered in .45 ACP, it is a reliable firearm. But it wasn't any easier to make than any other firearm (unlike the later M3 SMG) and with a wood stock, not compact. While it saw action early in the war, the Garand replaced it as soon as production could catch up. Defense plants, warehouses, docks, and military bases had to be guarded; for that, almost anything that hurled a bullet would do. And the government bought what it needed for those jobs.

Regarding the Garand replacing other firearms: The first units onto Guadalcanal, the first action we took in the Pacific on land against the Japanese, had the troops (Marines) equipped with Springfields. They were old hands, having been in the Corps for years, and well-acquainted with running a bolt-action rifle. They did exemplary work against the Japanese. Despite that success, as soon as Army units arrived and were equipped with Garands, the soldiers quickly learned that they had to guard their Garands if left in a rack unattended, or they'd be replaced with a Springfield. Yes, Marines were stealing Garands and leaving behind their '03s.

So, with that as a background, you'll have a better understanding of just how rigorous and epic in scale the production of Garands was in the over 1,800 steps it took to make a single rifle.

While a 1,000-yard rifle wasn't much use in the jungle, the ability of the .30-06 (especially the AP load) to penetrate chance obstacles was welcome.

The barrel threads, like the receiver threads, had to be timed so the barrel would torque up, so the front sight and gas port aligned.

If the barrel isn't timed correctly, the clip slots for the rear handguard will be tilted, and the handguard won't fit.

Initially, the rear sight had two unlocked knobs for adjustment. But it was found that the windage knob would loosen, so the locking bar was added to keep it tight under use. Later designs improved that, and the locking bar was no longer used.

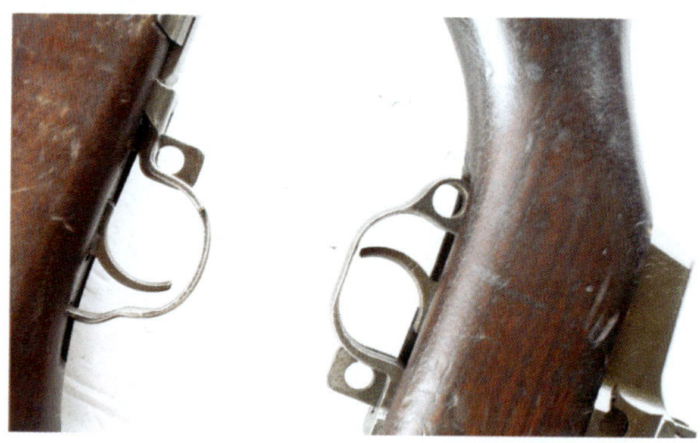

Like Springfields, Garands that came in for repair used stampings as replacements to speed up production. The triggerguard started as a milled part (right side) but was quickly changed to a stamping (left side), and they both work just fine.

GARAND PRODUCTION

Let's start with the receiver. Each receiver was a drop-forged block of alloy steel. This involved heating a piece of the proper alloy to a given temperature (red-hot to yellow) and then placing it in a steel die set. The top and bottom dies are shaped like the receiver-to-be, and the top one drops, with several tons of impact force, onto the hot steel, which forms it to shape, aligning the crystalline structure of the steel in the desired direction. (The design of such processes is an engineering art unto itself and is much overlooked in this era of additive machining.) Once out of the forge, each receiver is either left to cool or quenched.

The cooled forgings would be hauled to the receiver machining line and rows of milling machines, each with an operator and a fixture clamped to the table. The first line of operators would pick up a forging, clamp it in their fixture, and run the cutter through the steel. Depending on the cuts involved, the machine being used, and the operator's skill, this could require one, two, or even three cuts. The operator would then stop, unclamp the receiver, place it in the rack, take a new forging, and do it all over again. When the rack was full, someone would wheel the rack to the following line, where a different operator, with their own fixture, would make a different cut.

Once the receiver was nearly completed, there would be one last critical cut. Of course, there had been critical dimensional cuts made before. One, in particular, was the location of the locking lug seats and their distance to the receiver's front face. These had to be precise because they determined the headspacing of the assembled rifle.

Once the front face was machined and the locking lug slots cut, the barrel threads were cut. Now, let's consider cutting threads. Say you want to tap the hole in a plate to tighten a screw into it. Your thread does not have to be "timed." The "timing" of a threaded hole establishes where the onset of the thread slot or groove begins. If we take the top dead center of the Garand receiver as 12 o'clock, we can't have the thread starting just anywhere on the face of the clock, or every barrel screwed into it will torque at a different angle. And the barrel, remember, has the gas port, the handguard clip grooves, and other location-specific machine operations done to it.

So, the threads on both the receiver and the barrel were timed, starting at identical locations according to the drawings. As a result, an armorer with the right tools and training could unscrew a bent Garand barrel from an otherwise useable receiver, replace it with a new barrel, and not have to machine all the other details. Yes, if you wanted to be exact, you could measure the headspace and finish-ream the chamber, but in a combat theater, close enough was, indeed, close enough.

So, the barrels received much the same care. Each steel bar that arrived ready for production was inspected, lathe-turned, bored, reamed and honed, broached to create the rifling, and the handguard clip grooves machined, the rear of the barrel machined, and the gas cylinder band ground to dimension. Then, it would have the threads timed and machined, the gas port hole drilled, and the rear face of the chamber cleaned up.

In all the steps on these and other parts, the machinists had guide notes on the part dimensions. They would regularly measure parts and ensure the tooling hadn't worn or shifted so that they were holding tolerance. Every step of the way, inspectors checked parts to ensure they were made according to the drawings. You ask why there were so many drawings and revisions when the M1 Garand was the perfect rifle. That's because it wasn't perfect initially, even though it was really good.

In this context, perfect means not just the end performance but the steps in manufacturing. Let's take the bolt as a simple (well, not really simple) example. The bolt drawing specified the dimensions of every face but not the surface texture — at least, not all the faces. The breechface will be as smooth as the machining operation can make it, but the bolt body might just be left in the rough texture of the drop forge. Let's say (and I'm not saying this is how it went, but just as an example) the drawing and the designers assumed the drop forge could not forge to the final dimension. They would specify the bolt machined on the top surface. Then, a drop forge genius figures a way to forge to the bolt body dimension, no machining needed. That speeds up production but requires the drawing to

This is what the carbine was made for: a radio operator who works in a halftrack needs something handy and compact.

Approaching Omaha Beach, there are six M1 Carbines, one Garand and an '03 visible in this photo. The Garand was everywhere, but it wasn't everything.

be updated. So, we have bolt drawing number, dash-A or dash-1. Then, someone figures out a way to make the operation smoother by slightly changing the angle of surface "X," and we have drawing number dash-B or dash-2.

And this happens with each part. Now, if a part is significantly changed, it gets a new drawing number. Somebody figures out a way to use a cheaper, simpler or more-common alloy that is just as good. That warrants a new drawing number. And, on the significant parts, the drawing number also includes the manufacturer, so you'll see an "SA" on bolts made by Springfield.

What about production rates? At the peak of production, Springfield Armory produced as many as 4,600 rifles daily. Granted, Springfield Armory wasn't being bombed, but compare 4,600 a day to the 250 rifles the Japanese managed to make as copies of the Garand.

Wherever the Army went, its rifle had to work. Even in Sitka, Alaska, in the dead of winter, Garands had to function. They did.

SERIAL NUMBERS

Receivers got serial numbers at specific states in manufacture. The War Department issued serial numbers in blocks, so there would be no overlap. There were only two manufacturers in WWII, so this was relatively easy to manage. Since Springfield began production, it started with number 1 and made the first 100,000 before Winchester was assigned blocks. After that, it simply jumped from one block to the next.

These GIs are veterans. The clues? Unshaven, muddy galoshes, and weapons that do not leave their hands. The closest GI, Pfc. Berzon has a Garand, but the other two are packing Thompsons.

M1 GARAND ASSIGNED SERIAL NUMBERS, WWII

- 1–100,000 SPRINGFIELD ARMORY
- 100,001–165,500 WINCHESTER REPEATING ARMS
- 165,501–1,200,000 SPRINGFIELD ARMORY
- 1,200,001–1,357,473 WINCHESTER REPEATING ARMS
- 1,357,474–2,305,849 SPRINGFIELD ARMORY
- 2,656,149–4,399,999 SPRINGFIELD ARMORY

The reason was simple: the military did not want duplicate numbers. This was not the first rodeo for the War Department when it came to large-scale wars. The department had been through The Great War, and having the inventory system define the serial number and the manufacturer as a required detail was more than they wanted.

When it comes time to track rifles in inventory, all anyone needs to know is: "Rifle, M1 Garand, #1,000,000." Who made it doesn't matter. If there is some technical problem that the armorers must address, the serial number will suffice, and they can back that up with the markings (drawing numbers, etc.) on the various parts.

Now, if you want to know what month of what year your Garand was made, that level of detail can be tracked down. What matters for us is that, from a slow start in 1936 and with insufficient rifles on hand to equip the small army as it existed in 1942, we made 4 million more rifles in less than three years.

Remember our discussion about industrial bases at the end of Chapter 1? Well, that's what we had. We had enough production capacity to make all those Garands and everything else we produced.

Now, there's the plan, and then there's the reality. In reality, it seems that both Springfield and Winchester messed up. Springfield over-ran its assigned serial number block at 2,415,850; the last one is up in the 2,536,500s. These serial numbers were assigned to Winchester, but in the haste of making rifles, someone perhaps misread the chart and transposed some numbers.

Winchester also ran a batch from serial number 1,357,474 to 1,387,900-something, a series assigned to Springfield. Then it did it a second time! That was a batch of some 40,000 receivers that it made in 1943 but didn't assemble until 1945. Those serial numbers run from 1,601,150 to 1,642,000. They are called the "WIN13" rifles due to the heat-treatment number they received, which is stamped on the right receiver leg as the drawing number and heat-treat code: D28291WIN13.

IN ALL, SOME 190,000 RIFLES WERE PRODUCED WITH DUPLICATE SERIAL NUMBERS. WHEN THIS WAS DISCOVERED, THOSE UNITS WITH DUPLICATES IN INVENTORY WOULD (SOMETIMES) MARK THE DUPLICATES.

In all, some 190,000 rifles were produced with duplicate serial numbers. When this was discovered, those units with duplicates in inventory would (sometimes) mark the duplicates. So, a Springfield with the same number as a Winchester would have one of them stamped with an "A" as a suffix. Or not. If the unit involved didn't care, then it wasn't stamped. And as far as I know, no armorer update was sent to all units indicating that all Springfields (or Winchesters) with serial numbers in those blocks were to be stamped with an "A" suffix and noted in the inventory. That was too much even for the OCD members in the inventory system.

What does this mean for you? If you find a Garand with an A suffix, now you know why. Someone out there, someplace, has a matching pair, a Springfield and a Winchester, with identical serial numbers. Are they in trouble? Do we all need to stamp any rifles with serial numbers in those blocks? Nope. The ATF doesn't care. Not because it happened so long ago. No, they don't care because they know they can tell the difference. Having a Winchester Garand and a Springfield Garand with the same serial numbers is not much different from having a Ruger and a Remington rifle with matching numbers. For the Army, the serial number is what matters. For the ATF, the unique identifier is the maker *and* the number. That's why your Ruger firearm has a three-number prefix. It has a serial number of XXX-12345 to keep straight the vast number of Ruger models and provide a unique identifier for each of them.

As an aside, there are collectors (I don't know if anyone still does this, the task has become gargantuan) who collected each Ruger model as it came out, in "their" serial number. Back in the earliest days, if you happened to have bought a Ruger serial number 221, you could ask the factory to ship you all subsequent models of serial number 221. By today, that would be a serious pile of money tied up in hundreds of #221-marked firearms.

The chance of running into one of these Garands, even just one in the correct serial number range, is pretty small. We're talking 190,000 rifles, and even if we consider just the SA/Win universe of 4,500,000 rifles, that is one in 24. Add in the Korean War Garands, and it is one in 34 rifles. Not as unlikely as hitting the lottery, but not something to undertake as a collecting plan.

Then, on August 6, 1945, all the plans were set aside. Hiroshima was the recipient of the first atomic bomb, and two days later, Nagasaki joined the horrible club. With the sudden capitulation of Japan, the invasion plans were shelved. Invasion plans? The plan was to finish the war by invading Japan, requiring even more men, materiel, and time. The earliest plans had the U.S. invading in 1946,

The M1 Carbine was meant as a rear-area and crew-served weapon for defense, not up at the front, fighting. But the 15-round magazine (the 30-round ones came too late for most of the war) and its light weight made it attractive to the frontline troops.

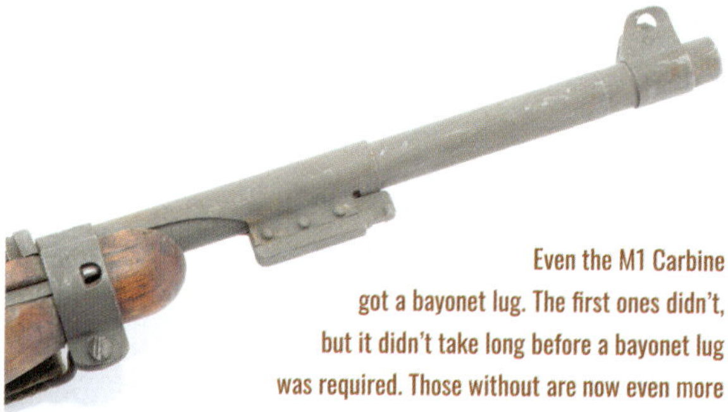

Even the M1 Carbine got a bayonet lug. The first ones didn't, but it didn't take long before a bayonet lug was required. Those without are now even more collectible than the M1 Carbine has become.

and with the experience of the Pacific, everyone knew what would happen. The Japanese had a good idea of the expected landing sites, and we knew the typical Japanese response.

My father's unit, just out of the European fight, was scheduled (I've done some research on the invasion, code-named Operation Downfall) and slated to be in Operation Coronet, the invasion of Honshu, in the third wave. The projections were that the third wave would experience "only" 90% casualties. The Japanese had already begun training and propaganda operations in June 1945

We fought WWII with three rifles: the Garand, the 03A3, and the M1 Carbine.

In this Signal Corps photo, note that the left-side GI has the belt with pouches for clips and three bandoliers of ammo. This is the 95th Infantry, the unit to which the author's father belonged.

to commit the entire population to resist the invaders.

The European vets weren't too enthusiastic about this, as they had already "won their fight," and the next looked even worse. But, with Japan surrendering immediately, that was that.

And the millions of GIs came home to start their lives over, working on converting the defense plants back into auto assembly lines, washing machine factories, and so on. The days of making new Garands were over, and now the task of refurbishing the old ones began.

Millions of Garands were turned in and recovered from battlefields (although I suspect a fair number of them still reside, unknown except by the owners, in various French and Italian farmhouses, chalets, and villages). Those guns had to be inspected, and any damage, wear, or faults corrected. Springfield kept busy making new barrels to replace the worn-out or damaged ones on suitable receivers. That was the start, and it added even more "churn" to the mix-and-match nature of the Garands we see today. If you're lucky, you may encounter a Garand made in, say, 1943, with a 1946 or later barrel.

Peace only lasted for a short while. It turned cold, then hot, and then cold again before getting hot in Vietnam. •

(Below) An experimental Garand, modified to use a box magazine and judging by the button above the trigger, also modified for select-fire.

CHAPTER 5

WHAT DO THE MARKINGS MEAN?

At the start of WWII, America was an industrial powerhouse. By the time the war ended, we had not only increased our industrial capacity, but the war had ground much of the world's industrial production into rubble.

The Garand was designed with a few — well, OK, more than a few — simple details that had to be attended to, and Springfield started with the plan to mark each part and ensure anyone with a handbook could tell what was what.

One detail that was almost unheard-of in the industrial world then: every bolt and barreled receiver was interchangeable. So, if you come across a 98K Mauser rifle or are offered one for sale, the description might include "matching numbers." That is, the serial number on the

bolt matches that on the receiver. When Mauser or whoever made that rifle, the headspace was correct for *that rifle with that bolt*; swap bolts, and the new pairing might not be correct. Well, the U.S. Army was having none of that sort of nonsense. The military had started with the Springfield '03 and didn't see any point in not doing so with the Garand. As such, each Garand was made so the headspace was correct from the front shoulder of the chamber to the locking lug surfaces on the receiver. And each bolt was produced with the correct headspace from the rear of the locking lugs to the bolt face.

As a result, you could put any Garand bolt into any Garand rifle, and the headspace would be correct. How precise of an operation was this? Time for a little bit of arithmetic. Headspace is the allowable variance of the room in the chamber for the cartridge. It's measured from the face of the bolt to the "datum line," a given diameter circle measured at a given distance from the bolt's face. The datum line is a line on the chamber's shoulder. (The shoulder angle can vary slightly, but the datum line is critical.)

In general terms, that distance can vary by six-thousandths of an inch (.006) in modern commercial production. In military use, the spread is larger, but not a lot, because too much means case separations, which is bad in combat. If we depend on two parts to always fall within that gap, then it is clear that the critical dimensions of each on its own cannot add up to more than a .003-inch variation. This means that when we get down to it, the critical dimensions of the two assemblies have a dimensional variance of +/- .0015 inch.

Yowza.

Why do this? Because the Army had an idea of how it wanted things to go in a war and implemented that plan. You see, rifles get abused in use, in combat. If only one part of a rifle was damaged, that part could be stripped off and replaced with one from the pile of useable parts, which would be taken off of other, more damaged rifles. For that approach to work, everything has to be interchangeable. And in the Garand, they were.

What if a Garand's barrel was the damaged part? Once it had been stripped of useable parts, down to the action, it would have been sent to an armorers' shop with spare barrels. The armorers would inspect it to make sure the receiver was still good. Then they would have unscrewed the damaged barrel, screwed in a new one, reamed the headspace to spec if they had to, and built it up with parts on hand or taken from other Garands.

And that's why the standard form of the Garand is a mix-n-match, and there is no such thing as an "all-matching Garand" or darned few of them. For it to match, it would never have gone overseas. There are few like that.

Each Mauser was headspaced correctly when made or rebuilt. However, it was common when accepting the surrender of many German troops to separate the rifles and bolts into big piles. So, it was common to find post-war Mausers with mismatched numbers.

One way would be for a Garand to be issued to a soldier or marine, used, and in its original form taken home after the hostilities were over. There was a lot of that in the post-WWII era. GIs who were done fighting but not done with owning a Garand (or M1 carbine, or 1911A1, or fill-in-the-blank) would stuff them in their duffle bag, box them up and ship them home. Or sample rifles that, for whatever reason, were gifted to arsenal employees, taken home for study, or issued for a match and then won as prizes in the competition. But most have been rebuilt, in some instances repeatedly.

BLUEPRINT MARKINGS

The Ordnance Department wanted to ensure it could trace all parts. Not that the department had to have serial numbers, but it did require other codes. One such code is the drawing number. Each blueprint, the document that laid down all the dimensions that mattered on a part, was assigned a number. Each drawing had its unique number. As a part was upgraded, modified, improved or altered, the drawing number would get a suffix, such as a "-1," added. If the change was significant enough, it might get a new number, not just a revision. There was a procedure to determine that step, as well. The existing parts did not get a new number, but the drawing did. Parts made after issuing the new drawing would be stamped with the new drawing number.

This way, if a particular design was found to have a problem, it was easy to check the drawing numbers on the inventory and yank out all the ones with the problematic number. If it proved necessary to make such a swap, this would be communicated to all the armorers at whatever level the swap was done, who would be tasked with checking inventory and updating all rifles that came through.

This IHA bolt has the drawing number, the IHA initials, and the letter "U" to indicate the heat treatment run.

HEAT TREAT MARKINGS

Some parts, like the receiver, required a particular heat treatment process. So, each process run would be assigned a number, and all of the receivers (or other parts) that went through in that run would receive the heat treatment lot number. Next batch, a different number. Why do this? To grasp this, we have to go back to the production of the 1903 Springfield. Back then, the workers in the heat treatment plant prided themselves on gauging the steel's temperature by eye. "Looks the right temp" would have been the signal to pull a rack of heated receivers out of the furnace for quenching.

In the goodness of time (a few years), some receivers turned up that were brittle — so brittle they'd break when fired. It turns out that when the light changed, like from a sunny summer day to a cloudy winter day, the perceived color could vary, and thus the temperature varied, and the steel could be too hot. (A sunny day was the primary problem, causing the temp to be higher when it was "eye-balled.") The term "low-number Springfield" indicates an '03 made before the arsenal changed to thermocouples for measuring temperature.

You can't risk shooting a low-number Springfield because it might break. And there is no non-destructive test to see if it is too brittle.

Garands were going to be made using thermocouples to measure temperature. Still, if there was some problem with a particular heat treatment run, the Army wanted a way to weed out those and only those affected. You see, the problem with the '03s arose during WWI. As a result of being unable to test them, the War Department had to remove some 800,000 Springfield and 285,000 Rock Island Springfields from service. That's over a million rifles because there was no way to distinguish the brittle and hardened ones. That wasn't going to happen with the Garand.

MANUFACTURER MARKINGS

The receivers were marked clearly with the manufacturer's name. Those included Winchester, Springfield, Harrington & Richardson, International Harvester, Beretta, and the new company Springfield Armory, many years, decades even later. But other parts would be marked as well, so if a particular maker was found to have problems with bolts, barrels, whatever, those could be pulled and repaired or scrapped.

ARSENAL MARKINGS

Garands went through inspections and rebuilds when returned from service, having been used in training or issued to an overseas base and replaced with a fresh batch. (Some batches never got returned and stayed overseas for years, decades even.) When a Garand was finished in one of the U.S. manufacturers, a military inspector would look over as many of them in a given lot as the regulations required, and if they passed, the lot would be stamped with acceptance marks. These could be marks on the barrel or the stock (called a cartouche) and then crated and shipped. Also, if a rifle came into an arsenal for a rebuild, it would sometimes be marked by that arsenal to indicate where and when it had been worked on.

ROLL MARKS

Up to this point, the typical process of marking the numbers on parts used a "roll mark" — a wheel with the reverse of the numbers or letters. This wheel was crafted by toolmakers of steel that could be hardened, when finished, to be harder than the steel being marked. (Obvious, when you think about it, right?) The wheel was pressed against the part, then rolled, sometimes back and forth several times. Why not just hammer the numbers in? Despite being hardened, the marking tool has limits. Hammer it, and it will wear faster, even break. Roll it, even at the pressures it takes to mark steel, and it lasts longer. And hand stamping with a hammer would be far too slow.

ACCEPTANCE MARKS

A few markings were applied by hand with a marking die and a hammer. The punch mark was sometimes applied on barrels when the receiver maker installed them. Another is the "P" proof mark each rifle received after test-firing. It was applied to the barrel when it wasn't feasible to disassemble each rifle, once tested, and use a roll mark. So, once all the rifles in the rack were fired, someone would walk down the rack with a die and hammer and whack each barrel someplace. That is why they are sometimes at such cockeyed angles and odd locations: it was wherever the hammerer could reach.

Another mark was the Defense Acceptance mark. This mark has the eagle and three stars in a cartouche and is seen on barrels and stocks. It was adopted in 1952 to replace a slew of other inspection and acceptance markings, like the crossed cannons mark and the "P" proof mark. It was also supposed to be applied to more than just rifles and bayonets, and the DoD approved the use of a steel stamp, a rubber stamp, and a stencil.

The Defense Acceptance dies are relatively easy to find. An unscrupulous owner could mark their Garands with it, and none would be the wiser. Of course, since they all got it anyway, is this a problem?

UNIT MARKINGS

Once shipped to a given depot for use by the units at that base or issued for combat, Garands would often receive what is known as a "rack number" added to the rifle for stacking in racks. Once a given serial number had been assigned a given rack number (let's say, Rifle, M1 Garand, Winchester serial number 1,000,000) had been assigned to Rack A, number 39, the inventory would have been easier to track if it had a rack number. To do a regular inventory once rack numbers had been produced and inscribed or painted, one merely had to walk down the aisles between the racks and ensure that the numbers were sequential, there were no missing numbers, and all the rack slots were filled. Done. (We will overlook the possibility that GIs in the field, cleaning rifles, had swapped stocks. Life was good as long as a rifle was marked "A39" in the slot assigned to A39. Of course, when the annual serial number inventory was done.)

A rack number could be added to the sling, but since slings were parts that could be readily swapped, worn out and replaced, it was common to paint the numbers on the stocks, where they could be easily seen in the racks.

So all the major parts on your Garand will have numbers of one kind or another. The numbers allow you to get some idea of the life's history of your Garand. Let's get to it in more detail, then.

Congratulations, you just bought an M1 Garand of your own. Get ready; you are in for fun and a good, solid

Rack numbers could be any place that worked for the unit and the racks they had. This one has the rack number inked on a piece of masking tape on the rear handguard.

This Springfield barrel, made in January 1955, has multiple proofs, and you can see the DAS on the far right.

One of the author's Garands, complete with a bandolier of the kind of ammo his Dad loved; .30-06 AP.

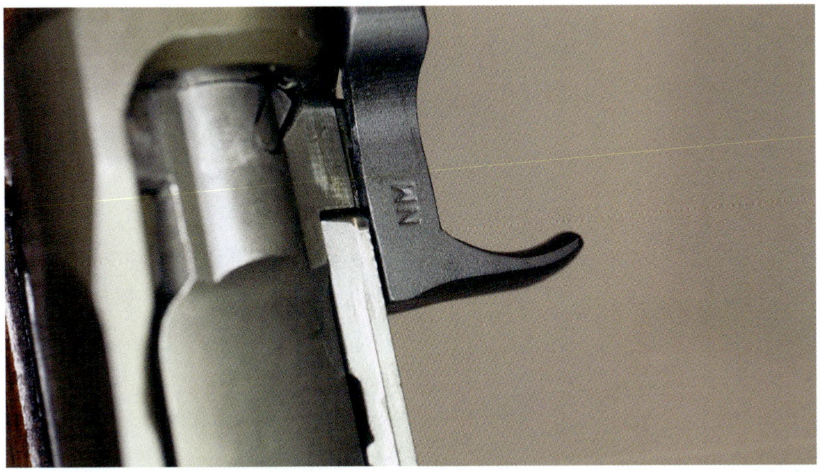

The "NM" marking on the author's Garand, indicating National Match grade op rod.

shoulder-thumping. As you pore over your new rifle, you will no doubt notice that it is marked all over the place with numbers and symbols. What do all those markings mean?

I bought my first M1 Garand in 1977. It was my second centerfire rifle (after a WWI SMLE, bought for a song), and it caught my eye because I had never seen a Garand with a glossy stock. It was in the rack of a long-gone gun shop at the reasonable price of $300. At the time, a Colt SP1 was going for the same amount of money, but it would be a decade at least before the shooting world got hot for the Stoner.

Why was the Garand so inexpensive? I looked it over. Despite being a match-conditioned rifle, with national match rear sight, NM op rod, glass bedded and everything, it was suppos-

You can make out the "NM" stamp on the rear sight assembly on Sweeney's match Garand. If you get one of these, you are doing good.

edly because "the bore was shot out." It had not been abused, there were no hammer marks or tire tracks, and everything seemed fine. I figured, shot-out or not, it was probably more accurate than I was at the time, and I could learn a lot by loading for it and getting in some big-bore practice.

So I shelled out the cash, took it home, and got some lessons from my dad, Sergeant James Sweeney, Combat Scouts, 379th regiment, 95th infantry division, aka Iron men of Metz. He had carried one in Europe until he moved on to tools better suited for his job, so I got the run-down. (Dad's job? For much of the war, and he spent more than his fair share at the front, he went out each night, found the Germans, and ensured they did not get a good night's sleep. His preferred tools for that job were an M3 "Grease gun" and a satchel full of grenades.)

The first thing to do with my new Garand was clean it. Even before effective bore cleaners, Dad had taught me what to look for. That first patch that came out of the bore was a revelation. The patch came out black as if dragged through a coal mine. So, I scrubbed it daily, taking care not to wear the crown, while I read up on things Garand.

One detail caught my eye: to truly be match-conditioned, the forward handguard must not touch the barrel. I stripped the rifle down and found that someone had manhandled it by the handguard, which was touching the barrel. I re-aligned it, finally got all the gunk out of the bore, and went to the range. Yes, it could shoot better than I could, and it wasn't "shot out." Between the fouled bore and the accuracy-harming contact, the rifle probably hadn't shot well for the former owner. Now, it shot just fine. With match loads, it came as close to 1 MOA as my skills at the time allowed.

Learning to run and shoot that rifle, I also learned about WWII manufacturing processes and reloading the .30-06.

As we have discussed, the Garand took quite some time to be developed and adopted, and this development time allowed John Cantius Garand to work all the bugs out of it and produce a fine rifle. It was designed to be modular and interchangeable. And America at the time,

Contact on the front handguard can take the gilt-edge off of accuracy, so if your Garand is match-built, check this.

The author's father, Sergeant James Sweeney, Combat Scouts, 379th regiment, 95th infantry division, aka Iron Men of Metz, carried a Garand in Europe until he moved on to tools better suited for his job, taking point or working at night. For that, he favored the M3 Grease gun. James Sweeney returned from the war as a Sergeant after earning a silver and bronze star. Of his original rifle company, he was one of six who did not receive a Purple Heart. In his words, "Not for lack of the Germans trying."

The lowest serial number the author has seen on a Garand in the wild.

representing the apex of modern manufacturing, could deliver on that promise.

Despite having started collecting them so long ago, I only own a few Garands. To provide more comprehensive coverage for this book, I contacted some guys in my gun club who have diligently collected Garands. They've been working with Garands for years and have an extensive collection. We looked over the racks and selected a few that would be illustrative.

A CLOSER LOOK

Let's start with your trigger assembly. With an unloaded rifle, pry the triggerguard downward, pivot it away from the stock, and pull the entire assembly out. The assembly is an integrated unit that can be exchanged with any other trigger assembly on other Garands. Remember what I laid out at the beginning of this chapter? This is an explicit demonstration of what the War Department, and the Army, wanted.

Service units could work over Garands literally within earshot of the fighting. A pile of battle-damaged Garands could be trucked in, and the armorers could strip them down, inspect, re-assemble and issue them back out. If the unit-level armorer took in 100 damaged Garands and could, in an afternoon, re-assemble 75 of them from the undamaged parts, he could send them back out and ship odds and ends of the 25 others back for more work, meaning the unit had 75 rifles still ready for combat. No hand-fitting, power tools, or need for anything but asking: "Does this trigger assembly work? Yes, put it in a rifle. If not, set it aside."

The Garand was lucky during WWII, with just two significant manufacturers, Winchester and Springfield, making them. The M1 Carbine, by comparison, had a slew of manufacturers and a mob of sub-contractors. But they still managed the same feat. Yep, that was American manufacturing back then.

Receivers had serial numbers marked sequentially on each receiver in turn. The lower the number, the earlier

The correct marking for a trigger assembly housing, made by Springfield.

A Springfield hammer inside a Springfield trigger housing.

the production sequence. Unlike common European practice, the other parts were not numbered to the receiver. The manufacturers (again, during WWII, just Winchester and Springfield) had blocks of serial numbers assigned to them. If they used up the digits in a block, they'd skip to the next block. So, as an example, if Winchester marked a receiver with the number 165,500, it would jump to 1,200,001 for the next one. All the numbers in between "belonged" to Springfield. So, if someone offers you a Winchester M1 Garand, number 170,000, there's something wrong. The last number assigned? 6,099,905. Does it still exist? No idea.

... THE GUYS DOING THE FIELD REBUILDS HAD NO TIME TO MESS AROUND WITH HEADSPACE GAUGES. THEY MIGHT USE EROSION AND CROWN GAUGES IF THEY HAD THE TIME, BUT IF A RIFLE WORKED AND HIT THE TARGET WITHIN "MINUTE OF NAZI," IT WOULD BE RE-ISSUED.

Now, notice the numbers by looking at the trigger assembly in your hands. The housing will have a number stamped into it. This is the drawing number, and all the major components of a Garand will have such a number.

As mentioned, the drawing number is the blueprint number to which the part was manufactured. For instance, a number such as D28290-12-SA would indicate drawing number 28290, revision 12, made by Springfield Armory. This nomenclature let the Quartermaster know what parts were made, when, and where. Let's say someone discovers that (just making a fictitious number here) parts with drawing number 10001 have a dimensional problem. Those parts were made to match that drawing, and they have a problem due to that error. It is an arduous but simple task to check that number on the parts involved, or rifles using those parts, and yank out of inventory those that were made to that drawing. But at least you don't have to scrap all of them, not knowing the drawing number, *ala* Springfield '03s.

If a particular part were found to not be within spec but built to the drawing, the drawing would be changed and given a new number, and parts made using that new number would be so-marked. The new parts, with drawing number 10001-1, are thus correct. If the dimensional problem allowed it, it would be possible for the parts to be shipped back, corrected, restamped with the extra "-1," and re-issued.

As I said, all major parts were marked with a drawing number, and smaller ones would be marked with the manufacturer if a subcontractor.

The drawing number, plus the manufacturer's internal codes, indicate extra details about the production.

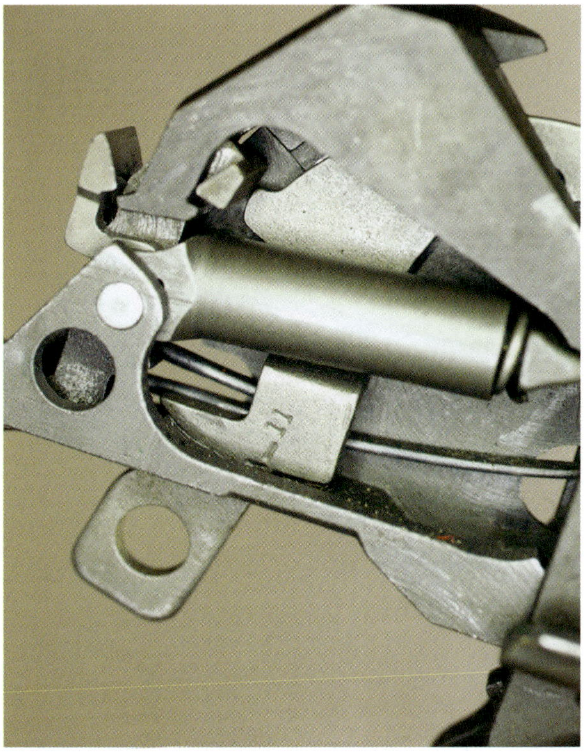

A Springfield safety in a Springfield trigger assembly. All proper.

The CMP has the drawing number lists — those approved, ones requiring parts removal, and others requiring modification. The CMP used these lists to ensure parts were correct on Garands, at least regarding the correct function. Historically, this wasn't always done. Why "historically?" Let's say you're the proud owner of Springfield Armory M1 Garand number 200,000. (Lucky you, that one was made in March 1941, before Pearl Harbor.) Suppose it arrived with a trigger housing drawing number with a revision not issued until 1944. If your Garand was a CMP Garand, CMP didn't care; if it worked, CMP shipped it. The arsenal rebuilding it back in 1956 didn't care, either. But, there's someone out there who does, and they went to the trouble of tracking down all the marked parts with drawing numbers and revisions used in March 1941 and assembling it "period correct" as it might have been. It doesn't matter that it might never have been that way; it makes them happy.

Why this level of marking on the various parts? Because, again, every part was made to be interchangeable. Let's say you're in a field rebuild tent, in the jungle of New Guinea, with a truckload of combat-damaged Garands. You don't care who made the trigger housing you need to replace. You want to know that all the other parts will fit into the replacement housing you stripped off of the Garand with the barrel bent into a "U" shape. However, you will have a list of drawing numbers noted as unusable. If it isn't on that list and works, it gets assembled into a working rifle and sent back to the front.

Unlike, say, a Mauser 98K, where the bolt will be numbered to the receiver, the Garand doesn't need that. More on that when we get to the bolts.

In no particular order, the receivers will have the manufacturer's name, serial number, and drawing number. If you pore over such lists, you can even determine that the drawing and serial numbers agree with the period the receiver was made. Some receivers will even have rebuild markings, indicating who (or, instead, which arsenal) worked on it at some period later.

The bolt will have a drawing number. This is important because bolts were meant to be utterly interchangeable between rifles. Again, the guys doing the field rebuilds had no time to mess around with headspace gauges. They might use erosion and crown gauges if they had the time, but if a rifle worked and hit the target within "minute of Nazi," it would be re-issued.

Bolts also had a heat treat batch number. The heat treatment of bolts and receivers was an essential opera-

A bolt with the drawing number, Springfield code, and heat batch number.

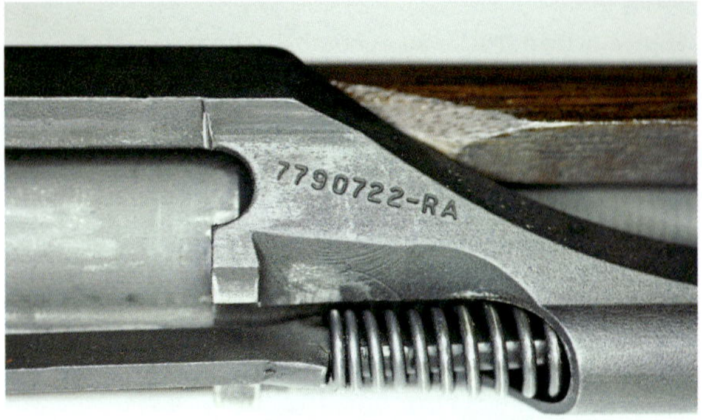

A National Match op rod, properly machined with the radiused "corner," so it won't crack under heavy use.

This barrel was made by Springfield in June 1953 and installed into an IHA receiver by IHA. The punch mark indicates such near the band between the "SA" and the sideways "P" proof mark.

tion. If a batch of bolts was later found with improper heat treatment, it was a simple, if arduous, process to eyeball every bolt in every rifle in inventory, and the spares, if any, and check for that heat treat batch number and pull out those with the defective batch number.

Because of how Garands were made, bolts headspace differently. Oh, the bolt was used to check the headspacing, but the actual measurement was from the receiver locking slot surfaces. That way, every Garand bolt made by any Garand bolt maker would drop into any Garand's barreled receiver. So, the European love of numbering all major parts to the last few digits of the receiver was unnecessary on the Garand.

Operating rods have drawing numbers, but they also could be sorted for proper function using other details — not something that was marked but made apparent. One such detail is the re-cut corner of the op rod where the spring tunnel joins the handle extension. When originally designed, the corner proved to be too square. The rod, in heavy use, would crack there. How much of a problem was this? Not enough to have been changed during the war. But post-war, new rods were made with a radius, and all existing op rods were modified with an end mill to make the corner a rounded notch, relieving the stress riser. The op rod would have been re-Parkerized, and none were the wiser. Oh, and a small detail: makers machined the op rods with two different radius cutters. Does it matter? Not one bit.

BARREL MARKINGS

Barrels can show a veritable library of markings. When the bolt is closed, markings are found on the barrel's right side and hidden by the op rod. You have to open the action to read the code.

First, the barrel marking has a drawing number with a D-prefix. So, you can track it by that. It will also have a manufacturing date, a month, and a year set. So, 2-44 would be February 1944. It will also have the manufacturer's marking if the manufacturer desired to mark it. Some, like Winchester, were so proud of their barrels that they would mark them even if the specifications didn't call for it. Springfield stamped them "SA" for the manufacturer's code, and later barrels, such as those made in Norway (yes, the Norwegians made barrels for their M1 Garands, post-war), had a crown-over-letter mark. There would often be a proof mark, a simple capital letter "P," and others received the U.S. Defense Acceptance mark, an eagle with three stars. Often jokingly called the "chicken and three stars," this mark was applied to barrels (and stocks) once the batch had been inspected and passed.

Other markings almost require a Dan Brown DaVinci Code-level of knowledge and inspection — for example, the top handguard held in by a steel clip. A center punch where the clip touches the barrel might indicate that the receiver's manufacturer installed the barrel. Or, both receiver and barrel were made at the same factory. This level of marking was done to keep the Ordnance Department informed, but it didn't matter to the unit-level armorer or the depot-level rebuilder.

STOCK MARKINGS

Stocks also got markings. These marks are called a "cartouche" (car-toosh) from the border that some Egyptian hieroglyphs received. (Properly speaking, a hieroglyph is only correctly inside the cartouche border if it is the name of a Pharaoh. No other use was correct, at least when Egypt was in charge of things.) The markings could be a set of letters representing the arsenal where the stock was first used, plus the inspectors' initials, the Defense Acceptance mark, or the crossed cannons of the Ordnance department. Unlike the drawing and other inspection markings, the stock cartouches used the inspector's initials as part of the stamp.

IF YOU LUST AFTER AN ALL-CORRECT, ALL-COMPLETE, WINCHESTER-ONLY RIFLE, THOSE ITALIAN PARTS ARE A BLOT ON YOUR PERSONAL LANDSCAPE. TO THE REST OF US, THEY ARE INTERESTING AND USEFUL PARTS THAT WE'LL BE HAPPY TO TAKE OFF YOUR HANDS FOR A NOMINAL SUM.

Cartouches are less commonly encountered than other markings because they were stamped in wood. The stocks and cartouches could be worn by use, sanded and re-finished, overhauled or rubbed flat from the Sergeant's instructions. Some markings will survive such changes because they are inside the stock. A subcontractor, Overton, made one stock we looked at for IHC. The numerical code is in the barrel channel where it was safe.

The loss of a cartouche is not necessarily a new thing. My father told me (more than once) about being issued his first Garand. They were soon issued brand new Garands in training, finally turning in the Enfields they had been drilling with. (These would have been M1917 bolt actions in storage since WWI and used only for initial training and drill work.) the Garands were encrusted in cosmoline. So, the parts went into the showers with GI soap and brushes and were scrubbed until the cosmoline was gone, oiled the metal with light oil, and reassembled.

"The drains?" I asked. "They had to be choked with cosmoline."

My dad wasn't concerned, then or later, when telling the tale. "We were shipping out the next day, we left that problem for the next platoon."

You can make out the edges of the inspector's cartouche on the stock. When you consider the heavy dents to the left of it, it is a wonder that any cartouches survive.

The Defense Acceptance mark on an H&R Garand's stock.

The marking for this Overton stock indicating use by the IHC was placed safely in the barrel channel.

This rifle was inspected and overhauled at the Red River arsenal in July 1966, marked with an electric pencil, and returned to inventory.

Now having new rifles to care for, they used linseed oil on the stocks until the stocks would not accept any more and then rubbed the stocks with the handles of their toothbrushes, both to compress the wood, which would seal the pores, and burnish the stocks to a sheen — bye-bye cartouche.

PRODUCTION CONSIDERATIONS

Garand production ended once WWII was over. We quickly went from nine million men and women in the Armed Forces to many fewer. How many fewer? The Army was only 600,000 men before the Korean War. Since we had made just over four million Garands and over six million M1 Carbines, we didn't need to make any more in 1946, or so we thought. We also could hand them out, practically willy-nilly, to allies worldwide. That's where some have gone, and a few are coming back from since Garands are so *passé* in the modern world. That attitude did not change until 1950, when the Korean War sprang up.

Then, the Department of Defense (recently re-named from the War Department) had Springfield restart manufacturing (Springfield had overhauled a half-million rifles in the interim), soon joined by International Harvester and Harrington & Richardson in making new Garands.

After WWII, but before Korea (which no one had a clue was coming), the War Department had the old supplies of Garands inspected, upgraded, rebuilt, and any worn, rusted or obsolete parts replaced. So, that pristine all-Winchester rifle assembled in 1944 and used enough to need a rebuild? It got whatever parts worked, fit, and

The Defense Acceptance mark, the eagle and three stars, on the front edge of the marking area of a barrel.

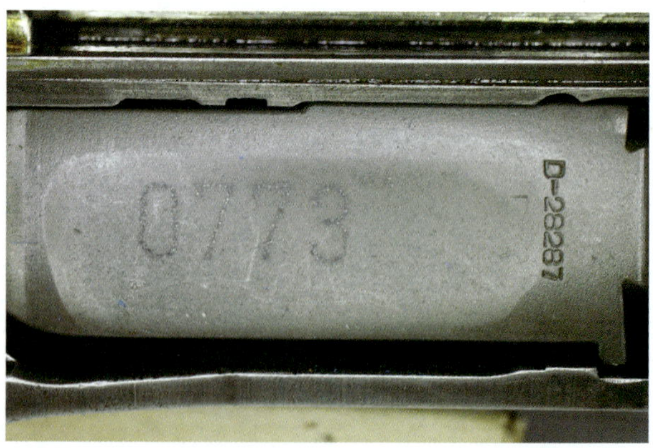

The Danes so desired putting serial numbers on individual parts that they used a surface grinder to put a flat on this bolt. They even removed the heat treat batch number to do so.

passed inspection. I know I keep harping on this, but of all the collectors, those who have gotten the Winchester bug are the most OCD.

THE NATIONAL MATCH

One question you might have is, "What is this National Match or NM you speak of?" At a time, shooting in national competition with service rifles was commonplace. You could show up, be issued a rifle and ammunition, and shoot the match. The idea was to encourage skill with the issue rifle. With any competition, there will be those who want to win. And those whose skills overmatch the vanilla-plain equipment (and much overlap in those two groups). So, in 1953 the Chief of Ordnance directed Springfield Armory to provide match-grade rifles for the annual Camp Perry competitions. Some NM-marked parts are selected for being (or made to) the closest tolerances. Others, like the sights, are made differently. The NM rear sight, for instance, has finer adjustments and a hooded aperture. NM-marked parts would fit a standard rifle, and, provided other details were attended to, a plain rifle with a good barrel could be made to Match Grade, which had been done to my first Garand.

Rack numbers might be stamped, painted, or in this case, written on tape with a felt-tip pen. They'd be shoved into the storage racks by their rack number; thus, it was easy to see if they were all there. If one was missing, it was easy to determine by the empty slot in the rack.

Sweeney's Fed Ord-marked import Garand. The metal may have some pitting but is not a re-weld of scrapped receivers.

MISCELLANEOUS MARKINGS

Then there were the rebuilds, the new barrels, and the international markings. Barrels came from many places, so it is not unusual to see a Winchester receiver, made between 1942 and 1945, with a Springfield barrel dated from 1965 to 1966. One my friend Rob and I looked at is an International Harvester with a Springfield barrel. However, the barrel had a punch mark, in line with the rear handguard band as described earlier, indicating that while Springfield made the barrel, IHA installed it. And you thought things were simple because there were so few prime manufacturers.

The Italians, as mentioned, made parts and overhauled them. The Norwegians produced barrels. The Danish modified and marked their rifles to suit their needs and practices. They all had their own marking practices and applied the marks and codes as their regulations required.

And then there are other markings. One of my rifles has a "Fed Ord" etching on the receiver leg. You might ask: "Didn't Federal Ordnance re-weld cut receivers?" Yes, but this one hasn't been cut. The etching is an importation mark. The receiver is a 1944 Springfield. And it was not the only one importing Garands. Rob has one in his

The en-bloc clips were marked with the manufacturer's name. Someone out there is collecting the entire set. (Good luck with that, and have fun.)

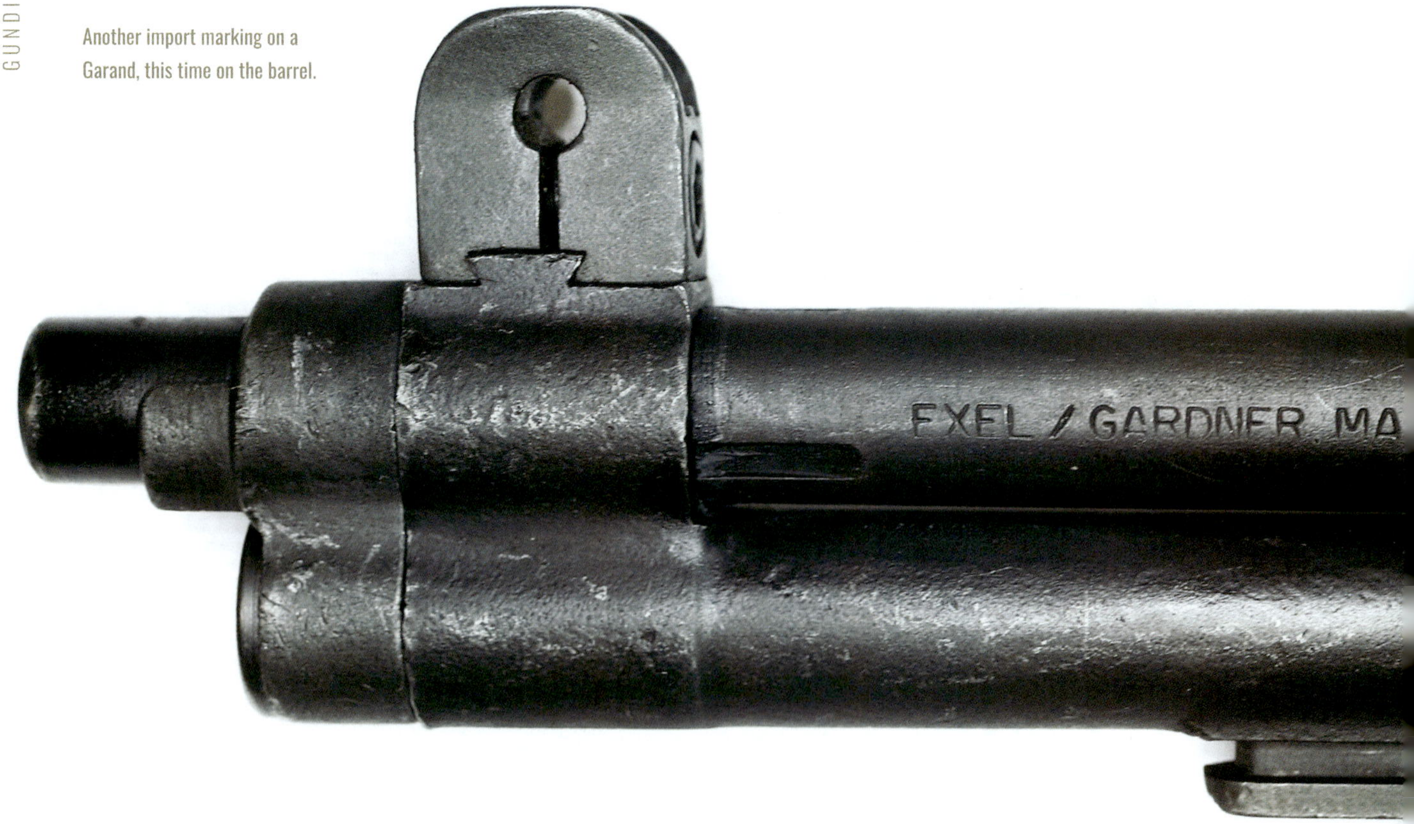

Another import marking on a Garand, this time on the barrel.

collection with a marking of "EXEL/GARDINER MA" on the barrel. So, made here, shipped overseas, repatriated, marked as an import, and now in the rack, ready to go home with you.

The last and most ephemeral type of marking you may encounter is the "rack number." This mark is an unofficial code used in arms rooms. Rather than try to track every serial number to control how many rifles are present, each stock would be given a number according to its place in the rack. These marks could be stamped, painted, or on one rifle we looked at, written with a felt-tip marker on tape on the stock. A quick visual check would tell if there was one missing or a problem with the inventory. "Corporal, where is rack number 71?" When the Sergeant asked that question, he wasn't asking about the rack itself but the rifle that was supposed to be in slot 71. You, the PFC, had better be able to account for it.

Now, as the collector, you have a rarity that you cannot trace to any particular unit, depot, or rack. Don't sand that number off. It is a part of history.

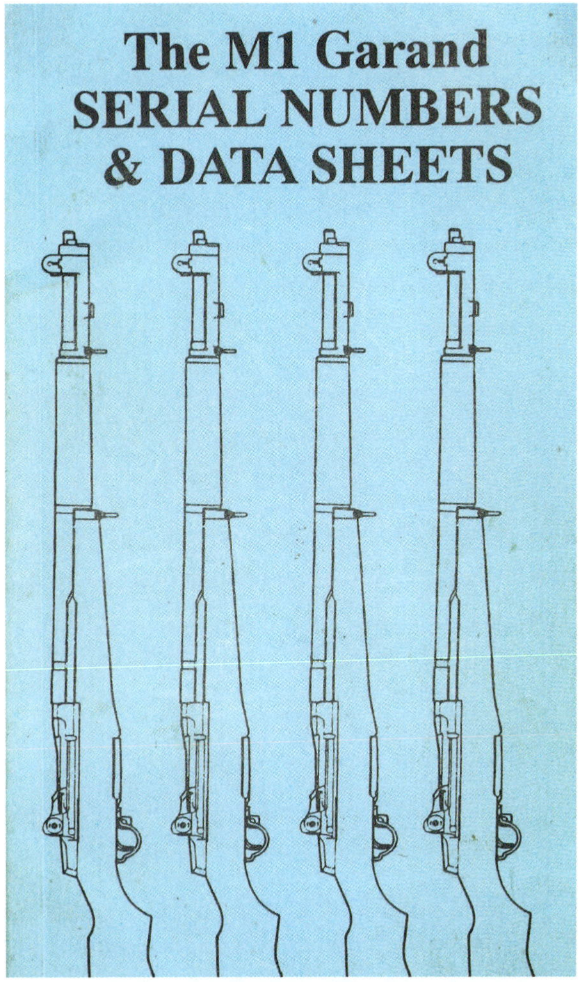

The Scott Duff Garand serial number book. Duff authors additional titles for other rifles as well as the Garand.

A "CORRECT" RIFLE?

This brings us to the question, "Is my rifle correct?" The simple answer is: yes. No aftermarket M1 Garand manufacturers were making non-GI parts to be fed into the consumer market. Actually, there were a few, but they are known, obvious, and easy to sort out. That happened to the M1 carbine but not the Garand. Springfield, Inc. made Garands for a short time, but they are marked clearly and parts-correct. They will interchange with your USGI Garand. No, you won't find the equivalent of the Universal or Plainfield carbines in the Garand, where a few parts might fit a USGI carbine, but most won't.

The Italians drive collectors crazy. Italy adopted the Garand (many countries did, post-war) and even went so far as to rebuild or recondition parts and rifles and make replacement parts when needed. This was done with U.S. approval, and the parts were made to be interchangeable. If you lust after an all-correct, all-complete, Winchester-only rifle, those Italian parts are a blot on your personal landscape. To the rest of us, they are interesting and useful parts that we'll be happy to take off your hands for a nominal sum.

Did Winchester produce all-Winchester rifles? Almost certainly. And just as certainly, the War Department didn't care. If on the next rebuild, or even in the arms room on a base, the Winchester trigger assembly got swapped out for a Springfield, IHA or H&R, the only concern was, and I know I keep repeating it, but it matters: "does it work?" If it did, it was correct, so stop your whining.

Oh, and while you're at it, take a look at the en-bloc

After firing, red paint from the primer sealing compound was left behind on the face of the bolt in the author's Garand.

clips you're using. Yes, they are also marked as to who made them. And yes, in case there was a problem with a particular maker, the War Department wanted to be able to track them.

With enough diligent work from books and online sources, you can find the origin and, within a spread, the production dates of almost every part of your Garand. It's just a matter of how OCD you want to be.

There are two modern books to get you up to speed on all things Garand markings and parts numbers. Since I'm not trying to write a collectors book — just give you a head's-up on collecting details — I'm happy to point them out. One, *The M1 Garand SERIAL NUMBERS & DATA SHEETS* by Scott Duff, covers (not surprisingly) the serial numbers and markings and includes data sheet info. The second is a two-volume set also by Duff, *The M1 Garand OWNER'S GUIDE* and *The M1 Garand POST WORLD WAR II*. With these books, you can parse out exactly when (within, say, 100,000 parts) the various bits of your Garand were made.

Hatcher's Book of the Garand is a historical reference chock full of helpful information. It details the Garand's history, development and testing and is current as of the original printing in 1948.

My father, trained on the Garand, later went to a tool better suited to his job in the infantry. Early in his unit's time at the front, he was in an assault at Metz. It had been raining for over a month, and he jumped into a muddy shell hole taking cover from the MG42 ahead. On his first shot, his rifle stopped working. The muzzle, packed with mud from jumping into the hole, had burst on firing. He took the Garand from the GI in the shell crater who no longer needed his and, after a few shots, realized that it didn't have the desired effect. He spent the next couple of clips plinking at the tile roof of a municipal building, zeroing his new rifle, before getting back to work. That is a demonstration of the advantage of the Garand's sights. The rifle he left behind? Probably picked up by a following unit, shipped back for rebuild, and re-issued.

Soon after that episode, he transferred to the Combat Scouts. As much as he loved the Garand loaded with armor piercing (AP) rounds, he remarked, "It gets into stone French farmhouses," it wouldn't suit his next job, where he spent the rest of the war either on point or working at night. For that, he favored the M3 Grease gun.

For myself, I started competition shooting with a Garand and then switched (for a short time) to an M1A, then to an endless array of AR-15s.

But all this time, my Garands, the original and later ones, have waited in the rack. Someday, they may be called on. I know for sure the wait won't dampen their abilities. In checking this out, I ran a bunch of ammo through the rack-grade Garand and was reminded of an observation I had all those years ago. When I first acquired the match Garand, the bolt face was covered in red powdery gunk. I had assumed at the start that it was rust and wondered if I had made a mistake. But it scrubbed right off, and I didn't give it another thought after that day in 1977. When I test-fired my Garand for this chapter, I went to clean it and, lo and behold, red gunk. It was the red primer seal paint left behind from firing.

So, red gunk is primer paint and an indication that the rifle has been fired with arsenal-loaded ammo. Remember that. •

CHAPTER 6

NEW WAR, NEW PRODUCTION & THE KOREAN GARANDS

When World War II ended, production contracts ceased. I know, not fair, with the manufacturers all set up to produce even more Garands, but we had won the war, and the Army would not remain bloated. In 1945, we had something like 9 million men and women in uniform. Since we would not conquer and turn the world into the American Empire, we didn't need that many. We downsized, and those returning wanted washing machines, cars, and refrigerators, in the new houses they would build, not more Garands, B17s, and artillery.

POST-WAR

But, there were many seriously worn Garands to tend to. So the initial work, once the other manufacturers had been told to get back to commercial work, was for Springfield to overhaul rifles. And the various arsenals around the country (this was decades before we even had the idea of Base Closing Commissions, essentially make-work for congressmen who can't even do a congressional job) would tend to the Garands in their inventory.

In 1946–47, Springfield manufactured roughly 330,000 new barrels to overhaul existing Garands. It also made whatever other parts it needed, except receivers, for updating and overhauling Garands.

Rebuilt Garands that were sent overseas, and those in National Guard armories across the country, received some interesting and, at times, cryptic rack numbers.

A NEW WAR

When the party bosses of North Korea decided to "re-unify" the peninsula, it came as a surprise to everyone. Then again, you must remember that this was 1950 when the world didn't know what to expect from North Korea or China, and everyone was busy cleaning up after WWII. The U.S. Army, still working on the assumption that having won the war, everything would work as it had before, set about stopping the advance. If you want to learn how not to start a military operation, study "Task Force Smith" and the unfortunate results.

Here's the short story: The 1st Battalion of the 21st Infantry Regiment was quickly shipped from Japan to Korea and positioned on a saddle-shaped hill straddling a main highway. The idea was to bolster the Korean forces with a show of American strength and to rebuff the advancing North Korean unit. Unfortunately, the post-war level of readiness that had been acceptable really wasn't … acceptable. And the American equipment had not been updated. The North Korean tank column motored through the defensive position, losing two T-34s and damaging two others of the 33 in the column. The next column surrounded the American unit and shot them until the command to retreat was given. (I would need the composure of a Buddhist monk not to point out that such unpreparedness would repeat, again and again, in American DoD planning down to today.)

...THERE WERE MANY SERIOUSLY WORN GARANDS TO TEND TO. SO THE INITIAL WORK, ONCE THE OTHER MANUFACTURERS HAD BEEN TOLD TO GET BACK TO COMMERCIAL WORK, WAS FOR SPRINGFIELD TO OVERHAUL RIFLES.

Having spent the years (not many, admittedly) since WWII gathering previously abandoned equipment and fixing the seriously used gear, the Army found itself in an awkward position: Despite having five times as much gear as it needed for the size army it had, it had no new equipment with which to fight a new war. The WWII-era artillery and bazookas were no match for even WWII-surplus T-34 tanks, let alone the newest ones coming soon from the Soviets. In small arms, that meant pulling Garands out of storage and finding out that while they had been put away with proper grading, inspection, etc., there was still a need for new rifles. So, the Department of Defense offered contracts for new rifles, and two companies stepped forward: Harrington & Richardson and International Harvester.

All this took time. The initial combat had the North Korean forces sweeping across the 38th parallel. In two months, they crowded the allied forces into the southeast corner of the Korean peninsula, the Pusan Perimeter. Then, the landings at Inchon (a port on the West Coast of Korea, halfway to the north) on September 15th, attacking the North Korean rear echelons, suddenly fought surging back to the north. The American forces and the South Korean army advanced almost to the Yalu river bordering China. The Chinese, not wanting the war to enter China or see their client state of North Korea fall, sent massive forces across the river and pushed the American and Korean forces back south.

The combat stabilized around the 38th parallel, with both sides settling into trenches and prepared positions. Meanwhile, the DoD was still negotiating contracts, and the winning companies were setting up the tooling and fixtures. It wasn't until 1953 that the first of the new Garands started coming off the lines, which is another example of why it proved difficult to convince manufacturers to produce defense materiel for DoD. The contracts were structured for high-volume combat and the resupply of forces engaged in the kind of expenditures of ammunition and consumption of rifles that the initial phases of the war had demonstrated. By the time the two companies delivered products, the war had settled into a low-level grinding trench warfare that used much ammunition but not the kind of rifle consumption as previously expected.

You'd think that with WWII ending just five years before the Korean conflict erupted, Springfield could get

The overhaul updated things like the old bar-lock sights. Not all Garands got the new sights; you can still find CMP and gun shop/gun show Garands with them.

Part of the rebuilding process was to take the old sharp-corner op rods and mill a circular relief cut in the joint as a stress riser.

back into the swing of things without too much fuss. No, it took the company until 1952 before it produced finished rifles. And there were other problems. Everyone had forgotten much in those few years, and Springfield had to reject many barrel blanks because they were made of the wrong steel grade. The Marlin company was contracted to produce barrels, which was short-lived, as Springfield soon straightened things out. The Line Material Co. of Birmingham, Alabama, another manufacturer, produced barrels. If you have a Korean-era Garand or one rebuilt during that time, you may notice "LMR" on the barrel, along with the proof mark, date of manufacture, and heat-treatment code.

We had also apparently forgotten how much materiel a modern war consumed (a lesson now being learned again in Ukraine).

Some parts were new, others old; some were updated, but many were not. And this is the dilemma faced by both DoD and manufacturers. From the DoD's perspective, if you filled warehouses full of the current equipment, you

The rebuilds continued for two decades after WWII. This Garand has a barrel made by Springfield in February of 1965. It could not have been rebuilt before February of that year.

Springfield made barrels and dated them while producing rifles. This is a 1955 barrel, and if your Garand has one with these markings, you're doing just fine.

would spend a lot of taxpayer dollars on gear that could be obsolete when needed. That the Ordnance Department was in the final phases of developing the rifle that would be the M14 when the war reached a stalemate was a demonstration of this. Why buy and store millions more M1 Garands when the new rifle would replace it? The money spent on Garands could be better spent on M14s.

From the manufacturers' perspective, there was no long-term plan you could count on with the government. So you had to either bid high to ensure a profit on the truncated contract or roll the dice about whether you could tool up, produce, and deliver the entire contract before the government could change it. The government has not found a way to solve this dilemma in three-quarters of a century since the Korean War.

Back to Garands. Since the various details of the Garand that needed updating or improvement had already been done, the H&R and IHA Garands all have the latest, newest (from the perspective of the 1953-57 timeframe) parts. And in subsequent rebuilds or overhauls, they should have received the current parts, not those from early WWII. However, there are no guarantees. Rifles received from the CMP will have been inspected and corrected, but if you happen upon an H&R or IHA rifle

Among the last Garands ever made, this one came out of Springfield in 1956.

International Harvester made rifles partly because it was in the middle of the country and not in "gunmakers valley" in the northeast. Spreading out production sites seemed like a good idea at the time.

Not a rebuild, probably, but a June 1945 barrel. If you come across a Garand with a barrel date like this, you have the start of a retro build that could be epic. If the receiver also dates to June 1945, you are in Garand collector heaven.

in a gun shop that never went through the CMP, it might have been "overhauled" in a foreign depot, and as long as it worked, no one there cared about parts upgrades. (After all, they might not have had the upgraded parts to select from.)

IHC had some problems starting up, and collectors have parsed out the details of IHC using receivers made by Springfield and marked as Springfield, but the format of the markings differs from IHC-made receivers. The problems IHC encountered, and the lessening of demand for rifles, led it to seek an early out of the contract, and it ended up only making 337,623 Garands.

Harrington & Richardson was a long-time firearms manufacturer for the DoD, even though the name is now a trademark and not a separate company making firearms. It was in New England, specifically Worchester, Massachusetts, in 1871. While H&R's product line had long been single-shot shotguns and top-break revolvers, it was a firearms manufacturer, and the DoD issued it a contract. Its products did not keep up with the shooting public's changing tastes, though, and being unable to innovate, it closed its business in 1986. The other company, International Harvester, had no experience manufacturing firearms. However, there were several advantages to

An LMR-marked barrel from the Line Material Company, which supplied barrels to HRA and IHC during the Korean War-era Garand builds. They were also used in later rebuilds.

A Springfield post-war barrel was used to overhaul a WWII-era Garand. While not exactly retro, this is an excellent find if plugged into your Garand.

One of the first 8,000 Garands that Harrington & Richardson produced — an early rifle, probably in 1953.

And confirmation of the H&R rifle, as the barrel (also made by H&R) is dated April 1953. It was assembled in mid-1953 and is now 70 years old.

issuing a small arms contract to a manufacturer in Evansville, Indiana. In the early and mid-1950s, the threat of nuclear war was high on the list of concerns. Most of our country's small arms manufacturing was by companies in New England; many of those were in a few towns clustered nearby. Colt, Remington, Winchester, even that new upstart Ruger, were close by, and a few nuclear strikes in a small area could wipe out the nation's small arms manufacturing capacity.

THE TWO COMPANIES DELIVERED 750,000 OR SO GARANDS FROM 1953 THROUGH 1957. SPRINGFIELD ADDED ANOTHER 661,000 TO THAT, SO ALL TOLD, ANOTHER MILLION-AND-A-HALF GARANDS WORLDWIDE.

Despite receiving a contract later than IHA, H&R, as an established firearms maker, could get up to speed and handle the various troubles along the way better than its competitor. Despite starting later, H&R produced 428,000 rifles. It also had to depend less on parts from Springfield to manufacturer Garands, so finding one with all H&R parts is not uncommon.

IHA was far removed from the rest in the wide-open cornfields of Evansville. And, as demonstrated in WWII, a company accustomed to manufacturing and assembly of an industrial product could be re-tooled to produce small arms, if needed. So, it got a contract partly because of those reasons but also because it agreed to costs, delivery times, and quality control requirements.

The two companies delivered 750,000 or so Garands from 1953 through 1957. Springfield added another 661,000 to that, so all told, another million-and-a-half Garands worldwide. Not anything near to the 4+ million made before and during WWII, but more than enough for the needs of the Army, Navy and Marine Corps, especially since the new M14 would replace all the Garands in common issue in a few years. (Oh, that debacle. We'll be covering that.)

There was a lot still going on, however. Since the Garand was still the service rifle, it was everywhere your troops were, even out in the Southwest deserts where atomic bomb testing was going on. On ships, at Army posts, Marine stations, and airfields, the Garand was there. And then, suddenly, it wasn't.

Here are the assigned serial numbers for the "Korean" Garands. Production was slow to start, and the

A pair of "Korean" Garands, one from IHA and the other from H&R. Do they have period-correct parts or were they rebuilt? Notice that the IHA has a rack number that is a Dymo label stuck to the rear of the receiver. How it has remained there all these years is a mystery.

H&R completed two runs of rifles under two contracts and two serial number batches. So no, the firm did not make over a million rifles — just under 450,000. The interesting thing is that the receiver roll mark changed in between runs. Note the ampersand.

Boarding the bus at Camp Desert Rock, 5:45 AM, for the coming atomic bomb tests. Poth is his name, and where he might be today (or even still alive, it has been 60 to 70 years) is unknown to the author. Garands were there when the atomic bomb was tested during the start of the Cold War.

last of them wasn't produced until well after the Korean conflict ended.

International Harvester	4,400,000 to 4,660,000
Harrington & Richardson	4,660,001 to 4,800,000
Springfield Armory	5,000,000 to 5,000,500
International Harvester	5,000,501 to 5,278,245
Springfield Armory	5,278,246 to 5,488,246
Harrington & Richardson	5,488,247 to 5,793,847
Springfield Armory	5,793,848 to 6,099,905

The gaps in the serial numbers assigned also indicate the expectations of production when the contracts were issued, the reality of slow production, and how the war progressed. By the time Springfield and the others were getting to the end of their contracts, it was clear to all that the Garand was done, and the replacement, the soon-to-be M14, would be the new service rifle. Little did anyone know how that was going to work out.

While the "Korean" Garands were made with new parts, once they got into the inventory, they would have been subject to the same use and rebuild program as one made, for example, in 1941. So, a collector looking for a period-correct "Korean" Garand has the same problem: identifying the parts in their Garand and replacing the anachronistic ones with period ones. •

CHAPTER 7

WHO ELSE USED THE GARAND?

Once WWII ended, the world moved on. Some countries did, some didn't, and most still needed weapons. One, for example, was the new West Germany. The police force had to be reorganized, and the army rebuilt once it was safe to have a German military again. This took time, and while that was happening, the issue weapon was the Garand. It seems odd, perhaps even alarming, to have police officers armed with military rifles. (Well, it did until the GWOT got M16s and AR-15s into squad cars.) From the perspective of Europe, a rifle was just fine. Police were not issued pistols except at the station for the shift and turned in at the end of the shift. Rather than having pistols on the street, rifles were easier to see and keep track of and less likely to be stolen or otherwise misappropriated.

A detachment of Austrian police officers instructed on the Garand's manual of arms. Many think of police officers as civilian, non-military organizations armed with handguns. In much of the world, the police are a detachment of the military and are issued rifles when they need to be armed.

When I planned this chapter, I figured, "OK, I'll have some fun telling tales of what I've found of the places that used the Garand." Well, no. The list of who got Garands as aid, sold, trans-shipped, or bought in bulk is longer than those countries that did not get Garands. With the shifting of international regimes, alliances and even religions, the list of which countries got Garands has some surprises, including Iran (yes, Iran)! Before the mullahs, during the Shah, Iran received something like 165,000 Garands. Those are rifles the American shooting public is never going to see again. Pakistan took in another 150,000, which will never see American soil. (I'm starting to get a bit sad here.) And then there are the 220,000 M1s sent to South Vietnam.

Those three sources account for almost more Garands than either International Harvester or Harrington & Richardson ever made.

So, instead, let's cover a few of those locales.

ITALY

The Italians, once WWII was over, wanted to provide for themselves. This first meant using supplied Garands, but they then acquired the tooling needed and produced them for themselves. This led to the development of the Italian BM59 program when the M14 production rate would be insufficient for anyone, let alone the U.S. and its allies.

Beretta made Garands, and when the Italians were done with the platform and had moved on, Beretta parts became available in the U.S. That took a while, but you can now find CMP and gun shop/gun show Garands with Beretta-marked parts. It would be a rare Garand that has a Beretta receiver, but there are some to be found, expensive now, with collectors having snapped them up. But they exist.

WITH THE SHIFTING OF INTERNATIONAL REGIMES, ALLIANCES AND EVEN RELIGIONS, THE LIST OF WHICH COUNTRIES GOT GARANDS HAS SOME SURPRISES, INCLUDING IRAN (YES, IRAN)!

Chilean soldiers or military, on guard outside an official building.

DENMARK

As with the rest of Western Europe, Denmark wasn't interested in joining the hot mess known as the various people's republics of the Warsaw pact. That is, they didn't want to be Soviets. A tincture of socialism, perhaps, but not full-on "one room to a family, one kitchen per floor" togetherness. So, they worked hard and depended on aid to keep themselves afloat. While they received less than frontline jets, for example (getting F-84s after they had been replaced here), what about the rifles? They were the best at the time: the Garand.

The rifles came mainly from the U.S., but some were made for Denmark in Italy by Beretta, which produced replacement parts for rebuilds. And, being steeped in the proper European gunsmithing tradition, various parts needed serial numbers marked as government property and where they originated. So, if you have a rebuild and some of the parts had been made in, or for, Denmark, they will be so-marked.

Denmark was the last NATO country to give up on the Garand, switching to the Colt M16 in the Canadian pattern (known here as the C7/C8, in Denmark as the Gevaer M/95 and Karabin M/96) in the mid-1990s.

SOUTH KOREA

With the border still "hot," the Republic of Korea needed an army to defend itself. After all, the Americans wouldn't stay there forever, right? The army that had existed before the war was not ready for the North's invasion (and one can ask, who was?), so after things settled down, they took the lessons learned from the war and built a military

The Beretta family home in Brescia, Italy. The factory is nearby, and the concern still produces firearms.

While the days of making Garands (or even BM59s) are long gone, Beretta still makes military small arms.

capable of defense. At the start, however, it depended on American equipment, including the M1 Garand. At the peak, the ROK army used just over a quarter-million M1s and continued to use them until we began supplying them with M16s in the late 1960s.

Then in the mid-1970s, it started making its own M16s, built under license, and the remaining Garands were either scrapped or put in storage, with some small numbers sold back into the U.S. through various import companies. If you have a Garand or an M1 Carbine with

With their experience from the war, it should be no surprise that the South Koreans took defense seriously. And since the Garand was the tool of the day, they used many of them.

A Beretta-made part, the clip latch, installed on a Garand, not of Italian make. So, a rebuild, done sometime in the recent past, probably by the CMP, since that is where this collector acquired it.

This Garand has parts marked as being in Danish service.

This Garand was a Danish service rifle. The Danish marking is evident, but the serial number indicates it was an Italian-made receiver for the Danish military before it somehow got to the USA.

The VAR-under-crown marking on this barrel indicates it was made in Denmark. A Danish barrel on a Garand doesn't necessarily mean it was used in Denmark, as there were more barrels than rifles, and it could have been used to rebuild a Garand that never left the States. But it's a quality barrel.

(Left) A staged photo of Danish soldiers training with Garands. While everyone in western Europe was concerned with defending themselves from the Soviets, rebuilding the economy was more important than making rifles, so everyone used the Garand.

the marking "Blue Sky Imports," that is a Korean return.

In the 21st century, there were efforts to bring back Garands from Korea, but those plans fell apart due to known and rumored problems. The known issues were President Obama in particular and Democrats in general. Through an Executive Order, Obama halted any reimportation of military items. The rumored issue was related to cost. If a rifle such as a Garand were sent as aid, it would return to the U.S. through the government to the CMP at shipping costs. We sent it there at no cost, or as aid, we expected it back at no cost. However, the Koreans bought a bunch of Garands (no reports on if they know the serial numbers or even have them sorted as such) and thus could ask for real money from importers to get them back here.

That made things difficult, as the importers needed U.S. approval for import and had to pay cash upfront for whatever showed up on the boat.

And even countries that didn't adopt the Garand in numbers often had a ceremonial guard who used the Garand. That's because, in part, they formed such units back when the Garand was the issue rifle and because it balances well and looks good. Plus, if you're issuing rifles chambered in 5.56, and .30-06 is not a standard or even allowed cartridge in your country, you can be pretty sure the ceremonial guard won't have loaded weapons. Four-foot-long rifles with bayonets, yes, but no ammo. •

The ceremonial guard in front of the Greek parliament building in Athens. Garands with bayonets, as are so many guard units.

M1 Garand rifle, USA. Caliber .30-06. Photo: Armémuseum (Swedish Army Museum), Stockholm

CHAPTER 8

THE M14 REPLACES THE GARAND

Even during WWII, there was interest and R&D on a replacement rifle for the Garand. While great for a 1930s rifle, the Garand was found to have some shortcomings in combat, and those who depended on a rifle wanted those shortcomings addressed. One was capacity. When the rest of the world had five-round magazine bolt-action rifles, a self-loader with eight rounds was a big step up and an advantage. But the M1 Carbine, with its 15-round magazine, and then the Stg44, with its 30-round mag, put the M1 Garand in the shade. The revelation of the AK-47 and its 30-round magazine put even more emphasis on capacity since we were in a Cold War with the Soviets. There was also the en-bloc clip problem. As we've discussed, if you've expended a few rounds from your Garand, you can't just top it off. You can only eject your remaining rounds and add a fresh eight-round clip.

With a rifle fed from a box magazine, you can quickly swap magazines and top off the saved, previous magazine when you can.

During the Second World War, there was some experimenting done converting M1 Garands to use the 20-round magazine from the BAR. One of the unfortunate aspects of those tests was a temptation I call the "something for nothing" lure. The testers invariably not only converted the Garand to accept a BAR magazine but also (usually) made the Garand a select-fire weapon. Having shot several of them, I'll admit that the BAR is a tad portly for what it is supposed to do. At 19 pounds, the M1918A2 is easy to shoot but had to be miserable to carry

During WWII, Garand tried to update his rifle. The T20 series was an attempt to add a magazine. The E2 here incorporated the lessons learned from testing the T20E1. A contract was issued in April of 1945, but Springfield put the first delivery date in "early next year." Well, we all know how that went.

in what amounts to a Squad Automatic Weapon (SAW) role. That would also explain my father's observation that he could tell when they were following a new unit on the march by the abandoned excess equipment they'd see by the roadside. The BAR bipod was one of those pieces of equipment. On the other extreme, a select-fire Garand, at only 10 pounds, wasn't controllable and quickly overheated.

One problem with using the BAR magazine, which Garand himself undoubtedly discovered, was that the receiver was too short. The Garand's receiver was the perfect length to properly feed cartridges from the en-bloc clips. A BAR magazine has a slightly different feeding geometry that needs more length to strip and position the cartridge as it is fed into the chamber. So, making the Garand take BAR mags means taking a perfectly functioning, 100% reliable rifle and making it less so. Not a good thing.

The search for a replacement rifle, post-WWII, also had a problem: range. The bright lights in charge of the research, testing, and development in the Ordnance Department insisted on .30-06-level performance. That is, a 1,000-yard rifle. Despite the experiences of those in the fight, who could have (if they had been asked) told them that they hardly ever shot at anyone past 200-300

The Stg44, the rifle that started it all. Made with stampings in a medium caliber, holding much ammo, and select fire, it was everything the modern method of warfare trended toward.

yards, and most of the time, inside of 100 yards. For them, problems 200+ yards away were what the BAR handled, and 300+ were for the M1919A6.

Advances in powder technology allowed for a propellant with the same power but in a denser form, thus using a smaller case. That is the origin of the .308 Winchester, aka the 7.62 NATO. By using a shorter case, the new rifle could have a Garand-length receiver, but shorter than the BAR magazines; at least, shorter in the length-wise dimension, even if it was just as tall as a BAR magazine, holding the same 20 rounds of .30-06, compared to the new rifle and 20 rounds of .308. This design eased the feed geometry, and by fitting the new magazine to the geometry they had to handle (the feed lips of the M14 magazine and the BAR differ), the designers could make the whole thing fit (more or less, we'll get to that in a bit).

The AR-10, a .308 rifle that briefly contended with the FAL and M14, was the predecessor to the AR-15, the rifle that now rules all.

The research focused on the gas system and involved removing the Garand's long, unsupported op rod. Unlike the Garand, the M14 uses a shorter rod with a support hoop attached to the barrel. It uses a piston inside the gas housing to tap the op rod into action. The piston valves gas with two steps. One, the slot that feeds

Gunner's Mate Seaman Patrick Cornwell fires an M14 semi-automatic rifle during a live-fire exercise aboard the nuclear-powered aircraft carrier USS Nimitz (CVN 68). Note the gas plume underneath the gas cylinder, venting gas as designed.

gas from the gas port in the barrel enters the piston through the piston slot. As the piston moves, the slot quickly slides past the port, shutting off the gas flow. Also, a vent port in the gas housing vents excess gas out of the system — a clever way to make an improved Garand.

It did, however, pose a problem some decades later when attempts to fit suppressors to the M14 were undertaken. The vent port expels gas at high pressure, which makes noise. There is only so much you can do to quiet an M14, and the vent port thwarts further action. An M14 can't be as quiet as a rifle based on the AR-10 due to the vent port and its additional noise signature. But, back to the history of Garand and the M14.

That there was no interest in any other design, in-house in the Ordnance Department, besides an "improved Garand" should give you a clue about how backward-looking the program was. Oh, and it was also select fire as well. The plan was that this improved rifle would replace four weapons in the small arms inventory: the M1 Garand, the BAR, the M1 Carbine and the M1A1 "Grease gun" SMG. That brings me to one of my favorite observations: the big lie that "One size fits all," which really means "One size fits none." While the M14 (as it finally came to be termed) could readily replace the Garand, it could not displace the BAR. It was too light to do the same job as the BAR and too large to serve the same roles as the M1A1 SMG or the M1 Carbine.

The British were following a different path. First, they were determined to go with a bullpup action. This is where you, in essence, lop the stock off of a rifle, put the buttplate at the back of the receiver, and then arrange a pistol grip and trigger forward of the magazine. This design shortens a rifle by 10 or 12 inches without shortening the barrel and cutting into muzzle velocity. They also went with a smaller medium-velocity 7mm cartridge, pushing a 139-grain bullet at 2,500 fps.

Garand wasn't immune to the allure of the bullpup and offered one to the U.S. government. (Or maybe he was hedging his bets, as he had during the .276/.30-06 indecision.) His T31 was innovative on several fronts, but the problems of making a bullpup were enough, and the extra improvement Garand added to the T31 proved a bridge too far. That, and his retirement in 1953, as the new service rifle program picked up steam. One detail that did come from it was the magazine, which ended up being the base for the resulting M14 rifle.

The Belgians offered the SAFN49 post-war, which the Garand-with-a-magazine would have been. Unlike the rotating bolt of the Garand, it used a tilting bolt, cammed by a bolt cover, inside the receiver, and it ended up being the action the FAL used in the 1950s.

The Springfield Armory Scout Squad. This is what the M14 would have been as a carbine had the program not been canceled.

But those efforts didn't matter because the U.S. wanted a new rifle, even if the Ordnance Department had to cook the books and rig the tests to prove the M14 was superior to its competitors, which they did. Getting there wasn't easy. The new rifle was given a designation at each step in the design evolution, and the "T" series was born. The near-the-end rifle that was thoroughly tested was the T44, meaning 44 variations and design changes, and they weren't done yet.

Oh, and there were other details that the Ordnance Department fudged. The program's promoters assured the congressional committees holding oversight that it would be a relatively low-cost conversion. They said that much of the same tooling fixtures used for the Garand could be re-purposed for the M14 and would not have to be made anew. These assertions proved to be incorrect. I don't know if that was because the officials in charge didn't know how tooling fixtures worked or didn't ask because they didn't want to know. But the entire tooling and fixture package of the M14 had to be built from scratch, except the rear sight and a few other parts. As a result, the M14 program went slowly. It took from the end of WWII until 1957, before the M14 was adopted. I mentioned this to a shooter, who did a quick mental calculation, and said, "That's less time … than from WWI to the Garand." True, that, but John Garand had to not only design and test his gun but also prove to the Army that a self-loading rifle was even possible as a general-issue weapon. By the end of WWII, that was manifestly obvious, and it was simply a matter of "which one?" for the future.

An M14 made by TRW — yes, the credit company — back when it was an actual aerospace manufacturer.

Springfield Armory was still the government arsenal when this M14 was made. The M14 was canceled in 1963, and the arsenal closed in 1968.

The FN-FAL rifle, a contender to the U.S. Trials, was given a raw deal in the testing and "failed" as a result. It was so bad that only the rest of the entire free world (close, anyway) adopted it.

(Left) An M14 with the "dummy" switch, or selector lock, to keep the rifles semi-auto even though they were built to be select fire.

Oh, and one more wrench in the works? The finally adopted, officially approved we're-going-to-go-with-this-one rifle? It still wasn't 100% reliable. The Ordnance Department had to coax Garand out of retirement to work his magic on the new rifle. But wait, if he accepted a contract to work on the T44, he couldn't also collect his government pension. I would have loved to have been a fly on the wall to hear how that problem was worked out.

Once adopted, the manufacture of the M14 did not proceed smoothly. Initial production was contracted to Springfield Armory, Winchester, and H&R. The first contract wasn't even issued for almost a year, and the first batch of receivers from a subcontractor arrived at H&R out of spec and had to be replaced. The error was corrected before they could begin production. So, having taken 13 years to be developed and adopted, and four years after volume production was supposed to have begun, the news of the Berlin Blockade revealed an embarrassing situation: the frontline American troops in the new Cold War were still equipped with the M1 Garand.

The selector lock, the special cover that keeps an M14 from being changed to Auto. It does not, however, remove it from the status of a machine gun.

By 1960, there had been only about 10,000 M14s manufactured out of the expected five million the Army would need. To grasp the level of outrage that this generated, remember that WWII ended only 15 years before that. (Perhaps take a moment and think about what was going on in your life 15 years ago. Not that long ago, right?) In that time, the Soviets had gotten their A-bomb, and schoolchildren had been engaging in "Duck and cover" drills for several years. The Soviets had also tested, adopted, and issued their new rifle, the AK-47. Not only did it hold 30 rounds to the Garand's eight, but it was also select fire — a machine gun. One last data point: unlike today, where so few of our elected representatives served in the military, in 1960, it was a rare congressman or senator who hadn't been in uniform. Many of them knew what they were talking about. In the ensuing reviews and committee hearings, it came out that the Ordnance Department had rigged the tests and abused the test FAL rifles that would have otherwise won the testing and contract. And other shenanigans after that.

But, the M14 was the current rifle, and production had to be increased, and right now. A new company got a contract, the Thompson-Ramo-Woolridge company, then an aerospace manufacturer. It ditched the traditional production method of rows of dedicated machines and instead adopted a new method: numerical control. Instead of rows of milling machines, think of a room-sized machine with a cutting station like the hours of a clock. The operator locked each receiver forging into its fixture.

The machine moved the fixture to each position on the clock face, where it made its cuts, and when it completed one entire cycle, the operator took the machined part out, replaced it with a raw forging, and hit "go," repeating the process.

TRW (yes, the same TRW that now does credit checks, a lot has changed in 60+ years) accepted the contract at a delivery cost less than the other makers, with the understanding that it would be making M14s for the next decade or more, and could count on long-term income from it. In the short term, it depended on the bonuses: It earned bonuses by delivering early and at a higher QC level than the contract required. The contract had TRW making M14s at a loss on paper, but the bonuses made for a tidy profit. The firm planned on being a rifle manufacturer for the M14's duration of service and viewed the "loss but a profit" arrangement as the cost of entry. Once it worked out some efficiencies downstream, it could make rifles at a profit even without the early delivery and QC bonuses.

BY 1960, THERE HAD BEEN ONLY ABOUT 10,000 M14S MANUFACTURED OUT OF THE EXPECTED FIVE MILLION THE ARMY WOULD NEED. TO GRASP THE LEVEL OF OUTRAGE THAT THIS GENERATED, REMEMBER THAT WWII ENDED ONLY 15 YEARS BEFORE THAT.

How far behind was the M14 delivery, and how long would it have taken? Looking at the size of the services in the early 1960s and the production rate of the M14 at the new and increased volume, it would have been 1976 before every Garand in issue to regular forces would have been replaced by an M14. The National Guard units would still have used the Garand even after 1976 until they could also be supplied M14s. Realistically, from production beginning in the late 1950s, it would have been 1990 before every Garand had been retired, replaced by an M14.

Still, the plan was to change to the M14, and as soon as it was adopted, it began to see service. One location was in Indochina, where we aided South Vietnam in its resistance to communist encroachment. There the initial "advisors," a mix of USMC units and CIA operatives, used an incredible assortment of small arms. The CIA ops used whatever they wanted, which would pass relatively unnoticed, and whatever got the job done. The Marines? M14s, and glad to have them.

That's when the then Secretary of Defense stepped in and changed everything. The military advisory effort in Southeast Asia was heating up by the mid-1960s, and by the late 1960s, it was apparent that a 1,000-yard rifle proved less useful in a jungle fight. Yes, the power was useful in penetrating light cover and chance obstacles, but in a close-range fight in the jungle, volume of fire often won.

Secretary of Defense Robert McNamara felt the Ordnance Department and Springfield Armory were so cumbersome in their operations and unable to deliver what was needed in time that they had to go. In 1963, he canceled the M14 contracts. In 1968, he closed Springfield Arsenal. And the new Armalite rifle was just the thing for the fight in Vietnam, so the M14 got pushed to secondary status, and the future went to the .223/5.56. The Marines continued to use the M14 until they were flat-out told to switch to the M16.

The M14 wasn't done, however. With a glass-bedded or synthetic stock, and a magnifying optic on top, it became the M21, a semi-automatic sniper rifle. But long-distance snipers were not entirely impressed. Even an accurate M21 wasn't up to the pinpoint accuracy of a bedded and tested bolt-action rifle. But it was the logical successor to the M1C and M1D Garand sniper rifle variants with which old hands were most familiar.

The M14 continued in service elsewhere, used as a line-throwing rifle by the Navy (an M16 doesn't have the oomph to throw a line from ship to ship, not if the ships maintain a safe distance) and as an actual rifle when needed. It also saw use as a Designated Marksman Rifle during Iraq and Afghanistan, when the various service branches

A Winchester M14, something that only the wealthiest of Winchester collectors can afford.

While the M14 program had been shut down in 1963, Springfield was still making parts, so this barrel, dated September 1964, should not come as a surprise.

found they had a problem. The problem? The M16/M4 had a limited range, partly because it was designed for short to medium distances (that was that jungle fight decision, coming back to haunt everyone). The Army has never taught marksmanship past 300 meters. (One could argue that the Army never taught marksmanship anyway, post-1945, but that's a different book.) The M24 sniper rifle could reach beyond 300 meters, but it was a bolt-action rifle with a five-round magazine and not speedily reloaded. Infantry units had the M240 belt-fed machine gun, in 7.62, but there were only so many of those. When a properly laid-out-by-the-enemy ambush got going, the GIs that were subject to the ambush would find themselves in need of more than one or two 7.62 weapons capable of reaching past 300 meters.

THE M14 WASN'T DONE, HOWEVER. WITH A GLASS-BEDDED OR SYNTHETIC STOCK, AND A MAGNIFYING OPTIC ON TOP, IT BECAME THE M21, A SEMI-AUTOMATIC SNIPER RIFLE.

So, M14s got pulled out of storage, had scopes mounted on them, and with some quick familiarization, turned into DMRs. While useful, this was not a realistic long-term plan. First, there were only so many M14s after the Clinton debacle. Second, there were only so many M14 magazines, and each rifle used up, and each magazine lost, could not be replaced, at least not easily. And finally, there was no longer a support system for the M14. There were no M14-trained armorers. And what about the gauges to inspect the rifles to ensure they were ready to go? In a warehouse in who-knows-where. Or they were sold as surplus and in collectors' safes. The various services struggled to replace them with variants of the AR-10, the original Armalite rifle in .308, which was kicked aside in the 1950s in favor of the M14, which was replaced by the AR-15, which was turned into the M16. If the repetitive circles of design, acquisition, use, replacement and return make you dizzy, welcome to the club.

On the question of "what were they thinking," the M14 was made to be a select-fire service weapon. Except that most weren't. Each rifle was built with select-fire parts as part of the assembly. So, the auto sear bar, sear release, and other parts were installed. But, in place of the selector switch, the arsenal installed a selector lock. This cylindrical part fits over the selector shaft preventing the user from rotating the selector shaft to Full from Semi.

A U.S. Navy crewmember on the USS Kitty Hawk (CV-63) fires an M14 rifle equipped with a line-throwing device.

A SEAL Team 8 member checks his M14 during Operation Desert Storm.

The idea, I'm sure, at least in the beginning, was to control how many of the rifles would be select fire. If one of them broke or was disabled, a unit armorer could swap the selector switch over to another rifle, and the unit could keep on keeping on. After all, if one rifle would replace four, you couldn't have specific select-fire ones with, say, heavy barrels and bipods, and the rest semi-auto-only-can't-be-made-buzzguns. So, every soldier and Marine would have a machine gun, except they wouldn't. And we were denied the surplus M14s that could have been.

While the Ordnance Department was spending years and millions of dollars, the Italians jumped into the fray when they realized they wouldn't be getting M14s soon. They began by rebuilding Garands to the new 7.62 NATO cartridge and modifying them to accept 20-round box magazines. Called the BM59, the next step was to make new receivers (since the new rifles didn't need the clip latch) and design a new gas system to go with it. Now, the new BM59s were also select-fire because that was the attractive thing to have back then, and you weren't serious about being the military if you didn't have select-fire service rifles. So, when it came time to retire the BM59s, they couldn't be sent to the one market where you could get real, serious cash for them: America. The solution was to scrap the receivers and import the parts kits, which (again, no great surprise here) Springfield Armory — the new company, not the government arsenal — did, assembling the parts kits on new receivers.

However, there were some brought in, built as semi-only rifles. Because they had to comply with the then-new import restrictions, these had things like the bayonet lug and tri-comp muzzle brake removed. Called the BM62, they were made entirely in Italy.

The BM59/62 used proprietary magazines, now as collectible as the rifles. You're not likely to see a BM59 or 62

A Marine fires his M14 during Operation Double Eagle, January 29, 1969.

at the range, and if you do, it will be either in the hands of a collector or someone who bought it a long time ago and doesn't know they have a collectible.

The M14 could not be handed over to the CMP (back then, the DCM) for issue to us taxpayers for a reasonable sum because it was a machine gun. Now, it would have been possible for something like that to have happened, and the 1.5 million or so M14s would have found their way to us if the government could have torch-cut the receivers and only the receivers and handed the parts kit over to DCM/CMP. The CMP could then have contracted someone to make proper receivers and assemble the parts kits on the new receivers. Some of that did happen with the new Springfield Armory company, where the Reese family bought scrapped M14 parts kits and assembled them on new receivers. I have one of its early rifles, where every part except the receiver is a USGI part, and it is a good one.

As those parts dried up, Springfield Armory started having the parts sourced and made, one by one, until today, it offers the same rifle, called the M1A, as a completely new gun. Since it makes or has all the parts subcontracted, it can offer variants, and one of them is what in earlier years would have been called a "tanker" M14/M1A. These are the M1A Scout Squad or SOCOM rifles. The Scout has an 18-inch barrel with a muzzle brake, and the SOCOM has a 16.25-inch barrel and muzzle brake.

But there was one big obstacle and one later develop-

An Italian-made BM62. Based on the Garand, and for much less cost and time spent fiddle-farting around, the Italians did what the Ordnance people couldn't.

You can see the Garand clearly in the bones of the BM59. That clip on top of the receiver is a stripper guide to load magazines with stripper clips.

The Garand bottom plate was sectioned out for clearance for the magazine on the BM59. The slot on the front is for the magazine, which rocks into place like an AK-47.

The magazine release is a simple tab, spring-loaded — no need for complicated parts here.

The British tried a bullpup, but NATO (read: the USA) went with the .308/7.62, which the British rifle couldn't take.

ment. The obstacle was, "it's a machine gun, so no." Getting the various bureaucratic minds to get out of the rut of "machinegunohmygod" and see it as simply a parts kit was impossible. And then, in 1994, President Bill Clinton ordered the disposal of "surplus-to-needs" weapons, and some 750,000 M14s were either sold overseas at $1 each or fed into industrial shredders.

And the British and the Belgians? Post-WWII, and facing the Soviets, the U.S. and the European countries formed NATO. But, since this was after WWII, and most

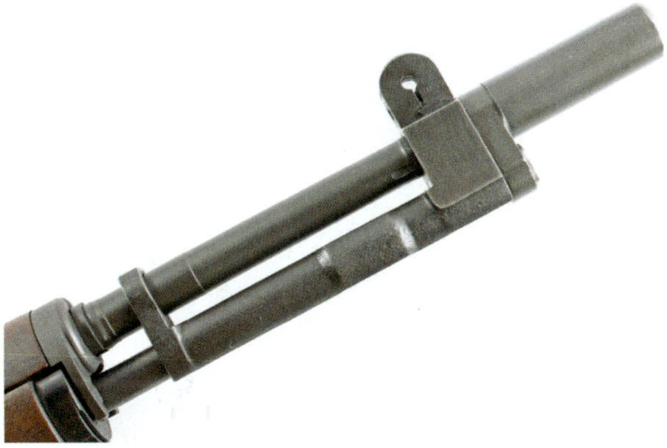

The flash hider on a BM62 lacks a bayonet lug and is missing the tri-comp of the 59.

A Beretta 59 shows the magazine tilt, unlike any other mag used in a .308 rifle.

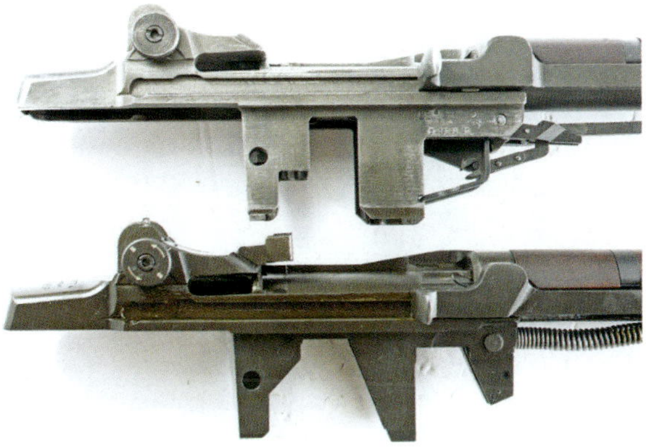

Top, a Garand receiver; bottom, a BM59 receiver. Note the changes made to accommodate a magazine.

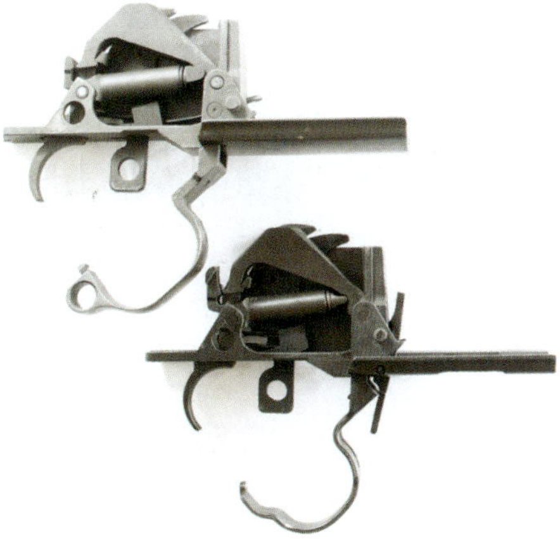

Top, Garand, bottom BM59. Not much has changed here, and some parts will interchange.

of Europe had to be rebuilt, the U.S. footed most of it. As a result, everyone else had to go along with what the U.S. Army wanted in small arms. This did not mean buying M14s, even if that had been possible. Everyone knew that depending on someone else for essential defense materiels was a fool's position, and they would make their own rifles. But, they had to be chambered in .308/7.62 NATO.

The British found that their 280 bullpup couldn't handle the .308. The new NATO round was too powerful. Having produced the SAFN49, the Belgians had also been

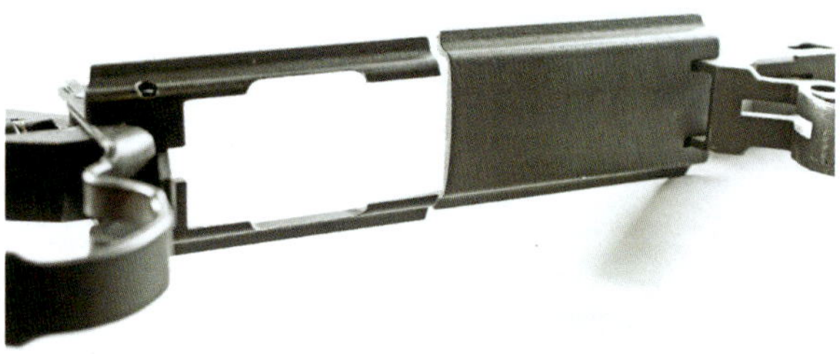

On the left is a BM59 trigger assembly, and on the right is the Garand. Other than the clearance for the magazine and the latch, they're the same.

The BM59 on the bottom has the magazine placed as it would be when the rifle was assembled.

A BM59 with the tri-comp flash hider, grenade sight, and bipod, as it was issued in the Italian army.

The British not only went with a bullpup but also tried to jump ahead and use a rifle with an optical sighting system. Half a century too soon, as it turned out.

Today's Springfield Armory produces a vast array of M1A variants. Its three flagship models include the (top) Standard Issue with a 22-inch barrel, (middle) Scout Squad with an 18-inch barrel and the 16-inch-barreled Socom on the bottom. Photos: Springfield Armory, Inc.

working on a variant they tested in various intermediate cartridges like the German WWII 7.92x33. With everyone forced onto the procrustean bed of 7.62 NATO, FN took the action of the SAFN49, added the pistol grip and other details and came up with the FAL. The British finally had to admit defeat on the 280, but when it came time to adopt a rifle, they had no other options. So they adopted the FAL, changed the blueprints from metric to English standards and called it the L1A1. (Unfortunately, the magazine locking tabs also changed, so the FAL and the L1A1 can't swap magazines, despite being identical.)

The West Germans (back then, there was a West Germany and an East Germany, one democratic and the other Soviet) also tried to come up with their own rifle, but they found the FAL was better than the designs they had. So they wanted to adopt the FAL. One big problem: the Belgians would not license it, but they would sell it. The Germans would not adopt a rifle they couldn't make and depend on someone else. (Again, Italy, LeMay, and others.) So the West German defense ministry lured the Germans who had decamped to Spain and were working on their roller-lock design. Soon they had their new rifle, the G3, made in Germany by HK.

If you were ever wondering how it came to be that NATO had all those rifles and yet the same cartridge, that's why. •

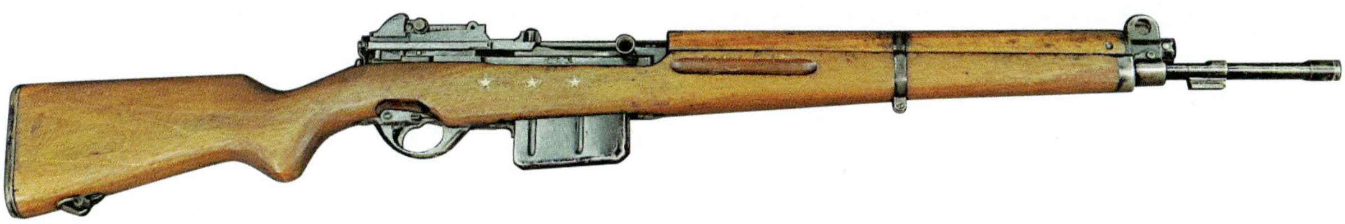

The Belgian SAFN49 was the last forged walnut-stocked rifle adopted in Europe. It would be made in various calibers, including 7mm Mauser, 8mm Mauser, .30-06, and 7.65x53 Argentine. While it didn't get much love, the action ended up being the FAL.

CHAPTER 9

SNIPER RIFLES: THE M1C AND M1D GARANDS

During WWII, it was obvious that more accuracy was needed in some instances. That is, sniper rifles. It's another instance of learning lessons from a previous war, forgetting them, and having to do it all over again. All the lessons learned in WWI were allowed to fade, and with Pearl Harbor, the Army had to get back up to speed. The Garand would be the new sniper rifle if the military could solve its problems with scopes. Until then, the existing rifle, the Springfield '03, would have to do. The conversion to sniper rifle was relatively simple by today's standards but a massive task in those days. But, by drilling and tapping the top of the receiver and installing a base and rings, the Army could wrestle together a rifle with a magnifying scope.

The first sniper rifle, the Springfield '03 with a Warner & Swasey scope, was used in WWI.

The military had done this once before, back in The Great War, when it installed a Warner & Swasey scope on the existing Springfield, the '03, and used it for sniping. The Marines went a different way and used a Winchester A5 scope in specialized target mounts. Optics were fragile then, and the mount for the Marines' rifle did not securely clamp the scope tube. Instead, the scope slid back and forth in the mount. On recoil, the rifle moved back, and the scope slid forward. The rifleman had to move the scope back to the rear position for each shot.

The existing WWII sniper rifle, the Springfield 03A4, was an updated (Remington upgraded the '03 with stamped parts) bolt-action rifle with a scope attached to the top, like a hunting rifle today. The mount locked the scope in place, unlike the Marine mount setup. You can see this in the movie "Saving Private Ryan" in the hands of Barry Pepper as Private Jackson. While it was more than accurate enough for what was considered sniping by the U.S. Army, it was still a bolt-action rifle. (The Western

The Marines used a modified Springfield as a sniper rifle, with a scope in target mounts. Delicate, but useful.

Front was not like the Eastern. In the East, snipers hunted each other and were considered high-value targets. In the West, the 03A4 was used more as a DMR.)

Let's consider accuracy. The existing Springfield '03 was inherently accurate. You'd get good groups if you mounted one in a machine rest and fired it. What hindered it was the sights. And its handiness. The sights were the late 19th-century idea of good target-shooting sights. The "combat" sight was a notch and post. So, you had a .30-06 rifle meant for 1,000 yards but used what amounted to pistol sights. If you wanted more precision, you had to stand up the rear sight, adjust the slider to the range, and use the peep sight. As far from your face as it was, that ended up being slow, awkward, and not combat-friendly.

... DESPITE BOTH RIFLES HAVING SIMILAR INHERENT ACCURACY, THE GARAND IS MUCH EASIER TO SHOOT ACCURATELY THAN THE SPRINGFIELD.

The Garand, as a rifle, was equally accurate. The '03 handiness? Well, a relatively lightweight .30-06 with a steel buttplate is not what you want to shoot a lot. The '03 tips the scales at about 8.5 pounds. The Garand is about 9.5 pounds. Add a pound of weight, and then soften the felt recoil by making it a self-loading, gas-operated rifle, and you have a much more pleasant experience. And while "pleasant" is not in the military's basic vocabulary, it does matter when you are trying to build skills.

While not the easiest variants to find, the Garand sniper rifles are popular among long-range shooters who compete in the Civilian Marksmanship Program's (CMP) Vintage Sniper Matches. Photo: CMP Archives

The big deal for accuracy was the Garand's sighting system. Placing the aperture near the aiming eye improves accuracy in several ways. First, the sight radius is longer, and that adds precision. Second, with the aperture close to the eye, the shooter does not have to move around as much behind the stock to get aligned with the rear sight.

The last part may seem like magic in the modern era with so many AR-15-experienced shooters using scopes or red-dot optics. If you relax and let your eye and brain work naturally, your eye will find the center of the aperture. Get comfortably behind the sight, focus on the front blade, and you will center it in the rear aperture.

As a result, despite both rifles having similar inherent accuracy, the Garand is much easier to shoot accurately than the Springfield. The value of an aperture sight was

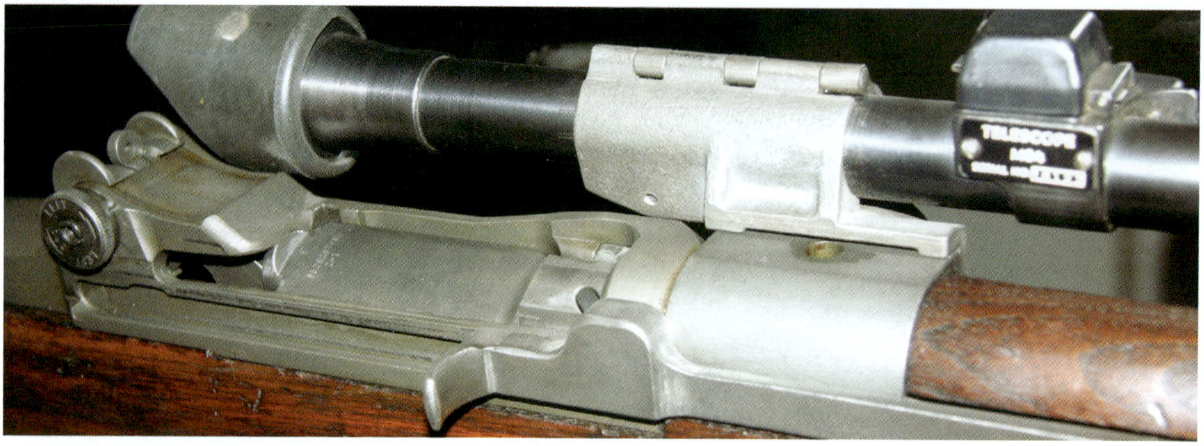

The Garand's scope offset to avoid clip insertion and ejection is apparent here. That meant a leather cheekpiece had to be tied to the stock, a small price to pay.

recognized quickly, and as a result, when it came time to scale up rifle production in WWII, something interesting happened. Remington, tasked with making sufficient Springfields to supplant the Garand production, reported to the War Department that the design was hopeless and the rifle had to be modernized. The War Department agreed, and Remington updated everything on the '03, making as many parts as possible, including heavy-gauge steel stampings, welded assemblies, and updated steel alloys. And it junked the elaborate '03 rear sight and installed a simpler aperture sight mounted on the rear receiver bridge.

ON THE M1 GARAND, THE SCOPE HAD TO BE MOUNTED TO THE SIDE OF THE BORE AXIS. ADD A PADDED LEATHER CHEEKPIECE, AND THE SOLDIER IT WAS ISSUED TO COULD USE THE OPTICS AND STILL HAVE A SELF-LOADING RIFLE.

The idea of the distances snipers can connect on these days would have been fantastical to GIs in the 1940s. A 1,000-yard shot was seen as a target-range distance on a six-foot-sized target. They were concerned with hitting a partial target, like a helmet, at 200 yards. For that, a magnifying scope would be handy.

The demand for a more accurate Garand with a scope was strong enough that the Army did what it could. Let's look at this from a technical perspective. First of all, there's the en-bloc clip. It has to go straight into the receiver. And after the last round is fired, it has to come straight out. You can't have a scope in the way. The Springfield had the scope on top, so it could not be reloaded with a stripper clip. The user had to thumb individual rounds into the magazine, fitting them under the scope. So, in a fast-moving, target-rich environment, you, the sniper, were armed with a bolt-action rifle, and when you had used your five rounds, you were out of action, behind cover for a minute or two, thumbing rounds into the magazine.

Meanwhile, your squad mates were hammering away: eight rounds, reload, and eight more.

On the M1 Garand, the scope had to be mounted to the side of

The Germans had lots of experience with snipers in the trenches and kept that knowledge current for WWII.

The M1C's mount was attached to the receiver and required holes drilled and tapped. Photo: Rock Island Auction Company

the bore axis. Add a padded leather cheekpiece, and the soldier it was issued to could use the optics and still have a self-loading rifle. There were two prototype designs to consider: the M1E7 and M1E8. The E7 used a Griffin & Howe side mount. This mount placed the scope to the side, and it was a known and well-regarded mount to add optics to a Garand. The M1C, as it was designated when adopted, used a Griffin & Howe mount with five holes in the mount and receiver. Three of the receiver holes were tapped, and two were left untapped. The three tapped holes were for the screws that held it on, and the other two were for tapered pins. The pins did two things: they provided mount location repeatability should it be removed and shear strength to keep the mount from loosening and coming off from the recoil of multiple shots fired.

The M1E8 did things differently. On the E8, the barrel was the mounting location, the mount clamped on a modified barrel, and there was a large knurled thumbscrew to tighten it in place.

For various reasons, the E7 was adopted as the M1C and put into production late in the war. Things did not go smoothly. The initial attempts had the non-heat-treated receivers drilled and tapped, the mount affixed, and the receiver heat-treated. When I first read that, a shudder ran through me. Two pieces of steel of different sizes and thicknesses, and almost certainly of different alloys, being bolted together and *then* heat-treated? The warpage must have been epic. After that attempt, the receivers were drilled and tapped, heat-treated, and the mounts fastened. While production was approved with a finalized design in June 1944, it wasn't until later that year that Springfield began production.

The M1C was made only on Springfield rifles, which only converted certain blocks of serial numbers. While those blocks fell within the 3,100,000 and 3,800,000 serial number range, the total number of M1C rifles made during WWII was about 8,000. Rare, indeed.

M1C production took so long that the sniper rifle saw little, if any, action in WWII. With its Lyman Alaskan

The M1D used a special barrel, no mods to the receiver, and was a better setup. Photo: Rock Island Auction Company

The M1D mount was attached to the barrel, so any Garand could be built or rebuilt as an M1D if you had the special barrel. And the scopes were, of course, serial numbered.

The British No. 4 was also made into a sniper version, but it required the receiver to be drilled and tapped (like the M1C), and a special mount with oversized thumbscrews held the scope.

scope (and all of its 2X magnification), it would have been very useful in the M81 with a crosshair or the M82 with a tapered-post reticle.

The E8, designed by Garand himself, was adopted as a substitute standard in September 1944, so the services would have a backup. Well, that was the official explanation. Me? I suspect those in charge got it wrong at the start and didn't want to admit it. Yes, the adoption of an existing scope mount system seemed prudent. But the heat-treatment mistake cost time. Plus, once you drilled and tapped a receiver to be an M1C, that's what it was. If you needed more, you had to make more from scratch, as drilling and tapping an already heat-treated receiver would have been a game of chance.

The M1D, on the other hand, was just another barrel. Once the tooling was set up to make the modified chamber area of the M1D barrel, you could make as many as you needed for years to come and stash them in inventory. If you needed more M1Ds, you swapped barrels in existing rifles. And, if something better for sniping came along, an M1D barrel, under a regular handguard, was just another M1 rifle.

Both the M1C and the M1D were issued with a laced-on leather cheekpiece that was padded to provide a solid cheek weld for the shooter, which aligned with the left-canted scope. The flash hider, M2, clipped onto the muzzle and gas cylinder like the grenade launcher but did not compress the poppet valve since there was no change in the gas flow when firing Ball ammo.

The Springfield 03A4 was not numerous, with some 28,000 made. But it served long enough to do well in WWII and see action in Korea. However, Korea changed things.

Just as with regular M1 inventory, the Army realized it needed more sniper rifles. So Springfield assembled them from existing receivers, but drilling and tapping receivers to make M1C rifles was a non-starter. So, the plant made new M1D barrels and installed them into existing rifles. This poses a problem for collectors. While the M1C rifles are M1C (I suspect there are more than a few fakes), the M1D could legitimately be any rifle. If Springfield grabbed an in-spec 1942 receiver and built it into an M1D in 1952, it was and is a legitimate M1D. Sigh.

The M1D suffered the same fate as the M1C, being too late to do much, if anything, in the war for which it was built. By the late 1950s, the new rifle, the M14, was set up to accept a scope mount (not designed yet, but one step at a time, right?) without going to extra measures. •

CHAPTER 10

THE NON-USGI GARANDS

The bulk of the Garands ever made came from the U.S. makers. That would have been during WWII, the Korean War, and a few years after. But other countries made them as well. The big one was Italy. The Italians were not at all happy about using Garands if the guns and the tooling to make spares, service, maintain, and inspect them were all in the hands of the U.S.

GARANDS WORTH COLLECTING

I can't help but compare it to General Curtis LeMay's situation when he ran the Strategic Air Command or SAC.

Beretta made Garands and BM59s once the Garand was replaced.

The U.S. Air Force had been split off from the Army after WWII when it was clear the two had different missions and focuses. That happened in 1947. During the 1950s, the Air Force formed SAC, the nuclear bombing arm of the Air Force. The Air Force had much stricter security on the bases where SAC wings were stationed. (Understandable, they had nukes, after all.) The SAC security forces were all armed with M1 and M2 Carbines. And the inventory of spares and parts, plus maintenance, inspection, and service, were in the hands of the Army, not the Air Force, and certainly not SAC.

That drove LeMay crazy. So when he had the chance to buy rifles for his security forces that were not U.S. Army, he did so. And that's how the AR-15 got into DoD inventory.

The Italians had a long history of making firearms and caring for them. So, the tooling from Winchester was shipped to Italy, where Beretta set it up and started producing rifles in 1950. You can identify Beretta-made parts by the "PB" stamp. They produced something on the order of 100,000 Garands.

You will also see Garands with the Danish crown and their own serial number range. The Danes didn't make them; they were produced for the Danish army by Beretta. The receivers have the crown and FKF stamp, but the small parts will have the "PB" stamp for Pietro Beretta. Beretta and Danish-marked Garands are first-rate firearms, as the Italians knew how to make rifles and used the Winchester tooling.

There's one small batch of Garands, those built by Century Arms. Scoring a batch of Italian Garands, Century found that the rifles could not be imported. (The technicalities are many, but if it was loaned to any foreign military, it was not permitted to be imported back to the U.S. If, on the other hand, it was shipped to the police, or sold, then it could be.) So, Century removed the receivers, imported each parts kit, and reassembled them on U.S.-made receivers. These are not FedOrd-level junk, but they also are not collectibles. They are solid shooters.

When it came time to change over to something chambered in 7.62 NATO, the 7.62x51 cartridge, aka .308 Winchester, the U.S. spent millions developing and producing the M14. The Italian options, in the late 1950s, to be on-board with their NATO commitments? They could try to buy M14s, but the U.S. government wasn't having much luck getting enough for themselves. They could buy FALs, but that meant sending money to Belgium and being stuck with FN as the service provider, which Italy had gotten away from having the U.S. in that role by making Garands. There was not yet a West German G3, so what to do? They decided to make their own.

The BM59 started as a modified Garand, and then Beretta made the receivers it needed and all the other parts — for a lot less cost and hassle than the M14 program.

The Danes used Garands and rebuilt them but didn't make receivers. This is a Garand receiver (and rifle) made in Italy by Beretta for Danish service use. Then it eventually came here, to the U.S.

They took the Garand, built a new gas system for it, modified the receiver legs to take a magazine, and designed a magazine that would fit within the space provided by the receiver. Violà! — the BM59. The clever aspect was the "make the magazine fit the receiver" part, instead of the M14 approach of "make a magazine, then modify the receiver to accept it," leading to many downstream design and fabrication problems.

That leads us in a roundabout way to the modern production of Garands by Springfield Armory, Inc., of Geneseo, Illinois. Robert Reese formed Springfield in 1974 once the government had closed its own Springfield Arsenal, and there would not be any confusion about who was who. (Confusion persisted because many people took a long time to forget that Robert McNamara had closed the first one.) Geneseo is close to the Rock Island Arsenal, where the government was scrapping tons and tons of military equipment. (A shocking waste of taxpay-

Left to right, we have a genuine Springfield, a casting from someplace with no markings, and a Fed Ord cast receiver that's probably best used as a paperweight.

ers' money, but what can you do? Once the medieval attitude of "bad gear must destroy" gets a hold in some people's heads, that's it.) He would buy the torch-cut receivers and all the parts for each rifle, strip them, and install them in new receivers of his own making. And that's how the Springfield M1A came about. You see, the M14 was a select-fire rifle. The ATF's attitude is "once a machine gun, always a machine gun." In most instances, reversing or negating the select-fire option is difficult. One example would be the M16. As long as there's a hole in the receiver to accept the auto sear, it can be changed back. Welding the hole might work, but the government can't count on the quality of a weld. "Oops, it fell out" would be a common welding "failure."

On the M14, the select-fire option depends on a lug on the bottom of the receiver to locate and create a pivot point for the auto-fire parts. The parts would no longer work if you used a surface grinder and removed that lug. The M1A receiver? It's an M14 receiver but made without the lug. No mechanical or functional difference exists between an M14 with the lug missing and an M1A that never had it.

IF YOU SEE A GARAND IN THE RACK OR AT A GUN SHOW, AND IT'S LISTED AT A FAIR PRICE, LOOK AT THE BARREL MARKINGS UNDER THE OP ROD. IF IT SAYS "SPRINGFIELD ARMORY, GENESEO," YOU'D BETTER SNAP IT UP BEFORE THE GUY LOOKING OVER YOUR SHOULDER BUYS IT THE MOMENT YOU PUT IT DOWN.

However, in the peculiar regulatory minds of the bureaucratic set, they are entirely different creatures. So, the M14 receivers had to be torched, but the parts were OK. At least until one William Jefferson Clinton became President. Then they had to be fed in their entirety into a crusher.

But, back to the 1970s. So, Bob Reese would buy the parts and build new rifles. While sourcing all the parts he could, he ended up in Italy, found the BM59s in storage, and bought and imported those as well. The story was much the same: the receivers, as machine guns, could not come in, but each parts kit could. In the course of asking, he kept pestering the folks at Beretta until someone finally admitted that, yes, it did have Garands. The parts that could be used also came over, and Springfield made new receivers and barrels for them since the originals had been hard-used and were mostly not up to commercial or retail use.

If you see a Garand in the rack or at a gun show, and it's

The proud owner of this Springfield (Geneseo) Garand has the box, the paperwork, and all the goodies it came with. We are all jealous.

listed at a fair price, look at the barrel markings under the op rod. If it says "Springfield Armory, Geneseo," you'd better snap it up before the guy looking over your shoulder buys it the moment you put it down.

THE UNDESIRABLES

Now, having gone over the good stuff, let's look at the bad stuff. There is a class of Garands known as "rewelds." The "re" part does not mean they have been welded again, having been welded before. No, it means they had been cut in half, and someone fitted two halves together and

Any receiver is made of a single alloy, properly heat-treated. If you mix chopped parts, you risk an alloy mismatch, and things can go seriously awry.

welded the gap back. This involved installing surplus parts on the receivers and selling them. It happened in the 1970s when you could buy a scrapped Garand for its weight in steel and sell a working one for a couple of hundred dollars.

The name to look for here is FedOrd, or Federal Ordnance. You can also find craptastic "surplus" builds under the names of Golden State Arms, National Ordnance, and others. In addition to welded receivers, they were also built on cast receivers from foundries outside the U.S., imported, then "cleaned up" (the few I've seen were so rugged and ugly it almost looked like they were dug out of the ground, de-rusted, and then built), machined to final dimensions, and assembled into rifles. They also did this with M1 carbines (the majority of their output, as the carbine was much less of an assembly job) and even '03 Springfields, Mausers, and Enfields.

Now, welding is not, as you might say, welding. Receiver alloys were not the same over time and from maker to maker. If you have a reweld with two different brands of receivers, and two different alloys, then add in the different "stick" used to weld, you will have a real mess.

Sweeney's rack-grade Garand is marked FedOrd, but that's because it was the importer of, in this case, an original Garand — not a "made on a new receiver" Garand. Yes, it looks like it was dug out of the ground, but it works fine.

One of the fine details of making a Garand receiver is receiver thread timing. Can we agree that a Third-World shop, back in the 1960s, '70s or '80s, wasn't going to be hip to that particular aspect?

All Tankers are rebuilt not from an arsenal but by a shop or company, not USGI. Some, like this one, are well done. Others are marginal at best.

Springfield used one alloy, Winchester another. (This was allowed because they did the appropriate heat treatments for each alloy in their manufacture.) Experts investigating this have found the mixed-receiver weld jobs — all of them horrible, none of them acceptable — referred to as "Winfield" and Springchester" for the "which is front and back" mixing.

Oh, and if you're going to weld two parts back together, you need a solid fixture with accurate alignment and must account for contraction once cooled. If you don't, you'll have an out-of-spec receiver, no matter how careful the weld was.

This is also the source of many of the "Tanker" Garands you might encounter. During WWII, there was an attempt to produce a shorter, lighter Garand. What, if anything, it had to do with tanks is anyone's guess, as it was an attempt in the field to lighten GIs' loads. If you could shave a pound off the full-up weight of a Garand, that would be good. If it became a bit handier in house-to-house and close jungle fighting, that would be good, too. But, post-war, there was no real impetus to make a "Garand carbine." No, that came from post-war surplus "builders" putting rifles together.

There is no real standard, no "this is the government drawing," so you should consider each one a one-off, custom gunsmithing project. If you give in to temptation and find your Tanker isn't reliable, you'll need the services of a first-class riflesmith. They will have two paths to follow, and I know which one they will recommend: the first thing they'll tell you is to take the barrel out, and replace it with a Garand barrel in .30-06, use the gas system if intact, replace if not, and get a new op rod and handguard or handguards. That will be the advice if it's an authentic Garand receiver. They will most likely pass on the project if it's built on a FedOrd or other. If you insist on making it work reliably as a Tanker, they might be willing to work on it but offer no guarantees.

While the FedOrd and other "new" receivers may have been an inexpensive alternative to a USGI Garand in the 1960s, '70s and into the '80s, they should not be fired. For one thing, there is no guarantee that the headspace is correct. Also, the alloy steel used? While they touted it back then, again, there are no guarantees. And heat treatment? Your guess is as good as mine. Imports of originals marked as imported by FedOrd are fine, though rough.

No, your options here are pretty simple: if the seller asks real-Garand prices for their FedOrd reweld or cast receiver rifle, pass on it. Just walk away. If they offer it for the price or value of its parts, and you have a source of an actual Garand receiver, then you can consider it a "project" gun to build or have built for you. •

CHAPTER 11

LOVE AFFAIR WITH THE GARAND

Growing up, I knew my father had fought in the war. The War. (There would be later ones, but growing up, it was singular and meant World War II.) While he had spent most of his time toting around an M3 SMG and making life miserable for the German soldiers his unit, the Combat Scouts of the 95th Infantry, would encounter each night, he had begun with a Garand. Since I could not own an M3 "grease gun," I was determined to own a Garand someday. I eventually did (recounted earlier) and looked forward to the fun.

The author's match-conditioned Garand, with a load it likes, iron sights at 100 yards.

The next time I managed to get to the range (I was working part-time as a counter guy at The Gun Room in Redford, where I was already embarking on my gun career), I test-fired that Garand and found it wasn't so bad. I had anticipated shotgun-like patterns on the targets. However, I was getting about two and a half inches at 100 yards on a good day, and that was with quality ammo. (My eyesight was much better then, so the iron sights were as much as I needed.) With service-grade FMJ, 100-yard groups just over three inches were well within the military specs for an issue Garand — one that was not match grade but not shot-out, either. So, I started doing some reading. (Which was another part of my gun career I had embarked on.)

I solved its various problems and scrubbed the bore out, and life was good.

What followed was a decade of learning to reload. Up to that point, I had been loading .38 Special, which was so simple compared to loading for the Garand that I could have taught the family Labrador Retriever how to load the stuff. It required lots of Sierra boattailed hollow-point bullets, varying from 150 to 180 grains (depending on the match), and several kegs of IMR-4895 powder. I reloaded because factory ammunition was too expensive to shoot, even in the glory days of inexpensive surplus ammo. I had a ready supply of once-fired .30-06 brass and could buy primers, powder, and bullets at cost through the shop. So, I didn't need surplus. Also, for accuracy: While surplus ball ammo was good for 2.5 inches, my reloads, with Sierra MatchKings, could get down to an inch at 100 yards when I was on my game. For that, I was happy to reload.

By the early 1980s, I was deep into IPSC competition, and in those early days, there wasn't IPSC/USPSA 3-Gun (or later, Multi-gun) competition. At our gun club, we started doing 3-Gun earlier than most IPSC clubs, and we also started bowling pin matches. In the club 3-Gun matches, using a Garand wasn't a handicap because we designed the stages to be equipment-neutral, so one rifle didn't have an advantage over the others. Not so, bowling pins.

The bowling pin match was the Light Rifle Pop and Flop, or LRPF, with actual bowling pins. The match was simple: you had a set period to run down range and set a series of 15 bowling pins onto their stands. You then ran back, loaded your rifle, and on the start signal, started shooting. Your score was how quickly you could knock them all off, the fastest time winning from the start of the shooting time. The running time was the same for all shooters and not part of your score/time. That is, unless you got back to the start line before the set-up time was over, you could catch your breath before the start of shooting time. If you didn't return by then, time started without you.

I was young, fit, and a fast runner.

In one match, I made it back, loaded up, slung up and caught my breath before time started. I dropped the fifteenth and last pin with my sixteenth shot.

I placed third. Third! The second-place shooter had used an AR-15 which was mildly embarrassing, but the winner? You have to know a bit about firearms hierarchy and history to understand the outrage I felt at that moment. He used a Universal carbine (not even a USGI carbine, oh the horror) with the telescoping, wire, "paratrooper" stock, and a crappy (even by the day's standards) scope in a side mount. He had used a pair of 30-round magazines, "jungle-clipped" together, and he had even reloaded, swapping magazines, in the short time he spent shooting. He beat us, and it wasn't even close. It was as if

The guy who beat Sweeney on the LRPF that day wasn't using classic iron like these. But instead, a shabby knockoff of the original, with the worst stock possible and a scope no one considered good even back then. Photo: CMP Archives

the rest of us had been using classic Detroit V8 muscle cars in a street race, and some guy in a Yugo showed up and handily smoked us.

I had just acquired a Springfield M1A, another smoking hot deal with a supposedly shot-out bore, and while I searched for a suitable smaller rifle for 3-Gun and pins, I took that M1A to the Second Chance Combat Shoot to compete in the LRPF there. I figured the 20-round magazine would give me a leg up from my beloved Garand. By then, the LRPF had changed to falling steel plates, with no running involved, and I was just left entirely in the dust by the AR-15 shooters. This was getting more than just embarrassing, so I settled on finding an AR-15 to use in the competition after that.

That M1A? It is a very early Springfield Armory, Inc. gun, which was still building them using USGI parts. The only non-government part was the receiver, made by the new Springfield Armory company. It, too, arrived with "a shot-out bore" and ammo cans of magazines, plus more ammo cans of surplus imported, amazingly dirty and craptastic ammo. Its bore was dark, so I paid a pittance for it. I figured I could get a good read on accuracy if I scrubbed the bore first, just in case I'd need to re-barrel it. Yes, the same plan as I had undertaken with the Garand.

The Grcck surplus came along long after Sweeney was over his initial Garand honeymoon period. Even when surplus ammo was cheap, reloading was cheaper, so that's what he did.

So I stripped it down and ran a solvent patch down the bore. The next patch came out so blue from copper that it practically glowed. Hmm, this seemed familiar. I spent the next two weeks at the shop (I was a full-time gunsmith by then), alternating between copper and powder solvent patches. When it stopped showing blue each time, I went with powder solvent, and when that stopped coming out black, I went back to copper solvent. When they both came out clean, I was done.

Test-firing a CMP Garand, in the snow, in the winter. Yep, it worked just fine, as anyone would expect.

The USMC Silent Drill Team demonstrating with Garands. So, four feet of 10 pounds of rifle with a sharp point on the end tossed back and forth. You should be impressed.

It shot to the high end of rack grade. So, I did more research and rebuilt it to USAMU specs for glass bedding, welding, etc. I also mounted a scope on it, and the first group after all that work was a one-hole cluster at 100 yards.

Alas, it was evident there was no place for .30-caliber rifles in practical competition, and I had already scored an AR-15 for competition. After the whole competition scene had shifted to AR-15s, there was a small movement to make a Division or category for .30-cal. rifles. Called Heavy Metal, it was the place for those who didn't want to give up their M1 Garands, M1As, FALs, AR-10s, G3s, and other rifles.

Life changed, we moved on, and while I still have both rifles, they don't get out much anymore because there just isn't a place to compete with them, at least not in what I do these days.

However, the Garand did get used. My father, who was then long past the war (and the bad memories faded quite a bit), would occasionally agree to come to the range on family range days. On one, the grandkids, knowing "Grandpa" had used a Garand in the war, insisted that he shoot one, just so they could see how it worked. At the time, we were on a pistol range at the gun club, but it was a "pistol range" only because it was 25 yards long, not because rifles were prohibited from use there. Dad fished a penny out of his pocket and used a target paster to hold it to the cardboard target. Back at the firing line, he loaded the Garand (smoothly, I might add), then, looking at the target, threw the rifle to his shoulder, paused for a moment, and fired. "OK, I shot it. Who's next?"

When we went to paste the target, the penny was nowhere to be found. After searching the range floor, someone found it — with a .30-inch arc torn off its edge.

Some skills take a long time to fade, and I suspect there were a lot of German soldiers who didn't make it home due to skills like that, from my father and other GIS, and the Garand as their GI tool.

Nowadays, Garands don't spend much time putting bad guys into the dust, but they do still serve. •

SECTION II

FUN WITH THE GARAND

CHAPTER 12

WHAT TO LOOK FOR WHEN BUYING A GARAND

Buying a Garand isn't like the AR-15. For the AR, unless there's been a recent gun control panic-buying spree (panic on the part of trying to ban them and buying on the part of those who don't), you can walk into a gun shop and see anywhere from two to two dozen of them. On the other hand, you can frequent a dozen gun shops and run into a Garand in the rack once in a blue moon. So, you walk in the door, scan the racks, and there it is: a Garand.

First, we'll review what to look for and what you can expect when checking out a Garand for possible purchase. Then, we'll go over the various tools and checks that low-volume dealers should be able to do, and finally, what you can expect from dealers with high volumes of Garands, who can check everything.

Be realistic; you can't check everything. Unless you have a complete set of inspection gauges (and the owner or gun shop is willing to let you disassemble it and gauge everything right on the countertop), there are things you can't check. Also, unless the gun shop has a range, test-firing your prospective Garand isn't in the cards. Heck, in many gun shows these days, the action will be zip-tied open or closed, and you may not even get a chance to dry

The markings "Blue Sky" means it was imported from Korea a few decades ago but was only part of the vast Korean stockpile proving difficult to import.

The alterations to this Garand included drilling and tapping for a tip-off scope. Unfortunately, they did not use the M1C drill hole pattern, so it can't even be "restored" to a faux M1C.

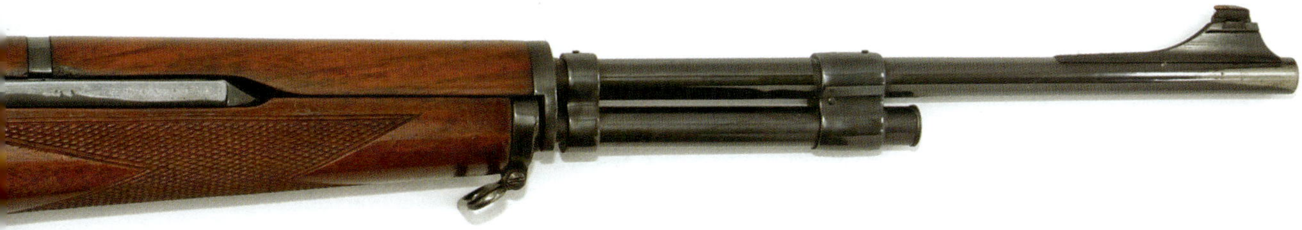

This is a rarity, a sporterized Garand. The design is not very amenable to being "sporterized." So when you see one, it will invariably be ugly and awkward.

The CMP muzzle gauge can be kept in your pocket when you find a Garand for sale.

fire it and test the trigger or peer down the bore.

Moreover, consider that the newest Garand you will ever see, the last one made, won't be new. It may look new if it hasn't been fired since 1956, when it was the last of its line to be test-fired and crammed into a storage rack. It may have spent its entire service life in a rack someplace, never fired, handled only for inventory purposes, and is in like-new condition. If that is the case, brace yourself before you turn over the price tag because it will be impressive. It may have traveled around the world and been owned by several countries on different continents. It could be on its second bolt, third barrel, or fifth action spring and may have seen more ammo than you could ever afford.

You should also be realistic that the Garand you are looking over will be no less than retirement age. In that time, previous owners may have done minor to heinous things to it. Some "fixes" could be or have been repaired, and some cannot be undone. For example, what about a Garand with a sanded and refinished stock? The stock can be replaced. One with a rubber recoil pad, inlays, and notches from hunts? A new stock. Some funky "I aim it better that way" front or rear sight mods? New parts will take care of that. A receiver drilled and tapped for some weird, bizarre, or out-of-production scope mount? You're stuck with the holes since they can't be welded (at least not without risking further unavoidable damage), so get it at an excellent price.

So first, we'll go over what you can check at the gun show table or gun shop counter. Then, we'll review what you can check at your gun club or range. Finally, a quick reminder about what may be causing malfunctions that you can see the cause of, if they can be corrected, or if the rifle needs to be returned. Then, I'll review the various gauges and inspections a well-equipped dealer or Garand maven could go through.

CONDITION

Firearms are described by their condition. This ranking has been done for a long time and is well-codified by the NRA, the Blue Book of Gun Values, and the Standard Catalog of Firearms, among others. Since I have spent a lot of ink and opportunities being snarky about people who re-invent the wheel and crow about it, I won't do that here. Regarding Garands, the preeminent authority would be the CMP, the Civilian Marksmanship Program. Previously known as the DCM, Department of Civilian Marksmanship, it is the agency tasked with selling surplus firearms into commercial channels. That is, from government inventory (ours and others) to us.

Photo: CMP Archives

Strange as it may seem today, the government used to encourage marksmanship training and competition. Along with the NRA (formed to encourage marksmanship, training, and competition in 1871 by Civil War veterans who were appalled at both the lack of marksmanship in soldiers and the poor training in marksmanship they had received from the Army), the CMP has solid descriptions of the condition of firearms. I'll give the CMP full credit here for its work on figuring this out and describe what it calls each grade. Then, I'll tell you the likely avenues you'd take in upgrading if you so wish.

A QUICK GAUGE PRIMER

The muzzle gauge is a stepped gauge that you poke (gently) into the muzzle, which gives a reading of the wear at the muzzle. The less wear, the better. The erosion gauge does the same thing at the throat, the start of the bore, just ahead of the chamber. And likewise, the less wear, the better. The Field gauge is a headspace gauge larger than a No-Go gauge but within the allowable use in wartime headspace. If a rifle accepts (the bolt fully closes) on a Field gauge, something is wrong, and you must have it tended to.

IMPORT MARKS

There are various eras and routes by which Garands were let loose in the commercial market here in America. First, there are those sold by the U.S. government as surplus, back when it still did that. There are also "bring-backs," rifles brought back by returning veterans of WWII or Korea. I put that in quotes because a bring-back is a foreign firearm that is a souvenir and has the paperwork to prove it.

Let's say your Great-Uncle Mort took a Luger off a German soldier in France in 1944. He could ask his commanding officer (at whatever level the unit tasked this process at) to provide him with a receipt or "bring-back

A stock cartouche is good and will bring a higher price when shopping.

papers" that showed authorization to own said Luger. Of course, many GIs, Marines, seamen and airmen didn't bother with papers. It was wartime, after all, and there was no paperwork required to own a firearm in the places they called home.

There were no bring-back papers for U.S. firearms. They were U.S. government property; you turned them in once you finished using them. Yes, well … we all know how that went.

The U.S. government wasn't too concerned as long as the gun wasn't a machine gun. A general amnesty on all "lost" firearms was the policy. If a GI wasn't caught with it, once he was discharged, it was his, and no one would come looking for it. Other than being marked as government property when manufactured, none of these would have extra markings of any kind. However, if an importer bought firearms overseas that were surplus, or foreign military, they had to be marked as imports after the Gun Control Act of 1968 (aka GCA '68). The size and imprint of the markings have varied over the years as the regulations got re-interpreted, "clarified," and generally made more onerous. It would not be overly paranoid to consider the latest markings as required in such a way as to "uglify" a surplus firearm and perhaps even hinder its performance. (I'm thinking of the large and deep imprint on barrels I've seen on some imports. Blue Sky comes to mind, and M1 Carbine barrels with "minute of barn" accuracy.)

A Garand brought in might have unobtrusive markings, like my Fed Ord import, stamped on a receiver leg, or it could have the marking stamped or etched, pin-punched or scratched with a file on the barrel or gas cylinder. The "no import mark" means just that. It wasn't one of those brought in by an importer and marred.

RACK GRADE, AKA FAIR

Most rack-grade rifles have been refinished or rebuilt several times while in military service and will have some parts from other manufacturers. Rifle wear will be exhibited by worn and mixed colors of the finish; there will be rust and pitting on the metal parts; wood will be sound but may be well used with minor hairline cracks,

The erosion gauge measures the Garand chamber throat wear. It is one indication of what a rifle has gone through. This measures 3, which is a relatively low mileage.

poor fit, multiple dings, scratches, and gouges; the wood may not match in color, type of wood, or condition. These rifles may have some foreign parts, and the wood may be walnut, birch, beech or other variety.

They do not have import marks. Bores will be dark and poor; the barrel crown may be nicked, and the muzzle may gauge more than "3" on the muzzle gauge. The throat erosion may gauge more than "5." The rifle is headspaced with a field gauge and function fired. The overall appearance and condition of the rack-grade Garand will generally be rougher than any other grade.

Translation: These are well-used rifles in rough condition. With good ammunition, they will certainly function and demonstrate "minute of bad guy" accuracy to 100 yards or more. This is not the rifle you want to enter a match with, but you could learn a lot using one in a match. You will have to do some stock repairs and perhaps refinishing, and some of the thinner wood parts or sections, like the handguards, might need more than just a jolt of glue into a crack.

The manufacturer of the receiver defines the rifle's name. For example, a Springfield will have a Springfield receiver, but there may not be another Springfield part on the rifle. These are definitely "mixmaster" Garands.

With some use and learning how to shoot, you will probably replace the barrel relatively soon.

FIELD GRADE: FAIR TO GOOD

The cosmetic condition will be fair to good, showing moderate to significant cosmetic wear. The finish may vary, exhibiting significant wear and color variation among the metal parts. It may have moderate visible pitting, frosting, or other cosmetic deformities on the metal parts above and below the wood line. The stock sets may consist of any species of wood (or a combination thereof); and exhibit significant dents, dings, scratches, and structurally insignificant cracks. New production commercial stock sets may be used and likely exhibit noticeable signs

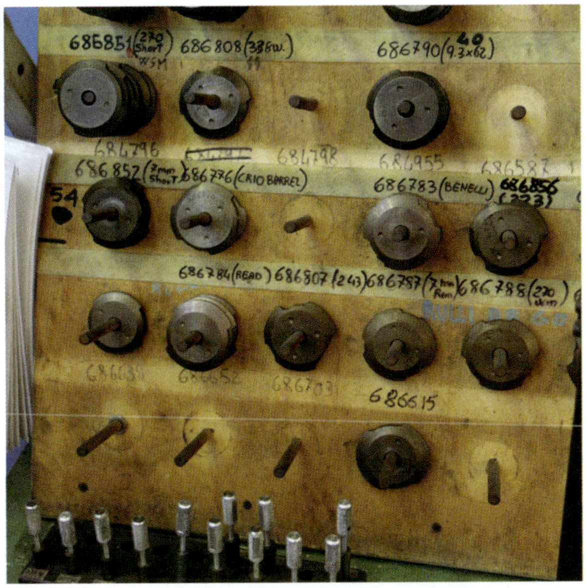

A rack of roll mark rollers. When each of these is needed, it is placed in a machine that presses it down into the steel and rolls it back and forth, creating the marking.

In a good shop or manufacturer, each roller is kept on its peg or drawer, and the number of times it has been used is logged.

of wear and prior use. Bores are generally bright and serviceable but may feature noticeable imperfections (pitting, frosting, etc.) throughout. The exterior circumference of the barrel crown may be nicked, dented, or dinged, but such deformity will not extend into the bore. Field Grade muzzles may gauge "3 or more," and the throat erosion will gauge less than 6. A reasonable allowance for gauge tolerances will be afforded.

Translation: The Rack Grade rifle's bore will be better, and the more wretched stocks will have been replaced with a used but serviceable commercial stock. Most crucial is the bore condition, which means you can expect decent accuracy, and, if you do some tuning, perhaps better than average. This will still be a hard-used rifle, and the stock and handguard would benefit from repair and refinishing. You can probably get an entire season of competition, maybe two, out of the barrel before your skills outdo the bore's ability to deliver accurate groups.

SERVICE GRADE: GOOD TO VERY GOOD

Service Grade Rifles will show less wear and a better cosmetic appearance than a Field or Rack Grade. The cosmetic condition will be good to very good. Rifle finish

Buying a receiver only and building it as a period-correct Garand by sourcing the correct parts is possible. Just buy a USGI receiver, not a welded one or FedOrd junk.

Avoid FedOrd-made receivers. These are all bad, ranging from crappy to dangerous. And does anyone think they made over 840,000 of them? Whom were they kidding?

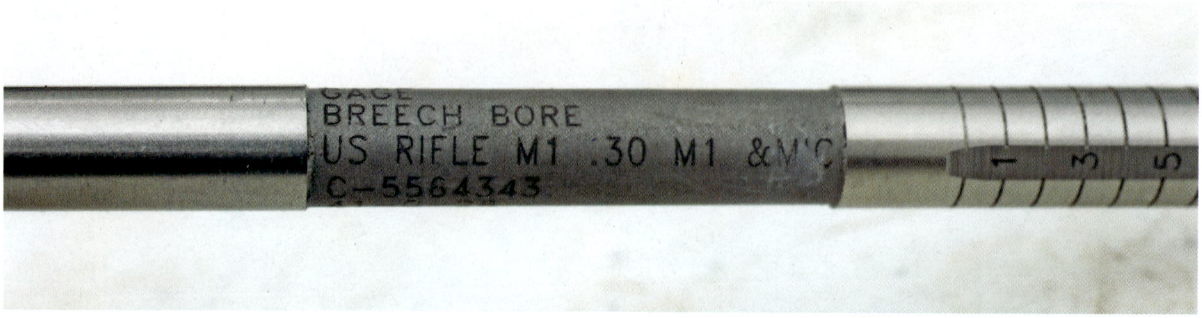

The markings on a USGI erosion gauge to measure from the breech end of the barrel for the M1, M1C, and M1D.

may vary, exhibiting normal wear and color variation among the metal parts. They may have some visible pitting, frosting, or other minor cosmetic deformities on the metal parts. Stock sets may consist of any species of wood (or a combination thereof); and could exhibit dents, dings, scratches, and structurally insignificant cracks. New production commercial stock sets may be used and likely exhibit signs of wear and prior use. Bores will be bright and free of any major defect that would be visible to the naked eye. The exterior circumference of the barrel crown may be nicked, dented, or dinged, but such deformity will not extend into the bore. Service Grade muzzles will gauge "3 or less," and the throat erosion will gauge less than 5. A reasonable allowance for gauge tolerances will be afforded.

A one-size-fits-all gauge used as a Go/No-Go gauge to check many parts. Better to have a chart and good digital calipers instead.

This muzzle is in excellent condition. It measures just over 1 on the gauge, and that is promising.

This rifle measures a 1 on the erosion gauge, so low mileage.

A set of headspace gauges: top to bottom, Go, No-Go, and field.

Translation: Here, the better-than-good rifles have less cosmetic damage, and the bores are slightly better. The sketchy stocks have been replaced, but the big deal is the bore, throat, and muzzle. With less wear on these, the Service Grade rifles will deliver better accuracy (all other things being equal) and would be a good bargain. You can probably get two full seasons of practice and competition out of this one, and by then, you'll have another Garand to use or build to be your match-shooting tack driver.

The rare and mysterious Garand gauge. Some have speculated that it is a locking lug/receiver dimension gauge. Nope. It measures the firing pin bridge to ensure proper firing pin lockout until the bolt is closed.

The Garand clip timing gauge. The clip has to lock in and release at the proper time in its cycle. This gauge tells you if yours does.

The two edges of the groove machined into the block are the timing indicators.

A bit of pitting is a sign that your Garand has been around long enough to have seen the world. A small patch like this should not be enough to kill an otherwise good price on a sale.

CMP SPECIAL: EXCELLENT

This is not a grade in the Blue Book, Standard Catalog of Firearms, or other rating methods. The CMP developed it to describe the condition of a rebuilt Garand. It is CMP's new grade of M1 Garand. This rifle consists of a new production stock and handguard set with a CMP cartouche, a new production barrel, and a new web sling. The receiver and most other parts are refinished USGI, but some may be new manufacture. The receiver may have pitting.

Translation: The CMP has taken the best receivers out of the worst rifles. With a bare receiver in good condition (a bit of pitting is allowed since it can hardly be avoided), it installs a new commercial barrel and puts it all together into a new stock set. The CMP cartouche lets anyone who cares know that this wasn't a homebuild or a USGI Garand that spent its time only ever in a rack in an arsenal, but a CMP-built rifle. However, note that while the stock and barrel are new, and the receiver is in good shape, the Garand you are ordering is not new. The parts it was assembled with will be serviceable, reasonably good-looking, and function properly.

Also, note that this grade is not always available from the CMP. It builds them when it can; if it can't, it doesn't list them. And CMP does not accept back-orders.

CORRECT GRADE: VERY GOOD TO EXCELLENT

Correct Grade rifles are similar to the Service Grade ones but will show less wear and use. Correct Grade have all correct parts for the date of manufacture with 80% or better overall original metal finish. The stock and

A rack number is another part of your Garand's history. Don't remove it, even if there's no way to determine its meaning.

handguards will be of walnut and correct for the rifle but will have some dings, dents, scratches, and marring of the wood finish. Stocks will have the appropriate original inspector's cartouche. The rifle bore will be very good with no significant defects, a throat erosion of less than 4 and a muzzle wear of 2 or less. Very good to excellent condition. This grade is rare and is only available occasionally in limited quantities. Because of the scarcity of these rifles, they will only be sold on the CMP auction site.

Translation: We are now getting into the serious collector level of cosmetic condition. These Garands arrived with excellent bores and receivers. The CMP matched them up as a retro builder would and, as far as possible, made them period-correct. They are used rifles and show it, but if the receiver was made in (for example) 1943, the rest of the parts will reflect a 1943 assembly as much as possible. It won't be a 1943 rifle with 1955 parts on it.

You do not go out and use a rifle such as this in competition until the bore is used up, and then rebuild to make it match-grade. That would be like street racing a clean, low-mileage 1971 Mustang Mach One or a 1971 Plymouth Duster 340. Collectors would hate you, and the rest of us would look at you as someone who had suffered a closed-head injury.

Photo: CMP Archives

COLLECTOR GRADE: EXCELLENT

Collector Grade Garands show almost no wear or use and have 95% or better overall original metal finish. Rifle bores are excellent with throat erosion under 3 and a muzzle wear of 2 or less. Collector Grade specimens have all original parts as they came from the manufacturer. The wood will have a few handling marks and minor dings and scratches. Stocks have the appropriate inspector's cartouche. Datasheets prepared by CMP armorers are included in the butt trap of each gun. Excellent condition — little or no use. Limited quantities are occasionally available. Because of their scarcity, they will only be sold on the CMP auction site.

Translation: You enter the auction for one of these and buy it for the satisfaction of owning a pristine original Garand and seeing the envy in the eyes of your gun club buddies when they handle it. And to be able to say, sorrowfully, "No" when someone asks if they can shoot it. This is a prestige possession, pure and simple.

NON-CMP GARANDS

Let's assume for the purpose of discussion that you're looking at a Garand at a gun show or in a gun shop and not one from the CMP that comes with an assurance that it is functional and correct. What to look for?

The first thing is to make sure all the various parts are there. It may sound trite, but really, you need to check.

Look it over from one end to the other, and ensure all the parts are present. Then, make sure the parts that are supposed to be tight are tight. Look for rust, pitting, dents, and scars on the metal. I refer to this as the "hammer marks and tire tracks" inspection. Look to see if the stock is cracked, dented, scarred, or has some finish on it that isn't proper GI. Some things might not be USGI, but they're fine if you aren't buying your Garand to be a period-correct collectible. One is the stock. Original stocks were walnut, with some of the replacement stocks or later rifles having birch or even beech, as those were good woods to use, and walnut was becoming hard to source. Today, a replacement stock can be had, made out

The unfired, original-grease Garand that the author reflexively opened to check the chamber. The owner wasn't too put out. "I've done the same thing. It happens."

of good ol' walnut, and you can even refinish it yourself if you want to. A company such as DuPage Trading can set you up there. Or, a replacement from Stocky's Stocks can be purchased with the correct finish applied. You could go with a laminated stock if the competition rules permit it. The advantages are greater weight (always a good thing in a target rifle) and environmental stability. The downside is, well, that it's laminated.

What items should you overlook, and which require a pass on the prospective rifle? The easy ones are cracks in the stock or handguards and a rusty bore. A cracked stock can be repaired (if you're handy with woodworking or want a project), and the exterior can be lightly sanded and refinished. How light? If you need to change any of the contours in sanding, that's too much to make it look right. Sure, a minor wood dent can be lifted by applying a hot iron to a wet patch placed on the dent, using the steam to lift the dented wood. Creased wood can't be lifted as much but can be improved. And an old, refinished stock looks like a refurbished rifle resting in the rack, ready for the next war, and should not be discounted.

Here we have a divergence from AR-15 purchasing. A Garand with a gouge in the stock that does not hinder its use, or compromise its strength, can be viewed as a combat scar. Or a training mar. Think of it as having been gouged while dragged over a stone wall in Aachen during an assault or the parallel scratches from barbed wire while repulsing a human wave attack one night in Korea. That dented lip on the buttstock? Perhaps gained from too much bayonet training at Parris Island back in 1961, preparing for the impending nuclear war triggered by the Cuban Missile Crisis. On an AR-15, such imperfections are reason to say, "Nope, the next one in the rack."

But on a Garand, it's a badge of honor.

Small, replaceable parts can be, well, replaced. So, on a Garand with a mangled rear sight, or a dented or bent front sight, you can replace those if the price is right and you know the part can be sourced. However, some Garand parts are rapidly approaching the "unobtainium" status, and you don't want to be at a loss if you need one. A rusted bore will require a new barrel, so bargain the price down accordingly, and things like a mangled gas cylinder screw, while it can be replaced, should be viewed with suspicion. Why? As discussed in the disassembly chapter, the gas screw can be removed improperly by holding the forward handguard or clamping the gas cylinder and transferring torque to those parts.

You'll want to look down the bore. Not just to "check for daylight" but to ascertain its condition. This inspection may take some practice, so if you already own a firearm, go to school in it. Can you see the sharp lines of the edges of the tops of the lands down the spiral? Dull edges indicate excessive bore wear. Breaks or unevenness in the lines means the lands have either had rust scrubbed off or are blurred by jacket fouling. Is the surface of the bore, both the bottoms of the grooves and the top of the lands, shiny? Once you get an eye for it, you can spot a "frosty" bore. "Frost" is a shiny but rough surface left when corrosion (left un-scrubbed, shows up as dark specks) has been completely removed from a bore. The rough surface, however, is not smooth, and the clean metal shines but does not appear smooth.

A dark bore could be several things. It could be jacket and powder fouling left caked in the bore. It could be rust, also uncleaned. It could be pitting from cleaned-out corrosion, but so rough it goes past "frosty" to now being dark. A dark bore is a cause for a reduced price.

Look at the muzzle. You should not see marks, scratches, gouges, or other mars on the crown. If you do,

Photo: CMP Archives

it means the rifle has had the muzzle struck by something — dropped on gravel, slid around in a truck, whatever. If the gouges don't reach to or extend into the bore, you can probably shrug it off. But it's a sign that the rifle was abused at one time. Look at the receiver rails. If you see gouges, scratches, or places where someone has been at work with a screwdriver, you can be sure that they had to pry fired cases out of the chamber, or worse, live rounds out of the feed way when it failed to feed. Those are signs of something amiss with the gas system, action spring, or follower arm.

Check the sights. Are they centered? Or are they cranked over to one side? Now, it's easy enough for someone offering a Garand for sale to center both front and rear sights and keep mum about it. If they haven't, and the sights are way off, casually ask if they've shot it. If you get a "dead-on" as the reply, red flags should go up. Something needs work if it's "dead on," with the sights set way off-center. And if they've left the sights as is but not shot it and are just shining you on, again, more red flags. Either way, tread carefully.

Now, work the bolt. If it's zip-tied shut at the gun show (I hate that), you won't be able to do it. Unless the dealer is willing to cut the zip tie, let you hand-cycle, and then zip-tie it again, which the show might not permit. Move the charging handle back slowly and smoothly. It should start the movement without hesitation, and the bolt should rotate and slide back, in turn, without hesitation, catching, or binding. Pull it all the way back until it stops, and then let go. It must stay back on its own. Give it an extra tug to make sure it is locked back and not just hung up on the follower. Give the charging handle a gentle bump toward the muzzle. It must not release and snap shut. (You gave it an extra tug to ensure it's mechanically locked open.)

If it snaps shut, the clip latch or some part in the clip system is bent or worn and must be replaced.

With the bolt back, grab the charging handle and try to pull it away from the receiver. This is not an "all you can give it" test. Instead, you want to see if you can get the op rod to jump the track with a bit of gentle persuasion, indicating the rod is worn on its guide tabs. This is not a critical failure, but it does indicate the need for a rebuild. If the price is right, you can buy the Garand and have the op rod rebuilt or replaced. But it will cost, and the price needs to reflect that. The work is specialized. It involves welding the worn tab, machining it back to spec, and re-Parkerizing the op rod. That process takes time, and if the part isn't period-correct, you can usually swap op rods with the shop that offers this service.

Look at the bolt face. Is it clean? If grubby, wipe it clean and look at the steel. The firing pin hole should be circular and flush with the face. If you see an oval or the edges of the firing pin hole are peened up, the bolt has seen a lot of use and dry firing. If there is an eroded circle around the firing pin hole, it has been fired a lot, and the leaking gas around the primer pockets of the rounds has burned small pits into the steel. There is no reason to reject such a Garand, but they indicate a high-use bolt. If the firing pin hole is peened, it might need to be dressed with a fine stone to make it flush to avoid piercing primers.

When the bolt is locked open is time to peer down the bore. Also, it's the only time you can check throat erosion and when you should use the muzzle gauge. I know we discussed it a few paragraphs back, but now is the time to give it a good, hard look. And we discussed non-USGI parts sometimes not being a bad thing. If the barrel isn't a GI part but a replacement, it could be good. It does, however, mean you need to either do a headspace check or get a return guaranteed agreement written on the invoice, should it fail such a check. There aren't many makers of replacement barrels for Garands these days, and they work hard to make sure theirs are correct, but you never know who did the installation. Someone might have misread the measuring tools or just did it by guess and eyeball when installing the barrel and adjusting the headspace.

MUZZLE AND THROAT

These are easy, and you can have the gauges in your pocket. They are stepped cylinders, and you gently insert them (each to their own, there is no "one gauge to measure them all" here) and note the number you can see. Lower is better.

The rest of the gauges, save for the timing gauge, are rare, expensive, and difficult to find. That's all the more reason to buy your Garand from a reputable dealer with the tools and gauges needed to check each one out. What might those be?

Before we go into those tools and their uses, I have to point out one important detail: Beyond the muzzle and throat gauges and the timing gauge, you have to detail strip the Garand to check with the gauges. Again, that is not going to be something you can do on the display counter in a shop, but they are something someone who deals in Garands should and can do before offering it for sale.

HEADSPACE GAUGES

Headspace gauges are steel cylinders with tapered noses that look like cartridges with no bullet or neck. They come in three sizes, of which you need only two if you want a set. These would be the Go and the No-Go gauges. The Go gauge is the minimum length the chamber can be. As long as your rifle accepts this, the headspace is not too short. If the bolt won't close on a Go gauge, your headspace is too short, and you will have problems with your ammunition, as the chamber isn't long enough. The No-Go gauge is just over the maximum allowable length of the .30-06 chamber. If your Garand doesn't accept this gauge, you know the headspace isn't excessive. If it will accept a No-Go gauge, your headspace is too long, your brass will stretch, and you'll only get a few loadings before cases break and separate on firing. (This is a bad thing.)

The third one is a field gauge. The Army was not going to be reloading fired brass. Each Garand left the factory with the chamber reamed to be between the Go and the No-Go lengths. As it wore, the headspace would increase. With this caveat, the Army used a field gauge to check each rifle for headspace: stretched brass didn't matter as long as it didn't break on its one-and-only firing. A tad unsafe, perhaps, but in a combat environment, an acceptable risk. In peacetime, the field gauge wasn't to be used, but in a combat theatre, rebuilding Garands near the front, as long as it wouldn't accept a field gauge, it was good to go.

You? This gauge teaches you nothing except that gauges cost money. A Garand that fails a field gauge would have failed a No-Go gauge. So you don't need both.

USING HEADSPACE GAUGES

Ideally, you want to use headspace gauges on a stripped receiver (and barrel, obviously) and a bolt without the extractor, spring and plunger, and ejector. Otherwise, the spring force of the action spring will close the bolt even when it does not have excessive headspace. (Yes, steel can be compressed.) Also, the extractor, especially the ejector, will make it difficult to feel if the gauge prevents bolt closure. (You have to compress the ejector to close the bolt on a round or gauge, which is bad here.)

TIMING GAUGE

The timing gauge is a block (steel or Delrin) with angled flats and ribs. It's used to check the bolt's clip release timing. To test, lock the bolt back on an unloaded rifle. (It seems obvious, but it bears repeating: you do not do gunsmithing work on loaded firearms.) The block has a wider section that is too large to fit into the receiver. With the bolt locked back, insert the timing block just as you would an en bloc clip. Press it down, watching the charging handle and the block. You'll see the "never release" stamped or molded into the block disappear into the receiver. As, or just after, the lip of the "must release" section disappears behind the rail, the charging handle must release. The timing block will stop it. If the op rod releases too early or too late, you have to find the worn, bent, or busted part and replace it.

Photo: CMP Archives

PISTON GAUGE

For military use, the piston gauge was simple: a hardened steel block with a slot of the No-Go size cut across the end, with the interior diameter of the slot just smaller than the "too small" diameter of a piston. If the gauge passed over a piston, it was too small, and the op rod was sent back to have a new piston head silver-soldered or brazed onto it. (It was if the rest of the rod passed its gauging. No point in replacing the worn piston on a bent or twisted op-rod, right?) Rather than tracking down a rare and expensive USGI gauge, use good-quality digital calipers or a micrometer. The cheap ones, able only to discriminate to a thousandth of an inch (.001), won't be enough to tell you anything; you'll need one that measures to ten-thousandths of an inch (.0001). Measure the diameter of the piston across three or four points around its circumference.

GAS CYLINDER GAUGE

To measure the gas cylinder, take it off the rifle. You can do it with it attached, but you'll need some way to securely hold the rifle in place while you test with the gas cylinder gauge. Now, you can do this with pin gauges from McMaster-Carr. You'll need .528- and .530-inch pins. The .528-inch one is your Go gauge, and the other is your No-Go gauge. The Go gauge should pass smoothly into the gas cylinder (the bore hole below the one the barrel passes through) and move smoothly into and out of the gas cylinder.

The No-Go should not. The front of the gas cylinder has a threaded section where the gas screw threads into it. Below that is a shallow shoulder, the beginning of the actual gas cylinder section. The No-Go gauge will pass through the threaded section, pass over the thread-free groove, and stop on the shoulder. If it passes past the shoulder, the gas cylinder is too worn for proper function. Yes, it is still functioning, but it is ready to quit at any moment. It will probably function because you have a full-sized piston in there. Lucky you.

The USGI gauge works a bit differently. It has one end that is both Go and No-Go. If it enters and stops with the shoulder outside the gas cylinder, it is a Go. If the indexing shoulder passes into the gas cylinder, it is a No-Go. The other end is a carbon scraper to clean the gas cylinder.

If the USGI gauge is a two-in-one type, why mention the pin gauges? Because a USGI gauge will cost you $200, and the pin gauges from McMaster-Carr are $6.50 each, plus tax and shipping. If you have to have the USGI one, go for it, but don't come complaining to the rest of us about not being able to afford ammo.

FIRING PIN PROTRUSION

The Ordnance Department made a special gauge to measure firing pin protrusion. The gauge is a cylinder with a sliding center. There's a tightening knob on the side. Start with the bolt out of the rifle. Measure the gauge length relaxed, and write that down. (The gauge should have its length stamped or etched on it, but always, always, always measure to be sure). Loosen the knob. Press the firing pin fully forward. Now press the gauge onto the breechface. The protruding firing pin will raise the center of the gauge. Tighten the knob. Measure the gauge again. The difference between the measured lengths is the firing pin protrusion.

Cumbersome? You bet. There's a simpler way. It does, however, require a digital caliper. Luckily for us, they are now quite common and easily found. With the bolt out, press the firing pin all the way forward. Take the calipers' tail, press the solid shaft against the firing pin tip, and let the sliding center move down to the bolt face. Read the protrusion from the scale, and you are done.

FIRING PIN TIMING GAUGE

This one is rare, expensive, and rarely needed. The firing pin timing gauge looks like a two-piece bolt with a handle sticking out of the top. It checks the bridge timing inside the receiver, which keeps the firing pin held back until the bolt has closed and rotated. The bolt appears to be in two pieces because the open area is the observation slot. By watching the movement of its firing pin as the gauge is hand-cycled in the stripped receiver, you can tell if it's properly held back until the bolt closes.

Why do this? Because a worn, altered, or incorrectly made bridge can lead to slam fires. How important is it to use? Not very. From talking to the few who own one, they have reported never seeing a USGI receiver out of spec, to some who have gauged hundreds of Garands over years of testing, finding one or two.

Why pass on owning one? Because they cost a bunch if you can ever find one. One owner was happy to have spent $500 for one, while another was gratified that he won an auction for one for less than $400.

That's a lot of money to find that your Garand is within spec, which was almost certainly the case even before you measured it.

FINAL NOTE

During any inspection, keep an idea in the back of your mind: all the wear should match. If you're handed a Garand with a worn finish, and there is some pitting here and there, but the stock looks absolutely new, and the cartouches are crisp and sharp, that rifle sits in a new stock — perhaps even a replacement stock with restamped cartouches. If offered as a "used rifle in new replacement stock," then things are good. If represented as, "Look at how the stock survived since 1949, untouched!" someone is trying to put something over on you. What else is wrong that you can't see immediately and that they aren't telling you? Not all dealers are trying to pass off something that isn't, and some don't know, but this is what we call a clue.

A dealer handling a lot of Garands will probably have all these gauges (and even some he has made for himself) to ensure each rifle is within spec and safe to shoot. •

WHAT'S THAT USED GARAND WORTH?

AN INTRODUCTION TO THE U.S. M1 RIFLE BY SIMEON STODDARD

Adopted in 1936, the M1 remained the standard issue rifle of the United States until it was replaced by the M14 in 1957. It was designed by John C. Garand, who worked for Springfield Armory from 1919 until his retirement in 1953. During this time, Garand concentrated his efforts on the development of a semi-automatic shoulder weapon for general issue to the U.S. armed forces. The M14 rifle, the replacement for the M1, was a compilation of his design work as well.

With the exceptions noted, all values given are for rifles which are in original, as produced condition. Development of the M1 was an ongoing project until it was replaced, as Garand never finished perfecting his basic design. Over 5,400,000 M1 rifles were built, with the majority of them going through a rebuilding process at least once during their service life. During rebuilding, rifles were inspected and unserviceable parts replaced. Parts used for replacement were usually of the latest revision available or what was on hand.

Major assemblies and parts were marked with a government drawing size/part number. This number is often followed with the revision number (see photo above). Barrels were marked, with the exception of early Springfield Armory and all Winchester production, with the month and year of manufacture. It must be remembered that this date only refers to when the barrel was produced, and has nothing to do with when the receiver was produced or the rifle was assembled. This barrel date on "original as produced" rifles should be from 0 to 3 months, before the receiver was produced.

Restored rifles, defined as ones with parts added/replaced, to more closely match what they might have been originally, are worth less money than "original as produced" rifles. This difference should be on the order of 30-40 percent of the values shown, and is due to the low number of rifles of this type. When in doubt, get an appraisal. To tell what parts should be correct, study chapters 5 & 6 of "The M1 Garand: WWII" and chapters 7 & 8 of "The M1 Garand: Post WWII" by Scott A. Duff.

REBUILT RIFLE, ANY MANUFACTURE

Many of the M-1 Garands seen on the market today fit into this category. Value shown is for rifles with a majority of its parts mixed/replaced. Depending on the type of rebuilding that a rifle went through, rifles could

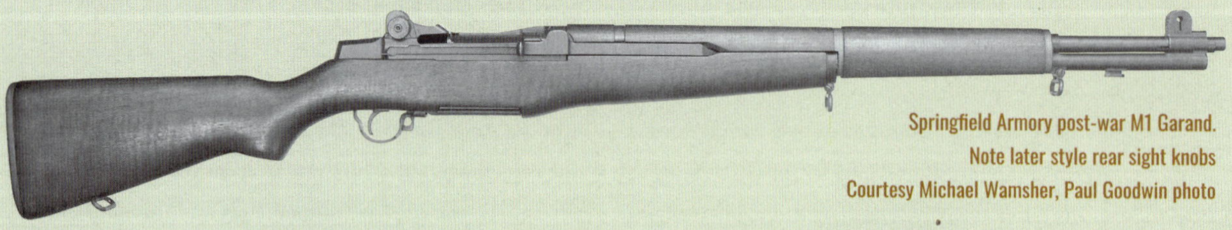

Springfield Armory post-war M1 Garand.
Note later style rear sight knobs
Courtesy Michael Wamsher, Paul Goodwin photo

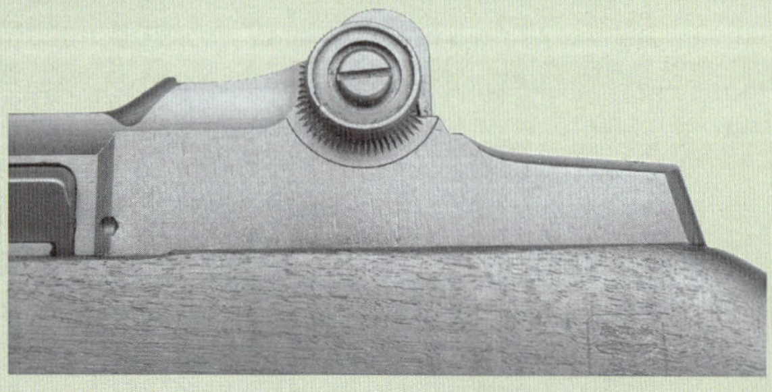

be completely disassembled with no attempt to put parts together for the same rifle. Valued mainly for shooting merits. Bore condition, gauging and overall appearance are important factors.

NOTE: *There were some M-1 Garands imported from Korea in the 1990s. These will be import stamped on the barrel. Most are Blue Sky Productions or Arlington Ordnance. These import marked rifles fit in the rebuilt category. There is no longer a major price difference with the import marked rifles, as this model is so much in demand. Bore condition is the main factor to consider when examining an imported rifle.*

Exc.	V.G.	Good
1000	850	700

NOTE: *Rifles built by Winchester will bring a small premium.*

CMP OR DCM RIFLES

The *Civilian Marksmanship Program,* formerly known as *Director of Civilian Marksmanship*, is operated by the U.S. government to promote shooting skills. It sells surplus rifles to qualified buyers. CMP M-1 Garands are offered in several grades including Rack Grade, Service Grade, Correct Grade, Rebuilt with new barrel, as well as several collectible variations including sniper rifles with or without scopes. These rifles should have the correct paperwork and shipping boxes to receive any pricing premium. DCM or CMP guns usually sell at the current market value for each variation. Contact the CMP for current pricing, availability and requirements for purchase. Web site: www.odcmp.com.

NAVY TROPHY RIFLES

The Navy continued to use the M1 rifle as its main rifle far into the 1960s. They were modified to shoot the 7.62x51 NATO (.308 Winchester) round. This was accomplished at first with a chamber insert, and later with new replacement barrels in the NATO caliber. The Navy modified rifles can be found of any manufacture, and in any serial number range. As a general rule, Navy rifles with new barrels are worth more due to their better shooting capabilities. Paperwork and original boxes must accompany these rifles to obtain the values listed.

U.S.N. CRANE DEPOT REBUILD

Exc.	V.G.	Good
1800	1000	1000

AMF rebuild

Exc.	V.G.	Good
1150	1000	1000

H&R rebuild

Exc.	V.G.	Good
1100	950	850

Springfield Armory Production

Exc.	V.G.	Good
1250	1000	900

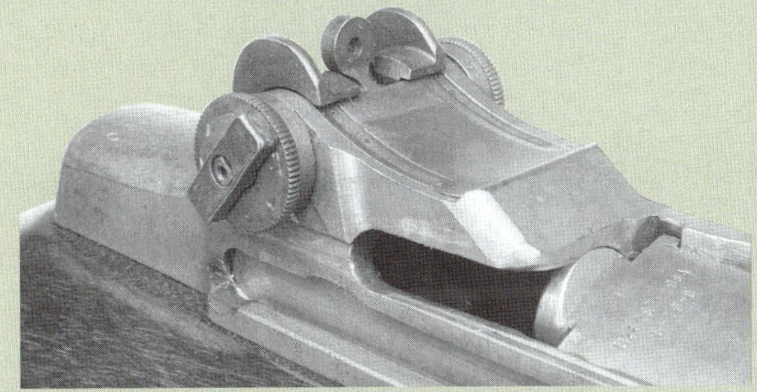

Springfield Armory M1 later style rear sight with bar type rear sight knob
Courtesy Michael Wamsher, Paul Goodwin photo

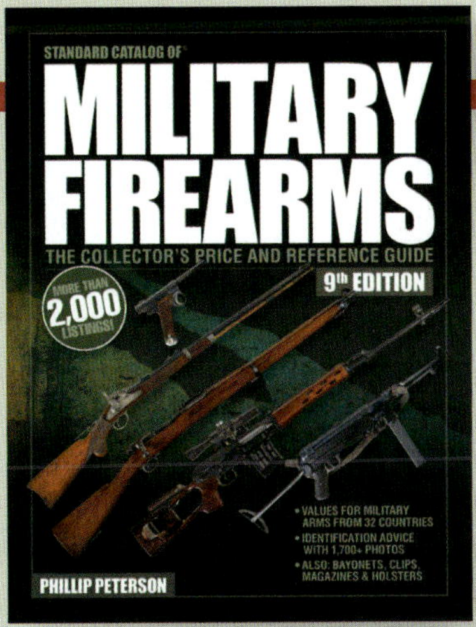

These Garand values are an excerpt from the *Standard Catalog of Military Firearms, 9th Edition.* To learn more, visit GunDigestStore.com.

CHAPTER 13

HOW TO MATCH-CONDITION A GARAND

When it comes to improving your Garand's accuracy and making it match-ready, I'm going to give you the tidbits of what not to do, what to look out for, and how to avoid problems based on my gunsmithing work on Garands, and from dealing with customers who got themselves in trouble. Taking a page from professional painters, most of the work is in the prep. The actual painting is the easy part. In other words, read and study before you apply power tools to or epoxy your Garand.

BEDDING THE STOCK

One of the best things you can do to improve your Garand's accuracy is bedding the stock. But heed warnings about using modeling clay and release agent seriously. If you don't, your Garand's action will almost certainly bond permanently to the stock, and you won't be able to remove

You need not attend Camp Perry to get practice. Many local clubs will have matches you can use your Garand in, but Camp Perry is the holy grail of Garand shooting.

the trigger assembly or get the action out. To start, disassemble every part of the trigger assembly and all the receiver parts. Then fill every gap where bedding epoxy is not supposed to go with modeling clay and smooth it flush with the surrounding surface.

Don't assume, "The epoxy won't get there" or "I've got the secret gel mix, and it won't flow to the wrong spot." Those are the famous words of customers who ended up in the shop.

Once the modeling putty is in place, apply the release agent. Let it dry, perhaps overnight. Then, inspect the coating with a close eye and a bright light. If you see any spots, lines, or joints where the release agent is missing or looks thin, apply more. Applying two coats is not a bad idea.

"But two coats make it thick, and I want a tight fit," some will say. It will be plenty tight enough, even with two coats.

When you press the receiver in, followed by the trigger assembly to lock it partially but not fully closed, epoxy will ooze out. Now is the time to use a wooden scraper and scrape the excess off. Do a good job here, as it's much easier to scrape liquid epoxy off than to cut, grind, sand, or otherwise remove hardened epoxy that you left oozed.

Then, once the epoxy is set (let it set for the whole time according to the packaging; there is nothing to be gained by taking things apart early), remove the receiver and trigger housing and inspect the interior for gaps. If there are voids, gaps, or missing epoxy spots, now is the time to address them. Use a degreasing agent on the epoxy, rough the voided spot and the area around it, mix more epoxy, and apply it. Re-apply more release agent and reassemble the receiver and trigger housing as before.

LEAVE THE TRIGGER ALONE. YES, THE GARAND TRIGGER IS GOOD, AND YES, IT CAN BE IMPROVED. BUT STONING THE SURFACES YOURSELF IS AN INVITATION TO PROBLEMS. GET IT WRONG, AND YOU'LL HAVE A DOUBLING OR SLAM-FIRE RIFLE AND GET HURT SOONER OR LATER.

Once set, take it apart again and inspect it. Is epoxy in all the right places? Now scrub the release agent off and clean out the modeling clay. Check the parts for a correct fit. If they fit, you are halfway there.

HANDGUARD FIT

The forward handguard is important. Do not get lazy or sloppy in fitting it to the steel ring to which it needs to be secured. Inspect the handguard fit every time you go to a match, as it must not touch the barrel. If it has been misaligned, straighten it and think to yourself how that could have happened, and don't do that again

.

PRO TRIGGER JOBS ONLY

Leave the trigger alone. Yes, the Garand trigger is good, and yes, it can be improved. But stoning the surfaces yourself is an invitation to problems. Get it wrong, and you'll have a doubling or slam-fire rifle and get hurt sooner or later. And even if you aren't hurt, you'll get dis-invited from the shooting range.

If you must have a better trigger, have someone who does it for a living attend to its improvement. You will avoid the hassle of an inoperative rifle and the cost of new parts. And, if you attend Camp Perry or shoot in an official match, you will have a trigger that will pass the trigger pull weight test. Yes, at matches above the club level (and even at some clubs), your trigger pull will be weighed, and if it's less than a specified amount, you will not get to shoot. Or, you get to shoot, but not for score/match standings.

RELOAD, THEN PRACTICE

Ammo only does so much. You can spend a lot of time and effort improving your ammunition, but your skills and the mechanical precision of your rifle will still limit it. What you especially don't want to do is exceed the loading limits for the Garand. You'll harm your rifle and gain nothing for it. Stay within specs and load for quality, not production speed or output volume.

CRITERION BARREL

Don't look to parts to improve your scores. Buying an NM or National Match sight set or a National Match op rod, and expecting some big jump up in your scores, or significantly smaller groups, is kidding yourself. Unless the original parts are seriously worn or out of spec, the improvements will be marginal.

One big jump up in accuracy will come from a new barrel, especially a match barrel from Criterion. Have Criterion install it properly. The bore will be better than any barrel made during the Garand's heyday. A matching-period barrel on an otherwise collectible Garand? Don't mess with it. Buy a beater. A rebuild, a non-period barrel on a mixmaster? Don't feel guilty about putting a new, better barrel in it for shooting. You can always have the old barrel plugged back in if you want a collectible.

EXPERT REBUILDS ONLY

Experts are worth it. Yes, there is a certain pride — and knowledge gained — by doing things yourself. But know your limitations, and where an expert would do it better, have them do it.

PRACTICE MORE

The best way to improve is to practice. Yes, it means using up a barrel and adding wear to the parts, but if you want to get good, you must put in the time. For serious shooters, this means two Garands. The "weekend" Garand, which looks good, is period-correct, and they can take it to the club on weekends and put a few clips through it. The serious one, the "shooting" Garand, is built on a pitted receiver with lots of mileage. Maybe it has been re-Parkerized, but it has a new match barrel, and everything is fitted properly. Since the barrel isn't a USGI, they can run it as much as they want and replace it when it shows wear. If it wears too much, you can have a new piston brazed onto the op rod and even a larger one if the gas cylinder is starting to enlarge.

This is true in shooting, car racing, and any skill-building enterprise or sporting competition. If you want to get better, you have to put the time in, which means putting wear and tear on the tools of the trade.

So, get to it.

Note: Besides these seven tips, you can learn more from USAMTU manuals, online videos, instructions from Brownells, and people who have done it. Don't listen to the guy at your club "who knows everything," but you suspect he hasn't done a tenth of it. •

Practice, that's the way. Get out and put in some trigger time. Yes, it wears the barrel, but it is the only way.

Buying parts to improve your score won't do much but hammer your wallet. These NM sights are cool but will only add a few more points to your score. Better to practice.

Photo: CMP Archives

CHAPTER 14

GARAND AMMUNITION & RELOADING

Why are we devoting an entire chapter to finding ammunition and reloading it for the Garand? Reason one: .30-06 is expensive. To a hunter who might go through a box a year (a lot of shooting for some hunters) or a box per presidential election cycle, ammo isn't that pricey. But for someone who wants to shoot a couple of hundred rounds a month, practicing and competing, it adds up quickly and to a lot of dollars.

Reloading saves money. Well, it doesn't, really, but it does mean that for any given amount of money you're willing to spend, you get in more shooting, which means better skills.

Reason two: not all .30-06 ammo is the same. You can buy "aught-six" ammo with bullets in weight from 110 to 200 grains, which leads us to reason three: The Garand is more sensitive to ammunition and the load used than any other rifle.

To fully grasp how the Garand works and understand what loading ammo for it entails, we must step into the Wayback Machine and go to France in 1884. Paul Vieille develops a useable "smokeless" powder. It isn't smokeless, but it produced so much less smoke than the billows of white smoke that blackpowder created (enough to envelop battlefields and obscure observation) that the name smokeless stuck. Smokeless is also much cleaner, which meant more reliability in the late 1800s.

Winchester is now making Garand-specific ammunition, so you have two choices for new, Winchester and Hornady.

The smokeless powder had several advantages over blackpowder besides less smoke. The first was efficiency. Blackpowder consumes only a tiny percent of its mass as combustion products and, as a result, leaves a lot of residues behind. Fouling, it is called. So much so that in the muzzleloader era, the amount of fouling had to be planned for and dealt with. Hence, the Minie ball could be shoved down a fouled bore, and the skirt would expand by gas pressure to grip the rifling.

By the 1880s, rifles used cartridges, and the bullets could be lubricated (the lube inside the case, not external, to attract grit) or wrapped in paper, called paper-patched.

The residue, however, was hygroscopic. That is, it attracted moisture. A firearm discharged with a blackpowder cartridge, even with the fouling mostly blown out by each bullet, if not scrubbed clean, would be rusted by the moisture the fouling attracted.

The next advantage of smokeless was that it was not explosive. Blackpowder is classified as a "low explosive," while smokeless powder is simply combustible. When contained, smokeless powder burns at increased pressure but won't explode like blackpowder. It has to do with the rate of propagation of the combustion front. Think of the classic old movie, where the line of blackpowder is run from the starting point into the building and burns, as our hero tries to fight off the bad guy's minions, save the lady in distress, and put out the burning blackpowder. Smokeless powder burns like blackpowder in that scenario. A line of high explosives will run along the line at 20,000 *feet per second or more*, not a foot a second, like blackpowder.

An example might make things clearer. Quarries produce rock, either as slabs or blocks or as gravel. Imagine a rock cliff face. Now, drill a line of holes straight down, parallel to the cliff face, 10, 20, or 30 feet back from the cliff face. Fill the holes with a high explosive like TNT, dynamite, or other. Detonate the charges, and your cliff now becomes gravel. OK, instead, pack the holes with blackpowder. The lower shock wave and slower burn rate will crack the cliff along the holes and push the slab or blocks away from the holes. Now, fill the holes with smokeless powder and touch them off. You will get merrily burning columns of fire jetting up out of the holes. Fireworks, in other words.

ARSENAL-LOADED AMMO IS SAFE, WITH ONE CAVEAT; CORROSIVE PRIMERS. IT WAS NOT UNTIL 1955 THAT THE U.S. LOADED MILITARY AMMO (EXCEPT FOR M1 CARBINE LOADS) WITH NONCORROSIVE PRIMERS. SO, ANYTHING EARLIER AND FOREIGN AMMO MUST BE VIEWED WITH SUSPICION.

The last advantage of smokeless powder is bullet velocity. It doesn't matter how much blackpowder you put behind a bullet. Your maximum velocity will peak at about 1,500 fps. To deliver a greater wallop, you must go with a bigger bore and heavier bullet. You can't make it up with speed.

As a result, by the 1880s, all the world's armies, and many hunters, had settled on a rifle cartridge with blackpowder in the .40- to .45-caliber bore. Any smaller, and you couldn't get enough *oomph* (technical term, that), and you also had much more significant problems with bore fouling due to the blackpowder. Experiments were underway with smaller-bore blackpowder rifles, but they all got changed right away when smokeless was invented.

In 1870, the French, still smarting after the Franco-Prussian War (a significant loss for them), kept their military advances super-secret, but it didn't take long for word to get out. Everyone else had also been practically flogging their chemists for decades to create a workable smokeless powder.

The first experiments were of bores smaller than .40-.45, which meant 7.5mm to 8mm. But, the bullet designs were still the old styles. This meant an 8mm cartridge, such as the German Mauser, used a jacketed round-

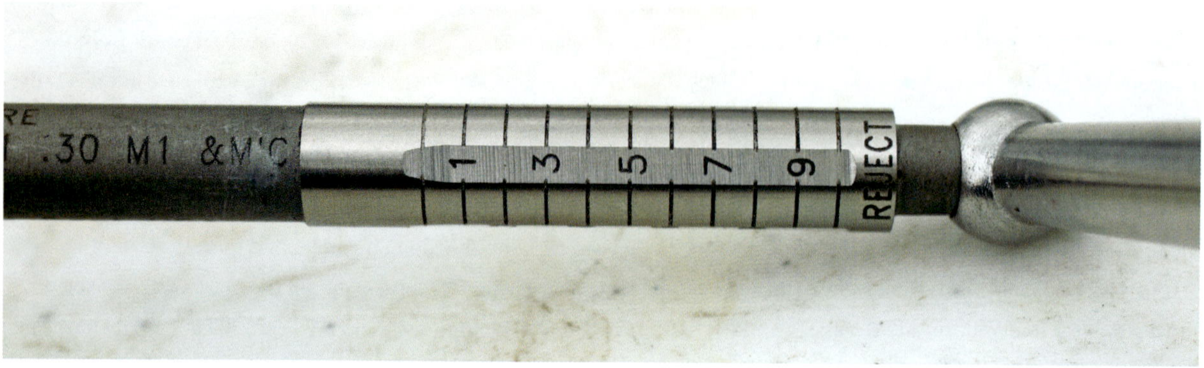

Sweeney's match Garand measures a "3" on the erosion gauge, meaning it's barely broken in.

nosed bullet in the 220-grain range. Even then, they cut the bullet weight in half from the previous cartridges used. The path to a workable cartridge wasn't easy. It is all settled now, but it had to be tested back then. So, bullet velocity jumped from 1,500 to 2,000 to 2,200 fps. A lead bullet can't do that, even adding alloying metals like Tin. So, the jacketed bullet had to be worked out. One such jacket material was cupro-nickel. The problem was that the cupro-nickel jacket's metal caused its own kind of fouling, which was detrimental to accuracy and could increase pressure if not cleaned out. The material we have today is called gilding metal, 95% copper and 5% zinc.

Oh, and the French? They didn't bother with lead cores in alloy jackets. They made solid bronze bullets on lathes for their rifle and machine gun cartridges.

The initial smokeless designs lasted a couple of decades at most. The French again thought up the next advance, the "spitzer" or pointed bullet. Instead of a cylinder with a round end, they made it pointed, lighter, and more aerodynamic. Why? Trajectory. A 200- to 220-grain .30- to 8mm-caliber (.323 inch) bullet at 2,300 fps — which was really booking, many were barely breaking 2,000 fps — has an arcing trajectory. Sure, it was much flatter than the blackpowder bullets it replaced, but range estimation was still critical.

If you take the U.S. Army .30-03 220-grain JRN bullet at a muzzle velocity of 2,300 fps as an example, and you zero the sights at 200 yards, your 100-yard point of impact (POI) will be 3.5 inches above the point of aim (POA). Your POI at 300 yards will be 14.4 inches below the POA. At 400 yards, your bullet will be just over 43 inches below your POA. Aim at a soldier at 400 yards, and hit the dirt before him. Maybe the ricochet will strike him, or maybe not. And while the U.S. Army .30-03 was booking along, others were slower.

The author's rack-grade Garand will swallow much of the muzzle gauge but still shoots well enough to learn and practice.

The next step was a bullet of around 150 grains, with a pointed tip and a flat base. These could be pushed fast, 2,600 to 2,800 fps.

Arsenal-loaded ammo is safe, with one caveat; corrosive primers. It was not until 1955 that the U.S. loaded military ammo (except for M1 Carbine loads) with non-corrosive primers. So, anything earlier and foreign ammo must be viewed with suspicion. Ammunition coming from the folks at CMP will be described as either corrosive or non-corrosive, and you can take their word for it.

The Garand barrel can only be cleaned from the muzzle, which is a concern. You can wear the muzzle if you aren't careful with the cleaning rod. One of my Garands (the just-barely-minute-of-zombie one) will swallow a muzzle gauge. But it still shoots well enough to keep using. My match Garand is still at the "zero" marking. On the other end, hard use wears the barrel throat, and Badger Ordnance makes a gauge to measure that as well. My match Garand reads "3," which is just broken in. My worst one measures "4," which is also the one that swallows the muzzle gauge. So, fair warning: you can lose more accuracy from cleaning than shooting if you aren't careful.

And the en-bloc clips? They are very durable. Unless you step on one, you can't easily damage it. They do wear, however, and many are now three-quarters of a century old and may have been used a lot. You can buy modified ones for two shots (NRA High Power use) and five (hunting) and find boxes of them at gun shows.

Let's now review the bullets that came quickly after with 175- to 190-grain boattailed bullets. Wait, "boattailed"? We were talking pointed bullets, and now we're talking tails? Yes, that is an additional aerodynamic change that increases ballistic coefficient (the measure of drag the bullet experiences due to air resistance) and thus flattens trajectory — specifically, the 220-gr. JRN has a ballistic coefficient of .300 (known as "BC," and the higher, the better) compared to the 175-gr. boattail bullet, which has a BC of .530. Along with the better BC, since the new bullet is lighter, we can generate more velocity without exceeding the pressure ceiling.

Photo: CMP Archives

The clips are marked with the manufacturer's name. Nowadays, that's not a big deal as long as you get USGI clips.

Our new load, going 2,700 fps and zeroed at 200 yards, has a POI at 100 yards of 2 inches high and a 300-yard POI of 8 inches low. At 400 yards, you are only 23 inches low.

The world's militaries used this new tool, the boattail bullet, to increase the maximum useable range without changing sights. If you train your soldiers to aim for the enemy's belt buckle and allow for a rise and fall of 12 inches, it's possible (theoretically) to hit an enemy soldier at 450 yards.

In today's age of optics, laser rangefinders, mortars, machine guns, etc., you are asking, "Why did they do this?" Simple: the world was different then.

In 1900, the world's total population was 1.6 billion. There was one person for every five today. The world was full of empty places, and the world's armies expected

The black-painted tips indicate a steel core, almost always indicative of corrosively primed ammo. Very accurate, it pokes holes like there's no tomorrow, but you must clean thoroughly after shooting.

to be fighting in those empty places. "Urban combat" was a rarity, not the norm. An infantry officer had … his infantry. That was it: no air support, on-call artillery, or squad machine guns. A company Commander, a Captain, would have between 130 and 180 NCOs and privates to call on to solve any problem he faced. Artillery was organized in batteries that officers directed at a much higher level than Captains. Machine guns were rare in 1900, and when the military got organized, it'd be organized in separate Companies that would, again, be under the command of other officers. Machine guns from 1900 until 1920 (and long after, in some armies) were viewed as small-bore artillery and treated as such.

So, more reach and a flatter trajectory were good for the Captain in question.

One anomalous organization at this time was the British army. While the militaries of Europe had a small cadre of professionals and impressively detailed schedules for calling up reservists and previously trained soldiers, the British had a professional army. And the British had gotten their butts kicked in the Boer War by the Boers and their marksmanship. Since the Crown's budget was not going to allow for the adoption of machine guns at anything like the rate they were adopted in Europe, the British army worked on marksmanship and bolt work. It was a matter of skill, and if you could not produce 10 aimed shots per minute out of an SMLE at an absolute bare minimum, you could not stay in that army. Most could do better, some much better. The 10-shot magazine, and the ability to load five rounds in seconds using stripper clips, made that easier than you might think.

In the 1890s, the U.S. Army used the Krag-Jorgensen, a five-shot bolt-action rifle that could not accommodate a stripper clip. It fired a 220-grain .308-inch bullet at a sedate 1,900 fps. The Krag was not strong enough for the bullet to be pushed faster. So, the Army decided to update its rifle and adopted its Mauser clone — the Springfield '03, chambered in the .30-03 cartridge, also known as the .30 Gov't. This rifle fired the same 220-gr. FMJ .308 bullet as the Krag, but at 2,300 fps.

A quick sidestep back to smokeless powders. The original powders were quite horrific as far as bores were concerned. They burned excessively hot, were abrasive, and were, by today's standards, not at all progressive burning. The pressure curve of a cartridge is a sharp upward curve that peaks and then drops like the slope on a ski-jump hill. A progressive or slower-burning powder extends that dropping curve at a slower rate. When looking at the effort a system creates, the engineering shorthand is "work is area under the curve." So, extending that slope forward from the peak adds work. Think of it as extending the push of the gases on the bullet, continuing acceleration.

A RUMOR CIRCULATED THAT THE GARAND WASN'T SAFE USING M1 LOADS. THE SCUTTLEBUTT STARTED BECAUSE OF THE COINCIDENTAL TIMING OF THE M2'S ADOPTION. HOWEVER, THAT RUMOR WAS FALSE.

The early powders didn't create much acceleration once the curve dropped off. The extra velocity gained came at the cost of barrel erosion. The initial work the British did with Cordite (yes, that is an actual powder name, and a powder it used for decades into the 20th century) would shoot out bores in a few thousand rounds. They were using an early polygonal rifling (no, Glock did not invent it), which wasn't all that resistant to erosion and ended up going back to "Enfield" rifling, the kind you think of with a gear tooth-like cross-section.

The bore pressure at the muzzle, when the bullet exited, was thus relatively low — still high enough to harm hearing and make you deaf, but not like the magnums of today that can cause pain along with deafness. Keep that in mind because the low muzzle pressure was a complicating factor when it came time to develop self-loading rifles.

The other problem was the primers. At the advent of rifle cartridges, the standard primers used fulminate of mercury. This substance made reloading cases (not that anyone did a lot of it then) problematic due to the mercury being driven into the case's brass on firing, and weakening the case, quickly and irreversibly. Cases would become brittle unless dropped into a solution to dilute the mercury-compound deposits immediately after firing. (Not such a big problem in the blackpowder days due to the enormous volume of blackpowder residue, diluting the mercury that could attack the case. Going smokeless uncovered it as a real problem.) By the end of the 19th century, mercury fulminate was going out, as it had a short shelf life. The replacement was a mixture of potassium chlorate and lead thiocyanate. The result, the residues of the combustion of the "new" priming mixtures (now over a century old and long-ago replaced) were potassium chloride and sodium chloride. Yikes.

So, having littered your bore with a high-pressure stream of table salt (sodium chloride), it would rust, pronto. Before non-corrosive primers, scrubbing your bore after you shot was critical to wash out the corrosive salts. It was the standard practice of the USMC to "clean the bore of a rifle on three successive days after firing" to ensure all the salts were removed. It helped that the cleaning solutions used were water-based.

In case you were wondering, the U.S. government switched to non-corrosive primers. The non-corrosive priming compound used lead styphnate with mixed abrasives and other hazardous materials. But it was not corrosive to bores. From the start, the M1 Carbine cartridge was specified to be loaded only with non-corrosive primers. All U.S.-loaded carbine ammo is fine. The .30-06 ammo depended on which arsenal loaded it, as it took time to switch over. Therefore, look at the headstamp. The first non-corrosive loadings for each arsenal were:

FA56
LC52
RA51
SL52
TW52
WCC51
WRA54
FN57

Headstamps matter. The "FN69" on this case indicates FN loaded it in 1969 and therefore is certainly non-corrosive

We have a simple "K53" on the headstamp. And a crimped primer. That's Kynoch, a British firm, and 1953 was still in the corrosive primer era. Plus, you'll have to deal with the crimp. In this case, it will be real work.

All dates after that for U.S. factory-loaded ammo will have non-corrosive primers. Before, most likely not.

Back to the U.S. cartridge. The .30-03 was obsolete before the military developed and fielded it, but the U.S. Army took a few years to make the switch. The 220-grain bullet at 2,300 fps became a 150-grain spitzer, a flat-based bullet at 2,800 fps. This bullet used a cupro-nickel jacket, another choice behind the times. It was known as "Cartridge, rifle, M1906."

WORLD WAR I DEVELOPMENTS

Then The Great War came along, and things changed. One thing that changed was rifle fire. The decade of

British bolt-manipulation practice paid off as a British rifle company could put out enough volume of fire (and accurate, at that) to lead the German units they faced to report the British as having far more machine guns than they had. The other change was the use of machine guns. They found use as long-range rifle-caliber area-denial tools. A machine gun squad would be set up in a particular location, and the guns would be aimed at a specific angle and direction. The streams of fire they rained down would make an area unsafe for use by the enemy. For example, this would be the reverse slope (the area behind a hill) 2,000 yards away. By doing this, enemy reinforcements could not advance, and counter-attacks would be impossible because the area would be constantly covered by machine gun fire. (I know we're taking some time to get to the Garand, but you need to know these things.).

The German, French, and British used cartridges with boattail bullets and spent time developing accurate firing tables. The U.S. had rushed into the war and didn't have enough machine guns to conduct training, let alone combat. The M1906 cartridge had been tested to 1,800 yards and then estimated past that. The estimated maximum range was 4,700 yards, but the actual maximum range was more like 3,300 yards.

After the war, it became necessary to get the correct info. The military chose Major General Julian Hatcher for that job. (Major General at retirement, in the early 1920s, he wasn't at that rank.) Hatcher was straightforward. He took everything he needed, crews, equipment, machine guns and ammunition to Daytona Beach. He would set up a machine gun on the beach (Florida in the 1920 census is listed as having a population of less than a million people versus 21 million today. Daytona Beach has 72,000 people, and the metro area has 600,000 today. In 1920, it was a small town with a broad, hard, flat beach popular with auto racers and aircraft builders.) Using survey equipment, Hatcher measured the exact angle of elevation of the machine gun barrel. Then he'd fire a long burst.

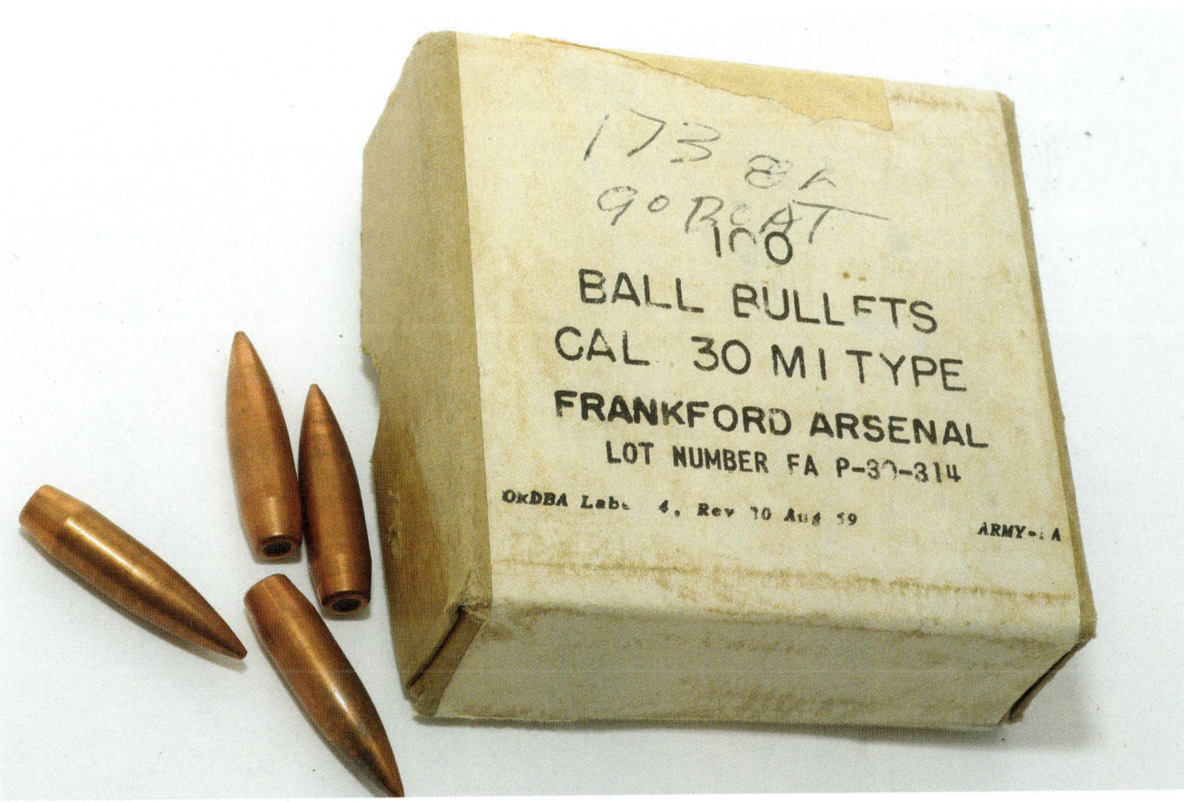

Bullets of the M1 production era for loading. They were manufactured in 1930, and because of this, the Ball M2 load was developed to keep range safety fans safe. The modern equivalent is the Sierra 175-grain MatchKing, which has superior accuracy.

Next, they unloaded and drove down the beach until they found the impact area and measured it, surveying the distance to the machine gun. After returning, they set up at a different angle and repeated it. What he found was awful: the range tables were wrong, so much so that they fell short by great distances, and at those ranges, it could put friendly troops in danger.

OK, more ballistics. The flat-based bullet has a lower BC, thus more drag, than the boattail bullet. The tables were developed by shooting to moderate machine gun distances and calculating the extra elevation needed beyond that. So, they'd shoot at 1,000 yards, then sit down with pencil, paper, and slide rule to calculate the angle of fire needed at 2,000 yards, 3,000 yards, and so on. The estimates had been incorrect. Making things worse was that the flat-based bullet, with its higher drag, slowed down past the supersonic speed sooner than expected. Accuracy got funky when it entered the transonic region around 1,000 yards, depending on atmospheric conditions, and the drag increased even more. Past 1,200 yards, it wasn't even staying reasonably accurate if there was any barrel wear or bore fouling.

A set of headspace gauges: top to bottom, Go, No-Go, and field.

The result was the "Cartridge, rifle, M1." It was a 175-grain boattail bullet with a velocity of 2,650 fps, and improved shape, to provide a higher BC. It stayed supersonic to a greater distance, on the order of 1,500 yards or so, and it stayed accurate even when it went subsonic. Its maximum range was in the 5,000-yard range, even mid-5,000 yards on a good day. It used a gilding metal jacket, not cupro-nickel, which became the U.S. Army standard in 1924. The problem was that vast wartime stocks of the M1906 were still on hand. How much ammo? How about two billion rounds? Today, that's enough to ease the ammo-buying panic of millions of AR-15 owners for a year or two. In the 1920s, that was a lifetime of ammo. So, training and marksmanship competition was still conducted with the M1906 cartridge, and it worked just fine out to the 600-yard targets at Camp Perry.

It wasn't until the early 1930s that the supplies of M1906 dwindled, and soon after, troops began switching

The left clip is standard, and the other two are modified for proper use while holding fewer than eight rounds. In hunting, you can't have more than five. In Service Rifle competition, you need at least one that holds just two rounds. The right-hand one is a "SLED" clip, meant to ease loading single rounds during slow-fire competition.

over to the M1. Trouble sprang up almost immediately. Consider that much of the military then was composed of National Guard units. Not so much Regular Army because there wasn't an all-volunteer force like today. Regular Army troopers cost money since they were full-time government employees. National Guard troops got paid for their two weeks of summer drill. And the Regular Army/NG shooting ranges were not the kind of range you are accustomed to. Today, you go to a range, and 100 yards away, there is a big hill. You shoot into the hill. Back then, and to a large extent even today, a military range is wide-open, with trenches downrange. Each trench holds targets that are lifted, fired on, lowered, and scored. Instead of stopping the bullets when they hit the hill, there is no hill, and the bullets continue until they fall to the ground. So, back then, a range could be 4,000 yards of empty space with nothing but flat ground.

Thus, a military range at the time would have a "safety fan." The safety fan is the area bullets can be expected to fall into when the range is used. Beyond that area, you're safe. Bullets can't travel that far. So, we have the old M1906 cartridge with a maximum target range of 1,200 yards. If the targets are 1,200 yards from the firing line, and you allow for a ricochet distance when they hit the ground, you are probably safe 1,500 yards from the firing line, 2,000 yards, for sure. Don't build anything within 3,000 yards of the firing line to be safe. You can erect buildings, construct roads, and practice maneuvers outside the safety fan directly downrange from the firing line. Today, troops get issued the M2, and the maximum range is now past 2,500 yards, and adding the ricochet extra makes it 3,000+ yards. The infrastructure built on military ranges in the 15 years since the end of The Great War — previously outside the M1906 safety fan — was now in a dangerous zone.

... IT DIDN'T TAKE LONG FOR THE ORDNANCE DEPARTMENT TO DEVELOP THE M2 AP OR ARMOR PIERCING CARTRIDGE. IT WAS A STEEL-CORED BULLET WITH A GILDING METAL JACKET AND A BOATTAIL SHAPE. THE AMERICAN FACTORIES MANUFACTURED BILLIONS OF THESE, AND WE WON THE WAR WITH THEM.

The Army quickly requested a new cartridge, the M2, with a 150-grain flat-based bullet and using a gilding metal jacket at 2,750 fps. This cartridge worked the same as the M1906, but with the proper jacket material, and stayed inside the safety fans that had been established.

OK, now for the Garand stuff. A rumor circulated that the Garand wasn't safe using M1 loads. The scuttlebutt started because of the coincidental timing of the M2's adoption. However, that rumor was false. The whole time John Garand was developing his rifle, the issue cartridge of the U.S. Army was (or was going to be, once the Army used up all the old M1906 stuff) the M1 cartridge. And the Garand works just fine with M1 and M2.

Now we enter WWII.

WWII LESSONS

The U.S. entered World War II with plenty of bolt-action riles in storage, machine guns and new weapons of many kinds in the planning stages. Or so we thought. It turned out that the need for materiel to conduct a worldwide war was more than anyone had considered. For instance, the Chrysler Corporation printed a book, *Bullets by the Billion*, detailing how the Evansville plant produced 3+ billion rounds of .45 ACP ammunition and an impressive volume of other wartime material.

To give you an idea of what it took, the Willow Run bomber plant in Michigan, run by Ford, produced a new and complete B-24 bomber every 59 minutes. One an hour. Well, that also required that the various firearms makers be able to produce and deliver 10 .50-caliber machine guns to install in those bombers every hour, in addition to all the ones they were making for the Army, Navy, and Marines.

Decisions had to be made. One was: what kind of rifle and machine gun ammunition would the military fight with? Well, if you consider bullets only by the million, not the billion, a 150-grain bullet, compared to a 175-grain one, requires less lead and copper — specifically, 3,500 pounds less per million rounds. So, 150-grain flat-based it was, and since there wasn't any long-range plunging machine gun fire anymore (no trench warfare, not with tanks in the mix), that was fine.

Things change. It turns out that while there wasn't a need for long-range machine gun fire, there was a need for better penetration and saving wartime resources. Steel is cheaper than lead, and steel-cored bullets penetrate better than lead, so the Ordnance Department didn't take long to develop the M2 AP or Armor Piercing cartridge. It was a steel-cored bullet with a gilding metal jacket and a boattail shape. The American factories manufactured billions of these, and we won the war with them. And, as it turned out, match shooters found that the wartime AP ammunition was more accurate than the lead-core stuff, so it became the go-to ammo for competition.

AMMUNITION CHOICES FOR DECADES

I'll compare the Garand to the AR-15 and others. To review, the Garand taps gas off near the muzzle, which means it's operating at low pressure. And, the gas system is, for lack of a better term, "lossy." The op rod piston head on the end of the rod does not fully seal the gas cylinder. As soon as the gas has pressurized the gas cylinder space, it's also flowing past the gas piston head and venting out of the cylinder. And a short time after the gas port is uncovered by the bullet, the bullet will have left the barrel, and the bore pressure will drop precipitously. That's all the gas flow the Garand has to work with. The AR-15 is not particularly lossy.

When the bullet uncovers the gas port, it pressurizes the gas tube, gas key, and interior of the carrier. It isn't until the carrier begins to move that it vents. The AK-47 is both lossy and venting, but the M14 is sealed and venting. In the Garand, the M14, and the AK, the op rod is given a

The Greek 1980 ammo uses a three-stab crimp. While this is just as secure as the ring stamp (even better, according to some), it's much easier to remove when reloading.

jolt, and the inertia imparted to it drives the system. To a much larger extent, the AR-15 has a carrier that is pushed, not jolted.

While the Garand was the go-to military rifle, anyone who loaded 150-grain FMJ ammunition, M2 or faux M2, loaded it to the specifications needed for an M1 Garand. And what were those? Simple: a maximum chamber pressure not to exceed the book specs, and a port pressure, the residual pressure in the bore at the gas port, as the bullet passes, were the limits. Generally speaking, we're talking 50,000 PSI max for the chamber pressure and 11,000 PSI average for the gas port pressure.

This requires a powder with a burn rate that falls within a relatively narrow band. The sweet spot is IMR-4895. What happens if you select a powder that is too far from the desired 4895? As you shift to faster-burning powders, you end up starving the gas port. Remember, the peak pressure is the peak pressure — the maximum ceiling permitted by the specs. The faster-burning powders will reach that ceiling sooner, and as the bullet moves forward, the Ideal Gas Law takes over. The bore pressure drops more quickly as the bullet moves down the bore with a faster-burning powder, and it doesn't take much to drop bore pressure below the port pressure that reliably operates the system. You can't add more powder to "pick up" the port pressure because more powder means a higher chamber pressure, and you don't want that. Remember, we're stuck with 50,000 PSI as our peak pressure allowed.

MILITARY AMMUNITION FOR THE M1 GARAND WAS LOADED WITH THESE PRESSURE LIMITS AND PARAMETERS IN MIND, SO YOU COULD GET RELIABLE FUNCTION, IF NOT ALWAYS MATCH-GRADE ACCURACY, OUT OF IMPORTED, SURPLUS AMMO.

A slower-burning powder will, in effect, "lift" the tail end of the pressure curve, and it won't take long before you have too much port pressure. This increases the thrust on the op rod and makes the rifle cycle faster — too fast, the impact of the bolt and op rod bottoming out at the rear becomes abusive. You can even bend the op rod, peen the receiver, or crack the receiver at the rear face.

None of this matters in a bolt-action rifle. As long as the peak pressure does not exceed the "book" maximum, the rifle will work fine regardless of the down-bore pressure. Now, there is a theoretical limit

Primo Greek ammo from the CMP, loaded in 1980, non-corrosive, and entirely suited for use in Garands. The primers will be crimped but non-corrosive, so while your cleaning will be easier, your crimp removal won't be.

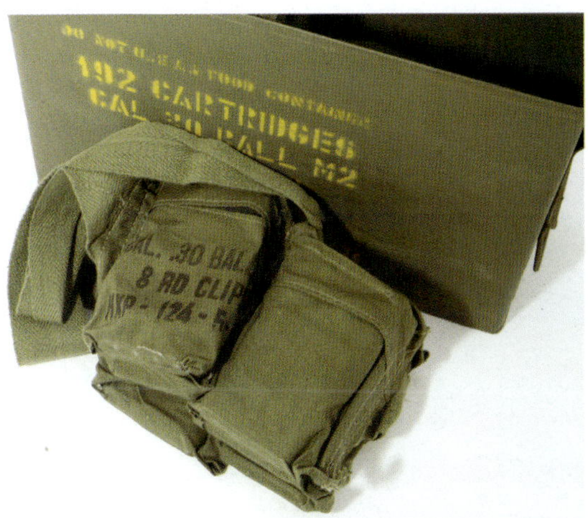

Even better, the Greek ammunition in this ammo can is already in clips, in bandoliers, and packed tightly for long-term storage.

When the military adopts a new cartridge, it must specify and load a wide range of types. This box of blanks uses paper "bullets" for training and ceremonial use with bolt-action rifles.

There was a time when gun shows had lots (relatively speaking) of ammo like this to be bought. Accurate for its day, you can load better if willing to do the work. And today, the box and its ammo are more valuable as collectibles than ammunition for the range.

here. Taking a moment to step away from the Garand and looking at the pressure curve, there's a physical property known as Work. The quick summary of Work is "the area under the curve." So, think of the plotted curve of your pressure graph as an area, and if you "lift" the muzzle end, you are creating more Work, which adds muzzle velocity to the bullet without exceeding the peak pressure limit. However, the bolt's locking lugs (whatever design they are) must support the load of the extra Work. The sustained load could, if the curve stays at peak to the muzzle (that would be an interesting pressure curve to analyze), create more load than the bolt lugs can withstand over a term of service.

But, all that is theoretical. And we're focused on the Garand.

Military ammunition for the M1 Garand was loaded with these pressure limits and parameters in mind, so you could get reliable function, if not always match-grade accuracy, out of imported, surplus ammo. Keep an eye out for the designation "M2" in the product specifications. This indicates it was loaded with the exact parameters the M1 Garand requires. The notable one, because it was the last big supply, was the Greek ammunition, with cases, boxes, and headstamps bearing "HXP" in the code. Back in the old days, there was German, Italian (both used the Garand), and Korean (big Garand users, obviously) .30-06 M2 ammunition.

But, with many shooters using readily available arsenal or surplus ammunition for competition, the seemingly inexhaustible ammo supply began to dry up after a few decades. First, the U.S. surplus Ball and AP dried up. The AP went first, mainly because it was more accurate and thus more desired. Then the imported surplus got shipped in, shot up, and supplies shriveled. We are left with two sources — American commercial production and reloaded ammunition.

COLLECTIBLE AMMUNITION

You may come across a special sealed container of .30-06, M2, AP, or whatever. This is a sealed metal can (not a hinged "ammo can," as you may be familiar with) in OD Green, with yellow (usually) markings painted using a mask or stencil. These are called "spam cans" in some circles, as they need tools to open. They come in one of two packaged contents: one will be 20-round boxes, and the other will be bandoliers of clipped ammunition.

The first thing you must know is this: Do Not Open Them. Not because they are defective, unsuited for use, or, no matter how old, out of date. No, you don't open them because collectors will pay you more than for brand-new factory rounds suited for shooting in your Garand.

The boxes of 20 are easy to understand, but bandoliers of clipped ammo? The reason: ease of supply. I have two reference points here, one that I read and one that I heard. The first comes from SLA Marshal, a slightly suspect researcher on things combat, from interviewing troops in Korea during that war. (Some of his other conclusions could be clearer, but this one is rock solid.) The troops reported that, almost without fail, someone would have the bright idea of hauling extra ammo up to the trenches in the "boxes of 20" storage and, during breaks, would re-load their expended clips with the boxed ammo.

Well, it never worked because of various reasons. The clips were hard to find in the mud, dirt, dark, and brush. Second, the troops were usually exhausted, and finding the time, dexterity, and focus to load clips properly didn't happen.

The one I heard was from my father. His infantry unit was resupplied regularly from the back of trucks or dumped supplies. They would radio or phone their need, and trucks would meet them in whatever town on the map would work. Or, the supply trucks would stop at a crossroads a mile or two ahead of their march location and dump supplies by the side of the road. My dad and the rest would pick up what they needed or wanted and leave the rest to be collected later. (Or, more likely, scrounged up by the French farmers or German locals and squirreled away in their barns.) The only GI interested in ammo in boxes of 20 was whoever was carrying an 03A3 Springfield, and he probably wanted grenade-launching rounds as much as anything else. Everyone with a Garand wanted only bandoliers of clipped ammo and most likely only M2AP.

Those spam cans of ammo are now primo collectibles worth more unopened than they are as shootable ammunition.

COMMERCIAL .30-06: THE GOOD, THE BAD, AND THE UGLY

If you go down to your Locale Gunne Shoppe, aka LGS, and look for .30-06 ammo, you will find (assuming they have caught up on supply) an overwhelming array of options. And most of them will be unsuited for use in the Garand. Why is that? Simple: powder isn't just powder. In a bolt-action rifle, the pressure curve is irrelevant. It would be theoretically possible (although interesting Chemistry-wise and horrific recoil-wise) to use a load that reached its peak pressure and never tailed off — a load that stayed at 50,000 PSI to the muzzle. This would be 100% efficient as a curve-power ratio. It would probably double the muzzle velocity, as there would be twice as much, or more, work generated. Hmm, a 165-grain bullet at 5,000 fps or more. Of course, that would double felt recoil, probably more than double it, and there's also the increased bolt thrust that the bolt would have to hold.

OK, not such a good idea after all.

But, some progressivity to the powder burn is a good thing, and that's how you get some really effective loads and impressive velocities. But the Garand's port pressure

Loading the top round left or right is a matter of which end the last round in the clip goes in from. Loading the last one from the camera end will make it top-left.

Properly built, your Garand should work fine with the top round on the left or the right. But many Garand shooters load top-left as a matter of habit and tradition.

would be excessive. Why are such loads OK in other self-loading rifles but not the Garand? In most instances, the port location matters most. If you shift the port from the muzzle to halfway down the bore in your rifle design, the difference in port pressure at that midway point between various powders is not significantly changed to cause problems. Also, modern gas system designs are made to be self-throttling. That is, gas is bled out of the bore, and once the system begins moving, the gas flow is cut off or vented out of the system. The M14 has such a design.

Quick detour here. Back in the early 1990s, The Steel Challenge competition expanded. It had been a handgun-only match with eight stages. There were some side matches, but in 1991 it became a five-match World Steel Championship, with the handgun portion, two rifle stages, and two shotgun stages. One of the rifle stages required a .30-cal. rifle. I experimented with my Garand and found it wasn't up to the task, primarily because optics were already ruling the ranges. There was no easy, elegant, or reversible way to put a scope on a Garand. So, I used my M1A. I found that if I pulled the 150-grain bullets from factory hunting loads and replaced them with 125-grain bullets, the M1A cycled 100% of the time, the recoil was significantly reduced, and it shot accurately. I used that combo to become the World Amateur Steel Five-Gun Champion. The M1A's gas system is self-throttling, while the Garand is not, and that is what let me get away with such changes. The M1A/M14 gas port doesn't drive the op rod directly — it bleeds into a piston that punches the op rod. The piston has a slot for gas to enter from the gas port, and once the piston has moved a short distance, it closes the gas path from the gas port, stopping the gas flow.

INSPECT THE HEADSTAMPS OF THE BRASS YOU'VE JUST VACUUMED UP OFF THE RANGE … USE A FLASHLIGHT AND PEER INTO THE CASE, LOOKING FOR THE FLASH HOLES. IF THERE'S ONE IN THE CENTER, IT'S A BOXER-PRIMED CASE. THAT IS RELOADABLE; KEEP IT.

The Garand will not stand for such sleight-of-hand changes, as the gas from its gas port hits the op rod directly.

GARAND-FRIENDLY FACTORY AMMO

Hornady has loaded Garand-specific ammunition in .30-06 for some time, duplicating the pressure curve and gas flow of the M2 ball load to run the Garand properly. If you're not reloading ammunition and don't want to worry about surplus, Hornady has you covered. Underwood also produces an "M1 Garand" target load, and as I was wrapping up this book, Winchester announced it would also offer an M1 Garand-specific line of ammunition. It, too, duplicates 150-grain M2 Ball ammunition with the proper gas pressure curve for the Garand. If you go this route, save your brass. You may decide to take up reloading later or find someone to do it for you, and you'll need brass.

POWDERS FOR GARAND LOADS

If you look at a powder burn-rate chart, you will see 175 powders listed. Lotsa choices, right? Nope. The Garand's gas system is spectacularly unforgiving of powder burn rate.

The powders you can use do not stray far from those used in the military .30-06 loads of the time; IMR-4895, H4895, Accurate 2495, and IMR-4064. Some have loaded IMR-3031, a faster propellant; others have gone as slow as Vihtavouri N140 or Varget. Those last two are a bit too slow for my tastes, but then I learned to load the Garand when your choices were between IMR-4895 or IMR-4064 or nothing.

When it comes to bullets, you are similarly limited. On the low end, you can't get lighter in weight than 150 grains; and at the top end, 190 grains is it. And again, my preference is not to exceed 180 grains, which stems from what was available when I was learning the craft.

The Garand also imposes other peculiarities on your efforts. As discussed in earlier chapters, the Garand's firing pin is free-floating. It does not have a rebound spring built into it. This means that when the bolt closes, it requires a case that will freely and fully chamber and not wedge a thousandth of an inch or so tight. The primer must be below-flush to minimize the firing pin "bump" it receives. So, case prep and primer seating are critical in the Garand. When all anyone used in the Garand was arsenal-loaded ammo in new cases, this wasn't a problem. But in reloading, you'll have to watch this, so let's go through the step-by-step process to ensure your ammo is proper for your historical blaster.

RELOADING STEPS

The rifle ammunition loading steps are as follows:

- Sort and clean
- Lube
- Resize
- Crimp swage (some cases)
- Trim to length
- Clean off lube
- Seat primers
- Drop powder
- Seat bullet
- Crimp case mouth

LOADING PRESSES

You can load on a single-stage press, but that will take much time, as each case will require multiple press-handle operations to get one loaded round. A progressive press speeds things up, but you must set up a pair of toolheads. One will be the case prep toolhead, and the other the case-loading toolhead. More on this in a little bit.

SORT AND CLEAN

First, sort your brass. Some Garand shooters use brass with the same headstamp, so it all came from the same source. Were you loading for match use and in contention for the top prize, I'd say go for it. But for the rest of us, who are loading plinking, practicing, and having fun ammo, all .30-06 cases are pretty much .30-06 cases. That said, there are a few things you want to watch out for.

Inspect the headstamps of the brass you've just vacuumed up off the range — if it's all familiar, great. But if you see headstamps you don't recognize, take a moment to inspect them. Use a flashlight and peer into the case, looking for the flash holes. If there's one in the center, it's a boxer-primed case. That is reloadable; keep it. If it has two or three, it is a Berdan-primed case, and you can't reload it. Turn it over, look at the headstamp, and then toss all the brass you have with that maker's mark.

Next, do the cleaning. My home range is a muddy and silty place, and brass ends up grubby. So I give it a hot water rinse to wash off the mud and silt, then run it through the Lyman Case Dryer to ensure it's dry. If cases have been on the ground long enough to be tarnished, I might sort them out of the batch, and when I have enough to make it worthwhile, give them a chemical cleaning to etch off the tarnish or at least some of the tarnish.

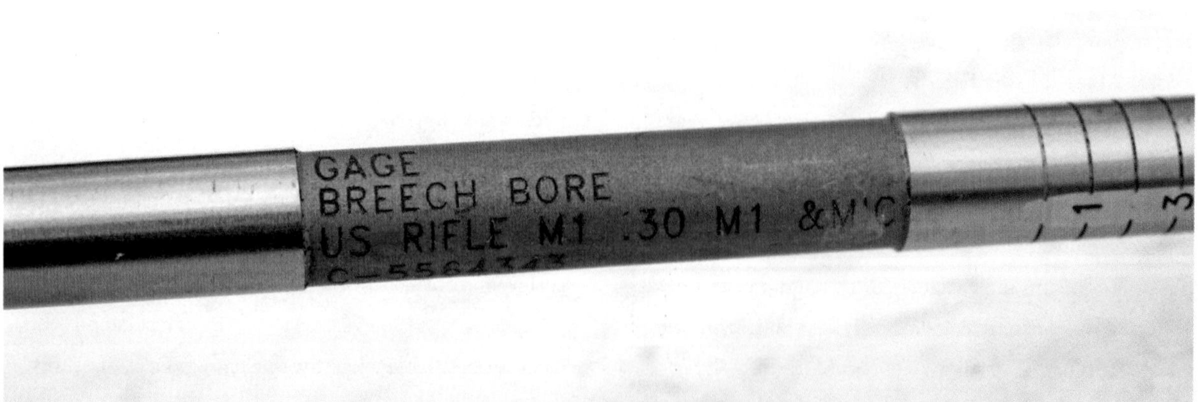

Erosion gauges are useful but use them at the beginning and end of a competition season, not weekly. Tracking throat wear at the OCD level will drive you crazy.

Then, once dry, it is into the tumbler for the brass. A couple of hours (or longer, depending on how dirty the tumbling media is), and I have nice, shiny brass.

Which tumbler? Which cleaning medium? What process? Long arguments can happen at gun clubs over this. Keep it simple: Get the largest tumbler you can afford or for which you have bench space. The .30-06 case is long, and you won't make much progress if you have a small tumbler (even though they vibrate, they are called tumblers) that holds 50-100 cases at a go.

The dry cleaning uses either ground corncobs or walnut hulls. Walnut hulls clean faster, but corncobs are cheaper. Use a cap full of polishing medium to speed up the cleaning. Two hours is typical, but I have a countdown timer, set it for four hours, and let it run until done.

The wet cleaners are either the ultrasonics, which do a fantastic job of cleaning off mud but not so much at removing tarnish and solution, and stainless steel pins. The steel pins are about the size of rice grains (which can also be used in place of the corncobs or walnuts above, but it just goes against my grain to use food to clean brass), and they clean quickly. The steel pin users typically decap their brass without resizing it. After all, it's dirty and would seriously wear sizing dies. The pins also clean the primer pockets, which the other approaches don't, at least not well, and only if decapped before cleaning.

Wet-cleaned brass must be rinsed and dried, so back into the Lyman dryer with them.

At this step, I can store brass for a long time in a sealed plastic container, waiting for the next step, which I generally do in batches. If you set aside a day for nothing but the brass prep, you can have — assuming you have that much — a year's worth of loadable brass sitting on the shelf ready to be loaded.

IF YOUR CASE IS TOO LONG (NOT SIZED ENOUGH), IT WON'T CHAMBER PROPERLY IN YOUR GARAND OR MAY CAUSE OUT-OF-BATTERY FIRING. IF YOUR CASE IS TOO SHORT (SIZED TOO MUCH), YOU WILL HAVE EXCESSIVE HEADSPACE AND A SHORT CASE LIFE.

SIZING

You have to resize your brass. This means using a sizing die with case lube and a case gauge to set things up. When you fire a round, the case is expanded from 50,000 PSI of pressure. The case grows to fill the chamber and presses the bolt back until the bolt lugs are in complete contact with the receiver lugs. The case is also stretched by the heat and gas flow, causing the case to lengthen. There's an additional problem (and all rifles suffer from this) in that the forward part of the case, having thinner walls, expands sooner and grips the chamber tightly before the bolt has been fully pushed back and seated. The case, in between these effects, stretches to fill the gap. Over time, repeated stretching thins the case at this expansion point.

Depending on how much excess headspace (or even if there isn't excess) your rifle has, the stretching is more or less pronounced. The worst offender is the British SMLE, which headspaces on the cartridge's rim. The chambers were reamed generously to ensure reliable combat function. Brass suffers heinously as a result, and the most loadings I've ever gotten out of .303 British brass was four before cases separated. I've gotten 10 loadings out of Garands without case separations.

But you'll need to size the cases and "bump" the shoulder back on each one to offset the stretching. This is where your case gauge comes in. It is a steel or aluminum cylinder with a minimum-sized .30-06 chamber reamed in it. The face has two machined levels or steps on the back end. The taller is the maximum length allowed, and the lower is the shortest. If your case is too long (not sized enough), it won't chamber properly in your Garand or may cause out-of-battery firing. If your case is too short (sized too much), you will have excessive headspace and a short case life.

Resizing requires lubrication. The easiest way is to spread your clean brass on an old cookie sheet and spray some lube. Roll them back and forth, dump them into the case feeder or a container, and fish each out to be hand-inserted into the press. You want the Goldilocks touch here. Too little, and a case will get stuck. Too much and you will get "lube dents" in the case shoulder — where too much lube built up in the sizing die, and since the lube is an incompressible substance, it dents the case where it built up.

Sizing your case also includes depriming, as most sizing dies have a decapping pin in the center. This is why you want to ditch the Berdan cases before they reach this point. A Berdan case has no central flash hole. The depriming pin will hit solid brass, bend, break, and maybe even bend the depriming rod. If that happens, assuming you can even get the case off the stem and out of the die, you will have to disassemble the die and replace the pin or stem-and-pin. That may not be easy, and you might find out that having slacked off on sorting, you now have a hassle, time spent fixing it, and even more expenses.

PRIMING

Once the old primer is removed, consider when you will insert the new one. If you haven't sorted for it already, this is when you look to see which cases have crimped primer pockets. The crimp is the stamped ring that locks the primer into the primer pocket, which was needed for machine guns. It was also the adoption that caused John Garand to change his rifle design since the original one used a primer setback to initiate unlocking. The crimp might not have kept you from pushing the old primer out, but it will prevent you from pushing the new one in. You'll have to deal with it.

The oldest reloading manuals I ever read discussed using a penknife (do such things even exist anymore?) to cut the crimp off. As if. It took me a while to realize that when the advice was being given, reloaders might prep and load 20 to 40 cases and use them repeatedly as hunting loads. So, what they had in mind was scavenging 40 to 50 empties from a Service Rifle match to be used loading for one's bolt-action hunting rifle. Those 40 cases would be an entire season of sighting-in and hunting for an avid

Seat your primers flush or below flush to craft safe ammunition for any firearm. In the Garand, it's critical because you can't replace a busted Garand. At least not easily.

You can readily load Garand ammunition on a progressive press. And if you pay attention to the details, it will be accurate ammo. You can't prep your brass (size, deprime, decap, time, etc.) on the press and load in one operation. Not even on a press with more stations than this Hornady Lock-N-Load progressive.

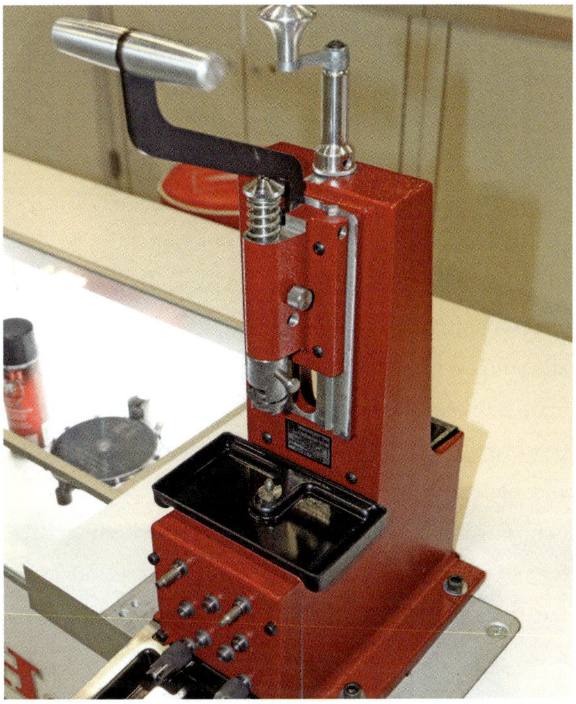

To prep your cases, trim them and address the primer crimp. This Hornady Case Prep machine can do both. You will be prepping them one at a time, but they only need the primer removed once, and trimming is something you can do every third or fourth loading.

hunter and several seasons for someone less motivated. The Service Rifle competitors? They used issued USGI ammunition in their Garands because that was what the government was handing them.

When I was reading that info, I was already loading ammo 200 rounds at a time for practice (handgun, I'll admit, but rifle ammo was soon behind), and the idea of hand-cutting crimps was simply absurd. There are two ways to deal with primer pocket crimps, both done by swaging. You can use a dedicated tool like the Dillon Primer Pocket Swager. It uses leverage to force a shouldered ram into the primer pocket and pushes the crimp out of the way. You can also use an attachment on a progressive press that replaces the primer seating parts to swage the primer pocket as part of the progressive press operation. Uniquetek makes an adapter for various progressive presses, such as the Dillon (550, 650 and 750) and the Hornady Lock-N-Load.

You can't swage primer pockets and seat primers in one pass through the press because there is only one station on any press to do either. And you've got to clean the sizing lube off before you produce loaded ammo. Otherwise, cleaning the stuff off of loaded ammo becomes a pain. You can't trim cases and drop powder because the vibration of the trimming tool would cause problems with consistent powder weights. This is why you assemble two toolheads for your progressive reloading press. With the primer pocket swaging adapter installed, the processing toolhead does the sizing and trimming. You then tear down the press, clean and lube, re-install the primer feed system, and use the loading toolhead to load ammo. Also, on the loading toolhead, you still have a sizing die at the first station, but not to size. Leave it screwed out a couple of turns from the sizing setting with the depriming stem installed. This way, if there is any tumbling medium in the flash hole, the decapping pin will knock it out. And if the case mouth was dented while cleaning off the lube, the expander ball re-uniforms it.

All this is predicated on the need to swage primer pockets to remove the crimp. If you're careful and pick up your brass and only your brass, you need only swage primer pockets once. If you find a motherlode of .30-06 brass at the range, you can sort and swage as needed. Here's a hint: if your gun club, like mine, has a "Leave it and you lost it" policy, *pick up the left-behind brass first.* Stash it in a separate bag, box, can, whatever, for later processing. Then, with a clean range, shoot your Garand and, once done, pick up your already-processed brass (which will still need cleaning, sizing, and trimming later, but not primer pocket swaging), keeping it separate from the motherlode you just scored. The motherlode gets processed separately later and enters your stream of "good to go" brass once fully processed.

To reiterate, brass must have the primer pocket crimp swaged (only if it was crimped) once, but it has to be re-sized and trimmed after each firing.

TRIMMING

Brass stretches on each firing. Sometimes not much, but it still requires attention. What happens if you don't? Well, a few things, none of them good. The brass could stretch enough to bump into the chamber neck area's front lip and be neck-crimped even more. This increases the force needed to unseat the bullet on firing and spikes pressure. In addition to excessive crimp, the brass has no place to go, and the bullet must force past the neck edge sticking up, which is bad for pressure and accuracy. Also, the case might be too long for the bolt to rotate down fully and lock closed. Firing out of battery is always a bad thing.

You've got two ways to approach this. One is to measure cases, trim the long ones, or trim a batch when some become too long. The other is always to trim. I prefer the latter, simply because with a progressive press, it's easier. Set the trim station to trim your already-sized cases to the book minimum. Then, they get fed through; if they're too long, they get trimmed. If they aren't, they don't, but now you don't have to do any measuring. To

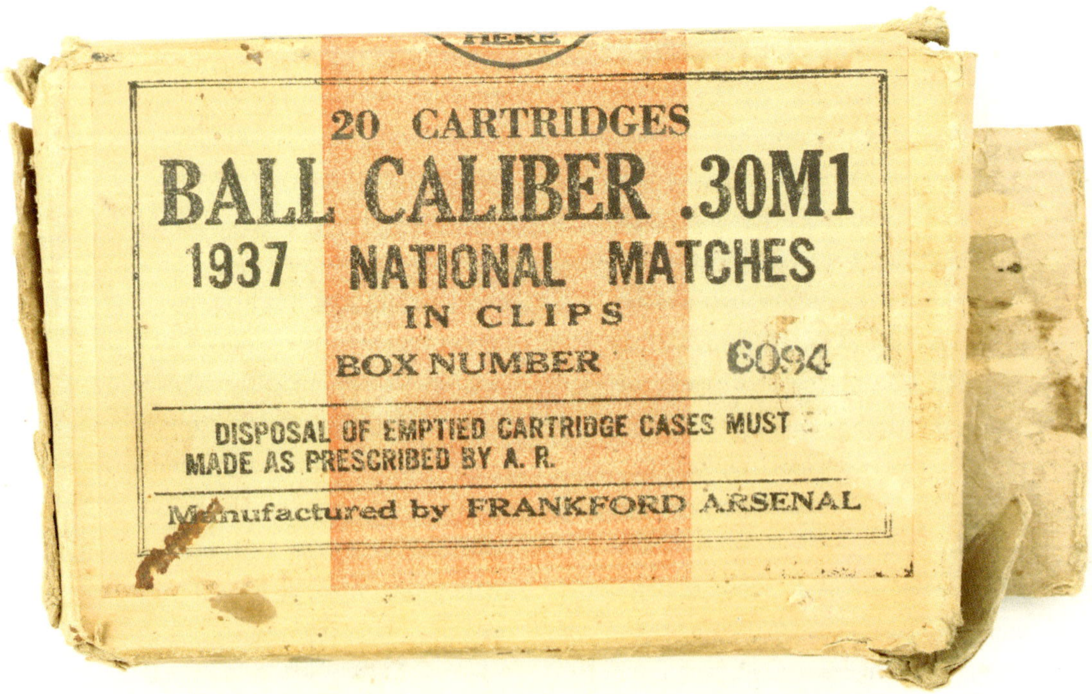

The ammunition issued for the National Matches was always good. The notation on this box, "in clips," means it is in stripper clips for Springfield '03 rifles. The Garand was adopted in 1936 but did not appear at the National Matches until 1940.

Here are enough Sierra MatchKing bullets to wear out a barrel from shooting. In fact, two barrels, as this cart holds 18,100 Sierra MatchKings.

steal a line from an old Japanese adage: the long cases get trimmed down.

Those not loading on a progressive press who want trimmed brass can use a tabletop hand trimmer (you will tire of it quickly) or a case prep station. Hornady makes the Power Case Prep Center, which trims and deburrs in one step. Use the Hornady Case Prep Trio to chamfer, deburr, and clean primer pockets. The only drawback to the Hornady tools is that they are not part of a progressive loading machine. But if you don't have or don't want one, they are the powered way to go.

DE-LUBE

This is a good time to clean the lube off your cases. How detailed you want to be or how industrial you want the process is up to you. You can wipe them clean with an old towel (horribly inefficient) or slosh them back and forth in an old bath towel, held like a hammock, after spraying them with rubbing alcohol. Me, I picked up an old roasting pot that had been left by the side of the street in a suburban neighborhood. I fill it with water, heat it to boiling, and then suspend a colander (also old, a yard sale find) full of brass in the water. Out, dump onto a wire rack to let the water drain, and then into my case dryer for a final, Sahara-like finish. If they have gotten water-spotted, giving them a quick hour in the tumbler to polish them up again is simple enough, and I'm ready to go.

But you must remove the case lube. You see, your rifle depends on it. Remember the case adhering to the chamber wall as part of the stretching? Well, the case adhering to the chamber wall reduces the case thrust — also known as the case head thrust — your bolt experiences. Let's do a little math. The case head diameter of the .30-06 cartridge is .473 inch. A little arithmetic tells us that this is .1757 square inch. If we multiply that by the chamber pressure, 50,000 PSI, we come up with 8,786 pounds of thrust as the potential maximum — 4.4 tons! That's a lot to ask of a pair of steel lugs, one of which has been drilled through to give the extractor a pivot point. So, whatever adherence the case does on each shot to reduce the case thrust is a good thing.

If you leave the lube on, you make it worse, and you do so in two ways. One, the incompressible lube doesn't let the case expand as much. You could boost pressure from 50,000 PSI to 55,000 PSI by not allowing case expansion. And since it is lube, there's no adherence, and all thrust gets delivered to the bolt. Ouch.

So, clean off the lube, and do it before you add the primer, powder, or bullet.

CRIMPED PRIMERS

The U.S. military went all-in on crimped primers after The Great War. This was to keep from causing malfunctions with dropped primers if the case failed, the headspace was too large, or other problems. If you have empty brass with crimped primers, you must, and I mean you *must*, remove the crimp before you can load. Do this after you have deprimed the cases because there's no other way to get in there and remove it. You can swage the crimp. This is done one at a time on a special swager, like the one from Dillon. Or, you can prep your brass on a progressive press. The Dillon 1050 has a station that does just that, but you can go to UniqueTek and find special add-on parts to convert your progressive to a crimped primer swaging press.

The other process is to cut the crimp away. This method is a lot slower and noisier. I did this when my loading group, The Gang of Four, cobbled together a machine. It consisted of an electric motor and collet holding a case deburring tool. We attached it so the pointed end was out and affixed a shield to create just enough protrusion of the deburring tool that it removed the crimp from .45 ACP empties. This was early in the IPSC era, and the .45 ACP was still in everyday use. One of the guys had scored a 55-gallon drum of once-fired military .45 ACP brass, and we needed to remove the crimps. The motor was noisy, so we wore hearing protection, sat in a comfortable chair with the machine in our lap, and held each case against the deburring bit after de-priming.

In all, it sucked, and I'd not do it again. Not even for free brass. I'll use the swager in a progressive press and spend less effort for the same result.

IF YOU WILL LOAD AMMO FOR YOUR GARAND ON A PROGRESSIVE PRESS, INVEST IN A BULLET PULLER … TO DISASSEMBLE LOADED ROUNDS WITH HIGH PRIMERS AND THEN DO A POST-MORTEM (SO TO SPEAK) AND FIGURE OUT WHY THE PROBLEM OCCURRED.

PRIMING

The primers you need are Large Rifle. Larger refers to the primer size, not the rifle size, although smaller cartridges than the .30-06 take smaller primers. But lately, the trend has been to use Small Rifle primers for all new cartridges, the 6.5 Creedmoor being the exemplar. (I can't help but note that the 6.5 Creedmoor can perhaps be described as a ".276 Pedersen Ackley Improved" cartridge, and the world might have been vastly different had the .276 been adopted, instead of the .30-06, in the Garand. Oh well.) The standard Large Rifle primer is acceptable for use in the Garand, but some shooters like to have an extra margin of safety and use a special primer.

For those self-loading firearms that have firing pins not constrained by a return spring, CCI makes the No. 34 primer, a Large Rifle primer with a slightly harder cup, to be less of a problem with firing pin bump. (It also makes the No. 41 primer for use in Small Rifle primer applications, such as the AR-15.)

Do you have to use these? How big of a problem is this? The problem, if it can be called that, happens once every several (or dozens of several) million rounds. A cartridge doesn't fully seat in the chamber, and the firing pin sets off the primer. It's more of a problem in the .308/7.62 NATO than in the .30-06, as the 7.62 is less tapered and more prone to stopping short.

It can also happen if your primers are not fully seated. When seating primers, make sure they are below flush. The specs call for a specified distance below flush, depending on the cartridge, the contract, the application, etc. Below flush is sufficient, so the primer is protected from the bolt face in feeding. What if the primer is flush? Probably nothing, and if everything works, you shouldn't have a problem. Above flush, now that's a problem. At the very least, it increases headspace (the cartridge's, not the rifle's), and the bolt can fail to close fully. If the primer is sensitive to the allowable specs, it can go off when the friction and impact are too great. This is very bad, as usually the bolt will not have had time to close and lock, and the case is unsupported. The bolt can be damaged, depending on where it is in the locking process. The receiver can be damaged, as the lug seats can be peened or chipped, or the rear receiver wall busted from bolt velocity. In any case, the cartridge case will blow open, as it is unsupported. The hot, high-pressure gas will jet like a cutting torch and break everything in its path.

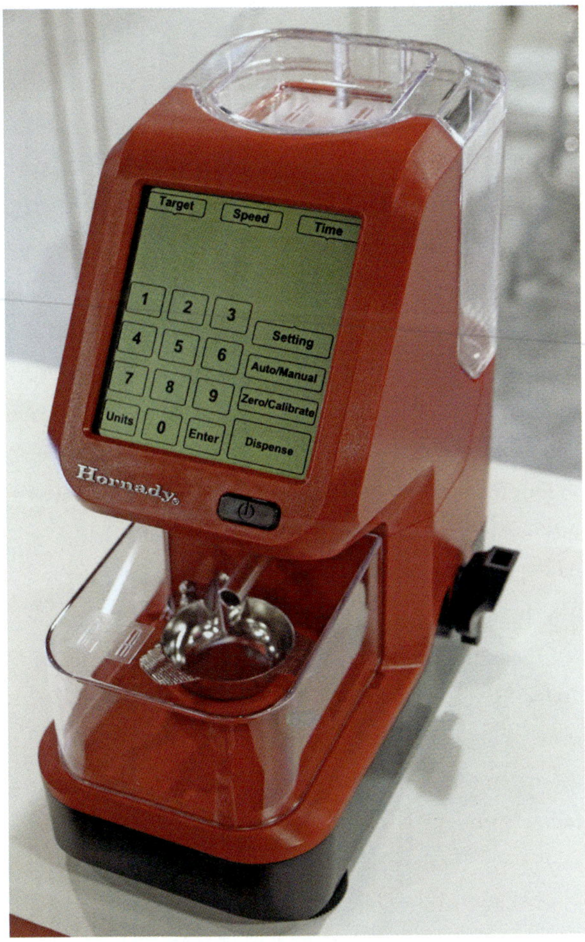

If you are really persnickety, you can use the Hornady Auto Charge Pro to weigh each powder charge. Sweeney loves his Hornady gear, but the consistency of a powder measure on a progressive press is plenty accurate for him and much faster.

The rifle will be destroyed, and usually, the shooter is unharmed. There can be injuries, and the shooter could have a severe flinch for some time afterward, which will take much shooting to dampen out.

How to avoid this? Ammo inspection. If you're loading on a single-stage press, inspect all your cases once primed to ensure the primers are below flush. If you find some that are not, you can re-seat them. You should also examine your process to see why you got some above flush. If loading on a progressive, inspect your loaded ammo. You cannot re-seat primers in loaded ammo. If there is a mechanical reason your primer wasn't seated properly, and you re-seat it and set the primer off (you're wearing hearing protection while doing this, right?) with just a case, you have lost a primer and get to disassemble the primer from the case and figure out the problem. If you attempt to re-seat a primer on a loaded round (Again, Do Not Do This) and set it off, you lose a primer. You launch a bullet. You burn up powder. And did I mention you launch a bullet, which will go you-don't-know-where? Murphy's Law being what it is, that "somewhere" is usually delicate, fragile, expensive or some combination of the three.

If you will load ammo for your Garand on a progressive press, invest in a bullet puller or a bolt-action rifle chambered in .30-06. The best would be a bullet puller to disassemble loaded rounds with high primers and then do a post-mortem (so to speak) and figure out why the problem occurred. If you have an ongoing problem with high primers, consider changing to stainless steel pin case cleaning, as this makes primer pockets squeaky clean and less prone to seating problems. The bolt-action rifle? Assuming your loads are safe but perhaps not as dimensionally correct as your Garand would like, you can always get practice and recover the brass (empty and fired once more) by shooting them through the bolt-action rifle. It's also a way to do a chronograph check on your loading without subjecting the Garand to the hazards of learning-to-reload ammo.

POWDER SELECTION AND USE

Precision shooters obsess over powder charge weight consistency. The idea is to produce weights of such regularity that the velocity spread is minimized. OK, waitaminit, what? The variations of powder charge weight mean variations in the pressure created, and thus the velocity changes. So, if loading for an average of 2,700 fps and the slowest one in a batch is 2,650 fps, and the fastest is 2,750 fps, that's a 100 fps spread. This would be noted in a loading chart as Es 100 fps. "Extreme spread, one hundred feet per second."

The case trim end of the Hornady Case Prep machine. You lower the held case down to the trim cutter, and once the stop adjustment is set, each one is an "insert, press down, lift, remove, repeat" process.

Is this bad? Well, that depends. If you're plinking at your gun club or shooting at a 100-yard match, then not likely. But at 600 yards, it would make a difference, so let's do some calculations.

The trajectory is calculated by taking the velocity, using the bullet's ballistic coefficient, and mathematically determining its trajectory in a Standard Atmosphere setting. Ignore wind, humidity, altitude, and barometric pressure; leave them all at standard values or none (like wind) and calculate the trajectory. Let's take a vanilla-plain 147-grain FMJBT bullet at our average 2,700 fps and see the differences with a 100 fps Es.

The closest I have to use as a reference is the Hornady Interbond, which is an excellent bullet. With a BC of .415, zeroed at 100 yards, the Interbond arrives at 600 yards with 1,562 fps velocity and a drop of 104 inches. Let's recalculate with 2,650 fps and 2,750 fps. At 2,650 fps, the drop is 109 inches. At 2,750 fps, the drop is 100 inches. If we assume that at 600 yards, your rifle can shoot 2 MOA (two minutes of angle) with no velocity variation, your hits will all be in a circle 12 inches across. However, on average, your rounds that tend toward 2,750 fps will hit up to four inches higher, and the 2,650 ones will tend toward five inches lower. (I've rounded things off a bit, which is why there's an inch difference.) So, your 12-inch circle now becomes an oval of 12 inches by almost 20. Oops.

If you have a more reasonable (and more common) 20 fps Es, the faster ones will be an inch high, and the slower ones will be an inch low, and the differences will get lost in the variances of your hold, trigger press, and follow-through.

So why do the precision shooters obsess over Es even more than that? Simple: their rifles don't shoot 2 MOA; theirs shoot .5 MOA. And they are shooting one-foot steel targets at 1,200 yards. They use a 6.5 Creedmoor or 6.5 PRC, and those bullets have BCs in the .640s, and at 1,200 yards, a 6.5 Creedmoor with a 5 fps Es has a variance of

Ammunition from the CMP comes in boxes like this when it can be found.

Not all Greek ammunition came in clips in bandoliers. Much of it came in 20-round boxes like this.

2.2 inches. You'd obsess, too, over 2.2 inches variance due to muzzle velocity on a 12-inch target because of powder weight differences.

That said, we have the other end of accuracy: benchrest shooting. Benchrest shooters shoot small groups at 100 and 200 yards. How small? In serious competition, the center-to-center spread of a competitive target will be less than .2 inch. They use special calipers to measure groups. Benchrest shooters do not weigh charges; they throw them with powder measures of the same basic design you will use. However, theirs are built to a level of precision that yours aren't, and they have tested to prove a particular measure delivers the goods, and the groups don't suffer due to powder weight variance.

All that said, how much should you worry about your powder measure consistency? Not much, if at all. Unless you're competing in matches that reach 600 yards, and your skills are up to the level that you can see (measured in your scores) that an excessive Es is hurting you, don't worry. The Slow Fire (one round per minute) 600-yard target at Camp Perry (where the National Matches are held each year) is called the MR-1 and has a 36-inch black

Much war-store ammunition was sealed into "spam cans," with the expectation that it would still be good no matter how long it took to open the can. And opening the can is work, says Sweeney.

center, the outside scoring ring (five points of the ten possible) is 60 inches across, and the target sheet is 64 x 72 inches. That means a group of 10 MOA stays within the scoring rings. The hardest part is getting a good zero at 100 yards and then learning how many clicks up your sights need to be set for the 200-, 300-, and 600-yard targets. Reading the wind is an order of magnitude greater problem than powder weight variances.

BACK TO POWDERS

You'll probably buy powder in the one-pound kegs when you experiment. That means a pound of IMR-4895, all 7,000 grains of it, at 48 grains per shot, will net you 145 rounds of ammo. With a similar powder, H4895, you can achieve the same velocity with only 46 grains. That's 152 rounds loaded. Once you find what powder works for you, your purchases will be in eight-pound kegs. (They are all plastic bottles now, but the bigger ones are called kegs. In the powder industry, real kegs are 30-, 40-, or 55-gallon fiber or plastic drums, which you will probably never have an opportunity to purchase.) This lowers your per-pound price, spreads the Hazmat fee across eight pounds, and means you'll be less likely to run out as you get on a loading roll.

When you get set up to load ammunition, you have two approaches to powder charging. One is for loading on a progressive, the other on a single stage. In either method, keep one type of powder on your loading bench at a time and store the other powders across the loading room. When you get set up, read the load data, then get the powder. Double-check the load data info against the label. Putting the wrong powder in your rounds can be embarrassing at the one extreme, and, at the other extreme, it can destroy your rifle and injure you.

Check the weight from your data source, and use your powder scale to confirm that your powder measure throws the correct powder charge. Of course, you have a scale to weigh with, but no one who is sane loads ammo without a scale to double-check powder weights.

With a progressive press, lock your powder measure onto the press and continue setting up each stage for loading. Once set up, load one round. Before you seat the bullet, remove the primed and powder-filled case from the shell plate, dump the powder into a pan, and weigh it on your scale. Yes, this is a triple-check, and you should do it. Assuming it is correct (if it isn't, find out why and correct it), use a funnel to dump the powder back into that case, seat the bullet, crimp, and then use a gauge to ensure it passes the chamber check. When you next do the volume loading, pull the tenth or twelfth round off the press, dump and weigh the powder charge, return it to the case, and continue loading.

If using a single-stage press, arrange your primed and empty cases in a loading block, and use the powder measure to drop a powder charge into each one. Take any of them at random, and once all are filled, dump the charge into the pan and weigh, just as above. Correct? Good, next step. If not, find out why. Then dump *them all* back into the powder measure and repeat it. With the loading tray filled with primed and powder-filled cases, stand so a bright light is over your shoulder or use a small flashlight and peer into each case to visually inspect the powder charges. They should all be filled up to the same level. If not, pull the ones that are different and find out why.

It could be that a clump of tumbling media was still in the case, and that's why it looks over-filled, or your powder measure ran low on powder, and the last one (or few) is short or has no powder.

OK, we've reviewed the essential details of loading ammunition for your Garand. Since the supply of surplus is now down to "collectors" levels, we come to the decision point: what powder, and how much?

As described, you have a limited window of powder burn rates to choose from to work well with your Garand's gas system. To that end, I have listed some loads that have worked for me and will likely work for you. As with all such processes, this worked for me, but there are no guarantees, and any mistakes you make are on you, not me. (Sorry to be so negative, but that's life in the 21st century.) We'll do this by bullet weight, keeping the following detail in mind: the overall length of all the loads will be the same, with minor variances only due to subtle variances in the ogive of the bullet being seated, compared to another.

Unlike other rifles, you can't adjust the overall length to improve accuracy because the Garand's action depends on a certain cartridge length for proper feeding. Once you've set your bullet seating die to the proper overall length, leave it for all the weights you test or load.

I won't give multiple grain weight powder charges

and muzzle velocities, just broad ranges; that is, a baseline powder weight for each propellant. These will be the performance equivalent of military-spec ammunition and work the Garand properly. If you want to adjust the powder charges up or down by a small amount because your rifle responds OK to a given load, but shoots much better with a half-a-grain-weight charge of that powder heavier or lighter, then go for it.

147- TO 150-GRAIN BULLET LOADS

Most likely here, the bullets of 147 or 149 grains in weight would be the surplus bullets, the "pulls" you can buy in bulk, while the 150-grain ones would be the new bullets you've bought from a bullet maker like Hornady or Sierra. If you want practice and plinking ammo, the surplus pulls will do just fine. If you're looking for more accuracy, then the new bullets are your choice.

Varget	47.0
IMR4895	49.0
IMR4064	47.5
H4895	46.5
BL-C(2)	50.0

These weights will give you around 2,800 fps, which is right in the ballpark for the Garand. I've seen published data for some powders and bullet combinations that push a 150-grainer to 2,900 fps, but I don't see the point. As you get closer to the pressure max, your rifle will be statistically more likely to "see" a load that tips over the max pressure. A pressure spike of 5,000 PSI, when running things at an average of 44,000 PSI, keeps you under 50,000 PSI. But if you increase things, the spike and the starting point also increase so that you could run at 50,000 PSI and then get a spike of 6,000 to 7,000 PSI. All that to gain another 50-75 fps on average. I don't see the value of the risk, but that's me.

The 147- to 149-grain weight bullets are the only ones for the Garand that you might find as "surplus" — which these days are pulls, bullets removed from ammunition broken down to recover the components, and not to be used as loaded ammunition. Note: pulled bullets are those removed from loaded ammunition because the ammunition, for a host of reasons, will not, or cannot, be fired. The usual, or classic, reason is poor storage conditions. If a warehouse full of ammunition is not kept under controlled conditions, the heat variance can cause the powder to change. This change may become unsafe. What to do? The ammunition could all be shoved into a smelter, but the smelter operators are often reluctant to introduce combustible products (powder and primers) into their plants. Plus, the lead in the bullets gets melted and mixed with the brass, making a pile of ingots difficult to separate.

THE 180-GRAIN BULLET IS AS HEAVY AS I'M COMFORTABLE LOADING FOR THE GARAND. I KNOW SOME SHOOTERS, PAST COMPETITORS, HAVE LOADED HEAVIER BULLETS, BUT THAT, TO ME, IS PUSHING THINGS A BIT TOO FAR TO TRY AND GAIN SOME SLIGHT ADVANTAGE.

Here, it's sold to a salvage operation, with all the legal niceties of "you must not sell this as ammunition." That outfit pulls the bullets, dumps the powder, sells the bullets and empty cases, and disposes of the powder. (It can be chemically recovered and turned into several other useful products by a chemical firm with the right equipment and experience.)

Those are the "pulled" bullets you sometimes see offered for sale. There is no "standard" product of pulled bullets; each batch is whatever they were when they were loaded into ammunition initially. You may find 147- to 149-grain FMJ bullets as pulls, but you are unlikely to find anything else. So, handloading ammunition for your Garand will consist almost entirely of selecting from one well-regarded bullet or another or the shelf full of premium bullets. There won't be any inexpensive "commodity-grade" bullets like you can load for your 9mm pistol. No, those .308-inch bullets were used up decades ago.

That's life, owning and shooting a Garand.

155-GRAIN BULLET LOADS

The 155-grainer is special and known as a "Palma" bullet. The Palma Match is a long-range target competition fired at 800, 900, and 1,000 yards. The Palma is a compromise bullet in that it's the lightest projectile that can be pushed to a sufficient speed and minimum BC to remain supersonic to 1,000 yards out of standard, non-magnum cartridges. Note that a rifle bullet starts supersonic (over approximately 1,050 fps) and loses velocity as it travels. When it drops below supersonic speeds, the transition can erode accuracy. That's why long-distance target shooters want their bullets to be supersonic when they've reached the target. You won't find these on the bargain table, as they are often a special-order item for shops that stock reloading components, and you'd have to seek them out. But you might want to give them a try, so here goes:

Varget	48.0
IMR4895	50.5
IMR4064	50.0
BL-C(2)	51.5
H4895	47.5

165- TO 168-GRAIN BULLET LOADS

Here we have match bullets that are the same weight as the classic M2AP that WWII and Korea were fought with and that match shooters used for a decade or so after the end of the Korean War. The shape and BC of the classic 168-grain match boattail hollowpoint are not much different from that of the M2AP bullet, in part because the designers of that bullet did such an excellent job of designing it. And, because the dimensions which bullet designers have to work with — overall length, neck length, case mouth location in the chamber, and feeding dynamics — mean bullet designers are hemmed in.

Varget	47.0
IMR4895	48.0
IMR4064	47.5
H4895	43.5
BL-C(2)	47.0

175-GRAIN BULLET LOADS

At 175 grains, Sierra makes a really good bullet that offers a better BC than the 168 and almost as good as the 180 without going up to that weight bullet. Does it matter? If your rifle says it does, then it does. If not, then acquire whatever bullet weight you can, and load it so you can shoot.

Varget	45.5
IMR4895	46.0
IMR4064	46.0
H4895	44.0
BL-C(2)	48.5

180-GRAIN BULLET LOADS

The 180-grain bullet is as heavy as I'm comfortable loading for the Garand. I know some shooters, past competitors, have loaded heavier bullets, but that, to me, is pushing things a bit too far to try and gain some slight advantage. What advantage? Wind drift, primarily. Since the target in a match is a known and consistent distance, the trajectory can be accounted for and clocked into the sights and left there. But the wind is constantly changing. A bullet with less wind drift better accommodates minor errors in judgment of the wind (a voodoo-like skill, by the way) or shifts between judging and shooting. But, like trying to gain a bit more velocity, going heavier than 180 grains increases the chances of bumping up against excessive pressures, which is not good.

Varget	44.5
IMR4895	45.5
IMR4064	46.0
H4895	42.5
BL-C(2)	45.5

VLD BULLET LOADS

You may be looking over the bullet selections and wondering, "There's no data for the new, hot, everyone-has-to-have-it VLD bullets. Why not?" Simple: they won't fit. Not that the bullet diameters, or weights, aren't in the proper ranges, no. But a bullet is made to be a Very Low Drag or VLD by elongating it and making the point pointier. The

The ballisticians who develop load data for your firearms are not doing this as a part-time job or out of their garages. They test pressure, accuracy, consistency, and reliability and report on what works. If a powder maker doesn't list a given powder for your application, there's a reason. The number of suitable powders for the Garand is limited but plenty sufficient.

curved portion of the bullet, ahead of the bearing surface, is known as the ogive. The shape of this curve determines, to a great extent, what the ballistic coefficient of a bullet will be. As a result of making them better in the wind, a VLD bullet tends to be longer in the ogive than a non-VLD projectile.

Remember our constraints on cartridge assembly? You are locked into a single overall length or OAL, and when you put a VLD bullet into a .30-06 case and make it fit the Garand OAL, the VLD bullet's ogive extends into the case mouth. You have just replicated the problem with the .30-03 cartridge and pointed bullets that the U.S. Army grappled with back in 1904-1905. If you want to use VLD bullets, you must find something else to launch them from beside your Garand.

POWDER SUMMATION

The suggested weights are in the same ballpark, regardless of bullet weight. That's due to the gas flow limits imposed by the Garand's gas system. And, of the bullet weight limits the gas flow requires.

You can use the powders listed without worrying about the proper gas pressure (with the correct powder charge weight), but you may see other powders listed occasionally. Yes, other powders might be made to work. You can use a special gas plug that vents excess gas or changes gas flow to use other powders. But why? If you happened upon a literal keg, a 55-gallon drum of rifle powder that was "pretty close to" but not precisely in the correct burn range for the Garand, then there might be a reason to experiment. (A quick calculation leads us to conclude that a 55-gallon drum of rifle powder is good for something on the order of 50,000 loaded rounds. Good find, if usable.)

But, if instead of finding such a trove, you are buying powder, well, you can purchase the proper powder just as easily as you can buy the improper powder, so why get the wrong stuff? Buy the right stuff. •

.30-06 Springfield (7.62x63mm/.30 Government M'06)

Historical Notes: The .30-06 Springfield is a United States military cartridge adapted from the .30-03 by employing a lighter, streamlined bullet and making other minor changes. In this it parallels other military cartridge developments of the era, with French and German versions leading the way. It was adopted, in 1906, for the Model 1903 Springfield service rifle, which was based on the Mauser bolt-action system. The Winchester Model 1895 lever action appears to have been the first sporting rifle chambered for the .30-06. The cartridge was added to the line in 1908. The Remington bolt-action Model 30, introduced in 1921, and the Winchester bolt-action Model 54, brought out in 1925, both offered the .30-06, among other chamberings. The Savage bolt-action Model 40 and 45 Super-Sporter rifles were also so chambered, when introduced in 1928. At present, in addition to the many bolt-action rifles, the Remington Model 7600 pump-action (24657) and the Browning BAR semi-auto line, include the .30-06 as standard chamberings. The Ruger No. 1 single-shot rifle is also offered in .30-06 as a distributor exclusive (1304). A number of British and European side-by-side or over/under double rifles can be ordered in this chambering, and so can some European rifle-shotgun combination guns.

General Comments: The .30-06 is undoubtedly the most flexible, useful, all-round big game cartridge available to the American hunter. For many years, it has been the standard by which all other big game cartridges have been measured. To say that a cartridge is in the .30-06 class means it is suitable for any game in North America. The secret to success when using this cartridge is to select the right bullet for the game and hunting conditions at hand. Lighter bullets of 100 to 130 grains should be used only for varmint and small game hunting. While these bullets can be driven at impressive velocities (well over 3,000 fps), they are designed to expand rapidly on small game and will not penetrate properly on large game. For deer, antelope, goats, sheep, or black or brown bear under most hunting conditions, the 150- or 165-grain bullet is proper and a good compromise for those seeking one load for medium to heavy game. For heavier game, such as elk, moose, or large brown bear, the 165-, 180-, 200-, or 220-grain bullets are the best choices. The '06 performs impressively with handloads using 250-grain bullets. Many experienced hunters consider the 180-grain bullet the most satisfactory all-around loading for the .30-06, because it can be used effectively on anything from deer to the heaviest game under almost any hunting conditions. As a matter of fact, the .30-06 will give a good account on all but the heaviest or most dangerous African or Asiatic species, under average hunting conditions. The 220-grain bullet is generally recommended for African game, although the 180-grain also has a good reputation. With the proper bullet, this cartridge can be adapted to any game or hunting situation in North or South America, whether in the mountains, plains, woods, or jungles. Few other cartridges can claim equal versatility.

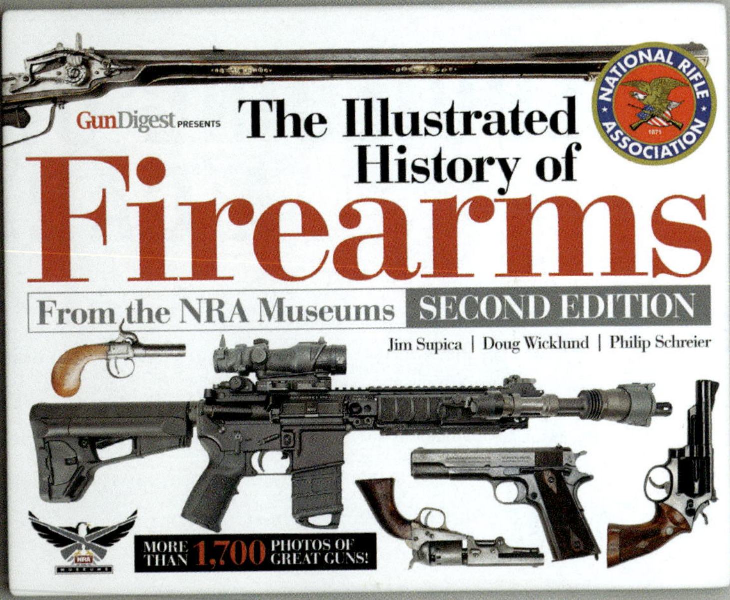

GunDigest PRESENTS
The Illustrated History of
Firearms
From the NRA Museums
SECOND EDITION
Jim Supica | Doug Wicklund | Philip Schreier
NATIONAL RIFLE ASSOCIATION
1871
MORE THAN 1,700 PHOTOS OF GREAT GUNS!

NEW TECHNOLOGY I
REPEATERS

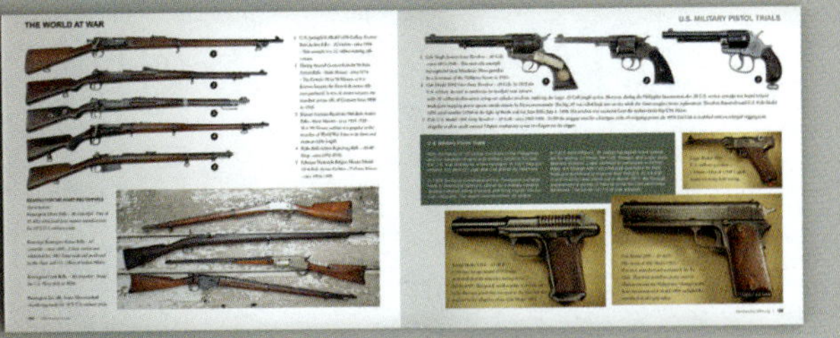

THE WORLD AT WAR
U.S. MILITARY PISTOL TRIALS

MODERN FIREARMS
HANDGUNS

CHAPTER 15

REBUILDING OR RESTORING A GARAND

What can you do if your Garand isn't entirely up to snuff — isn't as reliable or accurate as you'd like? Perhaps the barrel is genuinely shot out. Or parts are damaged, modified, ugly, or inoperative. What to do?

Rebuilding your Garand falls into two broad camps: Rebuild or restore. If you're looking to rebuild, to make your Garand operational and accurate, then you will be doing essentially what the armorers in the Pacific, Europe, Korea, or other combat zones did: replace broken or inoperative parts with correct ones to restore function. You don't care about timelines, who made what, or whether the shades of Parkerizing match.

To start a restoration, first, nail down the year or month the receiver was made. Then seek out parts appropriate to that time. Now, a part that wasn't changed over the Garand's life makes this easy. Say you have an

A new match-grade Garand barrel can turn your old warhorse into an accurate shooter, but the firearm will no longer be collectible. Photo: CMP Archives

oversized gas cylinder. Since there were only a few variants, replacing it will be simple. (Simple in that you have lots of choices, not so easy in that it might be expensive.) So, your 1943 Springfield receiver will be appropriately matched with any unmarked gas cylinder. No Korean-era gas cylinders will do, but if you come across one reasonably priced, you will find it useful to trade to a Korean restorer for something else.

Barrels are another matter. Your 1943 SA receiver needs a barrel no later than 1945, dated to be period-correct. (The real obsessives will insist on a 1943-dated barrel and perhaps spend the rest of their collectors' careers trying to find one.)

REBUILDING

The main rebuild elements are the barrel, the op rod, and the stock. Other parts wear and can be more readily sourced and replaced, but the big three are tough. Let's jump in with the barrel, as it's the most expensive and complicated. A shot-out or rusted-out barrel won't be accurate. The barrel is tightly screwed into the receiver, and new ones are pricey, depending on the quality. "How about a replacement original?" you ask. Good luck. Seventy-five years after it was a production item, the supply of new, unused barrels is about zero. And those that exist will be bid up by collectors restoring their collectible Garands. If you want a shooter, you must go with a new one.

New barrels are a "when available" item, as the barrel makers who can produce them are busy year-round with high-volume parts. They will typically calculate how many barrels it takes to satisfy their customers for a year and set up to make that many. If there's a run on Garand barrels, you'll have to wait until the next batch is made.

A new Garand barrel will not have any USGI markings, so installing one disqualifies your Garand from the collectible category. Of course, if you keep the old barrel, you can swap it back in if you want the historical accuracy, but you'll give up the target accuracy.

You'll need a properly fitting action wrench to unscrew the receiver from the existing barrel. Trying to do this with whatever you can make do with from your toolbox is just asking to bend an irreplaceable receiver.

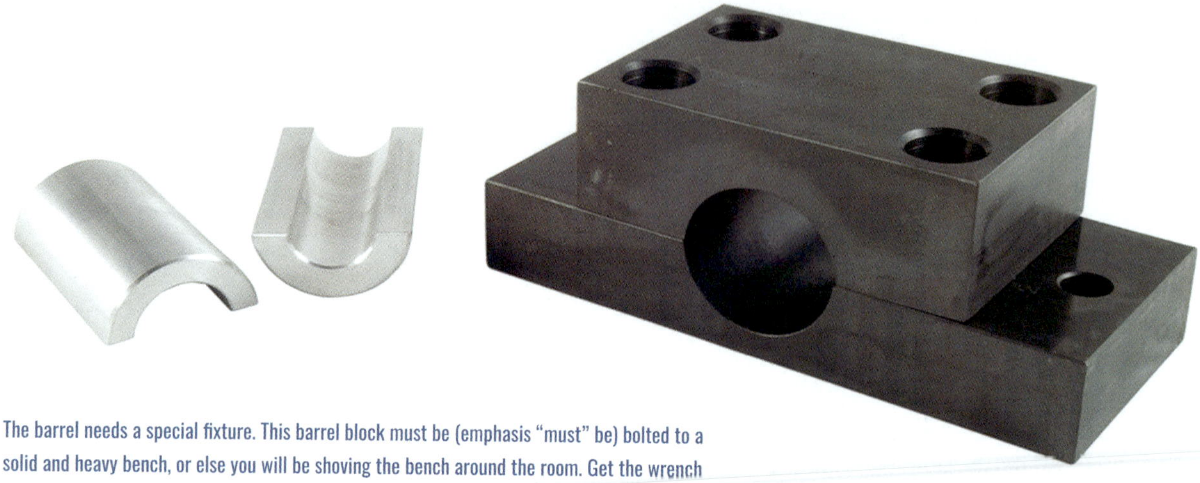

The barrel needs a special fixture. This barrel block must be (emphasis "must" be) bolted to a solid and heavy bench, or else you will be shoving the bench around the room. Get the wrench and barrel block from Brownells, the purveyors of all things excellent in gunsmithing.

A new barrel will run you from $150 to $300. That's just the barrel, which will have to be installed. "OK, I can do that," you say. Perhaps. First, the old barrel has been affixed for half a century or more. It was tightly torqued in place, and it hasn't moved since. You will need a proper action wrench and barrel block setup to get a good hold of it. A proper wrench, and the action blocks to fit your Garand, will run you $125 from Brownells. You will need a barrel vise, a steel block with a fitted adapter (the Garand requires special blocks), which runs much the same in price when available. You'll be wrestling a 3-foot bar, unscrewing a tightly fitted barrel. The barrel vise must be bolted to the sturdiest bench you can find. Not just any bench, but something big, heavy, anchored, and stout. If you don't own such a bench, or know someone who does who will let you drill the bolt holes to anchor your barrel vise, then you aren't going to be swapping a Garand barrel on your own.

Next obstacle: your new Garand barrel will not come headspaced. When the arsenals made Garands, they con-

A replacement barrel will be threaded and timed, but you should still check the timing and torque. If you don't, things will not go well.

trolled the dimensions such that barrel swaps were easy. (Relatively speaking, of course.) Today, there's no telling what the final headspace of any given Garand will be, so the barrel makers ship them "short" by ten-thousandths of an inch or so. That's why you will need headspace gauges and a chamber reamer to measure (you do have the proper digital calipers, right?) and then ream your chamber. And you'll also need a bolt disassembly tool to remove the extractor and correctly measure headspace.

In essence, you need as much as or more in the cost of tools as you would spend on a barrel. This is all to convince you that the gunsmith who knows what he's doing is worth what you are paying him.

Oh, and if you want to up the cool factor, you can spend the most and go to Criterion and get a top-grade barrel in a caliber other than .30-06. The choices (when available) are the .270 (a .30-06 necked down), or 7.62 NATO, which is what the Navy did when the 7.62 was adopted, and it could not get M14s. You can go bigger and opt for the .35 Whelen, which is essentially a .35-06, or you can get your replacement barrel in 6.5x55. The classic Swedish round offers lower felt recoil, much better ballistic coefficient, and superb accuracy, given the quality of today's bullets. The high BC of these 6.5mm bullets means they stay supersonic to 1,000 yards, which is not always possible with a Garand-approved .30-06 load. (I must admit that the Venn diagram of 1,000-yard shooters using Garands and looking for a 6.5x55 is pretty tiny, but what a cool group to be in.)

YOUR 1943 SA RECEIVER NEEDS A BARREL NO LATER THAN 1945, DATED TO BE PERIOD-CORRECT. (THE REAL OBSESSIVES WILL INSIST ON A 1943-DATED BARREL AND PERHAPS SPEND THE REST OF THEIR COLLECTORS' CAREERS TRYING TO FIND ONE.)

OP RODS

If not bent (bending is an arcane craft in its own right), op rods need service at two points. Luckily, both are relatively easy fixes. At opposite ends, we have worn or undersized pistons, guide lugs worn, and op rods popping out of the guide tracks.

The worn pistons can be replaced, as the piston is brazed or silver-soldered into the end of the hollow tube that is the op rod. This is not a home-gunsmithing task; either send your op rod off in exchange or have it re-brazed and returned. If yours is period-correct, send it for work and wait. If it isn't period-correct, and you aren't concerned, send it in for an exchange.

The worn guide lugs require proper welding and machining to correct dimensions; this is also not a home-gunsmithing job. It requires the proper alloy of fill stick, machining to the correct dimensions, and then Parkerizing. You don't need me to advise you if you know how to do all that. If you do not, then experimenting is not advised.

As an aside, if your op rod or piston is so worn that it needs service, then the action spring is probably tired as well, and you should measure it and replace it if too short.

STOCKS

Original stocks are, like everything else, over half a century old or more. Finding a pristine, original stock to restore your Garand is like searching for a winning lotto ticket: the odds are not in your favor. You can, however, replace it with a new stock and even have it stamped with the period-correct cartouches.

Stocks are not too difficult to find or replace, as we've grown new wood since the old days, and making a Garand stock is not that different from making other types. The CMP might have what you need, or you can check Boyds, DuPage Trading Company, or Bardalls, which can apply a period-correct cartouche on your replacement.

Once your Garand is returned from Shuff's, take care in assembly so you don't scratch the brand-new Parkerizing, like here, installing and removing a rear handguard.

This little hole in the barrel (the gas port) resulted from so much work on the part of John Garand. Had the powers-that-be not had a stick up their [never mind] about the subject, he could have gotten the job done years sooner. Oh, and that diameter that is bright? It needs to stay bright and be an exact size, which is why it was precision ground to spec in 1944.

PARKERIZING

The chemical finish applied to the steel provides a rust-resistant surface. Parkerizing is either a zinc or manganese phosphate deposition on the steel's surface. Manganese was used from the start and well into the war, but the Parkerizing of parts was changed to zinc phosphate in the summer of 1944. However, both were used, off and on, in post-war rebuilds and Korean production. The phosphate coasting looks like a sponge at the microscopic level, and filling the gaps with oil or grease makes it most rust-resistant. That is also why freshly "parked" parts appear light gray (zinc looks lighter, and manganese is more charcoal), and aged ones look green, brown, or other colors. The colors come from the oils oxidizing in the Parkerizing, making it even more resistant to the world.

Parkerizing is a specialized process, and you need someone who does not only Parkerizing but works on military firearms of this period. Shuff's offers full Parkerizing for Garands, and as a bonus, since they have to remove the barrel to properly Parkerize your rifle, they can install your new barrel for you. While they're at it, if your stock is in good enough shape (and you have shipped it), they can also apply the correct cartouche for the receiver and its period.

IN ESSENCE, YOU NEED AS MUCH AS OR MORE IN THE COST OF TOOLS AS YOU WOULD SPEND ON A BARREL. THIS IS ALL TO CONVINCE YOU THAT THE GUNSMITH WHO KNOWS WHAT HE'S DOING IS WORTH WHAT YOU ARE PAYING HIM.

AUTHENTICITY

Now, as someone who comes to this from when all the items we're discussing were new, original, and correct, I have to be concerned about all the services offered. Someone can go to the trouble of buying a new barrel and stamping it with hand stamps (and a lot of care, because it won't be easy) with whatever maker and date they want to. They could create a stock with cartouches and have an early receiver and parts Parkerized.

They now can assemble a pristine, early, "original" Garand and pass it off as a "grail gun" to a would-be collector. That makes me a bit uneasy, but I have to think that most collectors could spot such a counterfeit. However, as time passes, the knowledge of what to look for will fade, the quality of the re-work improves, and the desirability of the pristine original increases, so we might see more of that. And in the year 2036, the Garand's centennial, a restoration might have the status of "as good as new." In that, I find the example of Turnbull Restorations to be comforting. Turnbull takes originals that are not abused (and sometimes even abused ones) and restores them to their original condition, and everyone knows this. A Turnbull Restoration can be valued more than an original, and if that comes to pass for the Garand, well, more power to us all. •

CHAPTER 16

GARAND COMPETITION, CMP, AND CAMP PERRY

In the old days, you had one way to shoot your Garand in competition: Across the Course. This event is a series of stages that date back to the origins of the National Matches. The stages are: Standing at 200 yards, sitting at 200 yards, prone at 300 yards, and prone at 600 yards. As if that wasn't enough, the shooting rates are mixed up.

At 200 yards standing (the 10-ring is seven inches across, the aiming black is 13 inches) is fired slow fire. That is, you have ten minutes for your ten shots. Each shot must be loaded and scored individually, so you can adjust for the wind and light and note the hits in your logbook. (Yes, serious shooters note each shot fired in a logbook, with the wind, light, etc. noted.)

CMP-sanctioned matches are a great opportunity for you to get practical marksmanship training with your Garand. Photo: CMP Archives

The 200-yard sitting stage is a standing start, and it is fired rapid fire. It has the same target, but the time? You have 50 seconds to get into your sitting position, aim, fire, reload during ten rounds, and finish. Bolt-gun shooters get 60 seconds, but that's not you with a Garand. And yes, competitors use specially modified clips to hold two rounds to start, then reload with an eight-round clip to finish. During reloading, the serious shooters will take a moment to look through their spotting scope and see where the first two hits are, in case they have to correct for wind, light, etc.

At 300 yards, you again start standing (so you have to go prone in the time allowed and fire), and the 10-ring is the same seven inches, but you get a break with the aiming black, as it is 19 inches across. You have the same 50 seconds for shooting and reloading.

The 600-yard target seems generous with a 10-ring that is an entire foot across with an aiming black that is 36 inches, but at 600 yards, those are awfully small to the naked eye. You start prone and shoot slow fire at that distance, so 20 shots in 20 minutes. This can be work, lying in the sun for 20 minutes, with each shot loaded, fired, and scored individually, constantly assessing the wind and light, and shooting to hit the center.

That's 50 rounds, and this isn't easy. And it's even more challenging when you consider that it was developed as a course of fire suitable for combat training soldiers in 1903 when the first match was held. That match was in Sea Girt, New Jersey, until the event moved to Camp Perry, Ohio, in 1907, where it has been ever since.

Not all gun clubs or ranges have 600 yards available, so those with shorter distances use scaled-down targets. It is possible to fire a Service Rifle match, Across the Course, on a 100-yard range.

And today?

Camp Perry has a schedule of pistol, rimfire, airgun, smallbore rifle, rifle and Junior Highpower matches that would fill your summer. And empty your ammo vault. Can you use a Garand? Yes, you can, quoting a

Seasoned Camp Perry and other CMP match competitors sport all the specialized gear you can imagine, toted to the firing line with shooting carts. You don't have to start with all this stuff; begin slowly and acquire what you need as you gain experience. Photo: CMP Archives

In the Vintage Sniper Match, you'll see many Springfield 03A4s and other bolt guns. But there are plenty of M1C and M1D Garands as well. Photo: CMP Archives

politician in a way that would probably aggravate him. In the Service Rifle category, you had best be prepared to receive a thorough and proper thumping. The Service Rifle is now the M16, and there, you will be in the same position I was in back when I had to switch from the Garand or M1A to an AR-15. You will be up against someone shooting a 15- to 17-pound AR-15, softer-recoil ammo loaded with high-BC bullets, and they will clean your clock. Once the Service Teams adopted the M16 and tuned it, such was the case.

The various matches — Garand, M1 Carbine, Vintage sniper, etc. — are amazing, limited only by range time, number of participants, and the creativity of the match organizers. However, while there are Divisions, categories, and special matches, and you can find your scores compared only to other Garand shooters, provided you

USPSA matches are over-run with AR-15s these days, but you can still have lots of fun with your Garand.

enter the correct matches, there's a catch with all of them. Fair warning, however: be sure you know the equipment rules. For instance, in some matches of the Service Rifle type, you cannot have NM-marked parts on your Garand, and it cannot be glass-bedded. Show up with a Garand like my NM-built one, and you'll be shooting for fun, not for score. The same goes for the other equipment-specific division, matches, or categories.

AMMO UPDATE

You have a few limitations at Camp Perry and other matches like Across the Course. Use what you want as long as you aren't firing tracers (you might set things on fire) and your ammo isn't dangerous or damaging to the equipment. Of course, this must be within the equipment specs laid out for the match or division.

Before the government withdrew support for the National Matches after 1967, when the political heat got to be too much, you could enter the Service Rifle category and be issued a rifle and ammunition to use in it. Today, you must bring your own rifle, ammo, and whatever equipment or gear you need to use. That's why you'll see many carts, wagons, and such, like a gathering of heavily armed shopping ladies.

PRACTICAL

The USPSA/IPSC world is completely overrun with AR-15s and their clones. If you plan on entering a match with your Garand, you must do so in a 3-Gun (not many of those these days) or Multi-gun match. The difference? In 3-Gun, you use a rifle, pistol, and shotgun, each in its own stage or stages. In Multi-gun, you use two or three of them in each stage. You'll be dumping your Garand, muzzle first, into a padded barrel, so don't take your glass-bedded, match-conditioned rifle; use the rack-grade one.

Also, you'll be entering the Heavy Metal Division if the match has one. (If you're alone, there won't be a Divisional recognition. That's life.) That means you'll have to use an iron-sighted pistol and a 12-gauge shotgun, And the two Heavy Metal Divisions (Tactical and Limited allow optical sights on the rifle. Well, that leaves you out. So you'll be doing it pretty much for the fun of it. Of which there is a lot to be had. Oh, and the Power Factor for Major in USPSA rifle? 320. Since an average load for the Garand posts a PF of 395, you have nothing to worry about.

There are much better Heavy Metal .30-caliber rifles to be used, but not many are classier than a Garand. •

Be prepared for your Garand to share the rack space with lots of plastic and aluminum. It will stand out.

CHAPTER 17

COLLECTING THE GARAND

When it comes to collecting, the time to collect is before everyone else becomes a collector. Well, that time, for the Garand, passed a couple of decades ago. They were relatively inexpensive, as full-sized .30-06 military rifles go, until the beginning of the 21st century. That's when prices shot up.

This was reflected in the prices at the CMP (back then, the DCM) in auctions and at gun shops when you could acquire a good-condition Garand for under $1,000. It wasn't unusual to score a rack-grade Garand, and maybe even some ammunition with it, for $800. There was a time when you could buy eight Garands a year from the CMP, at the grade or grades you wanted, and see what showed up. Then things changed, and the political situation got

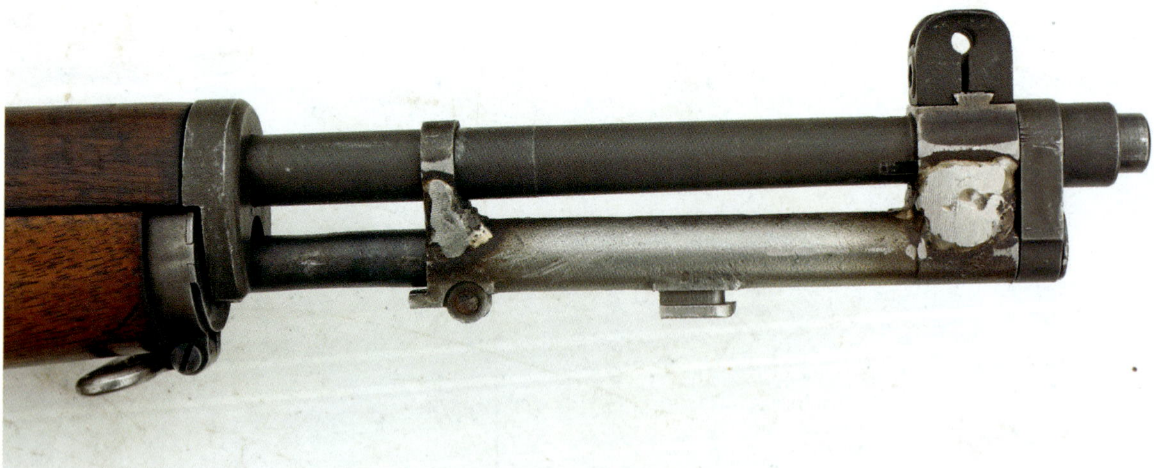

Every chopped Garand is a crime, and each "Tanker" is a missed opportunity to build a proper Garand.

more fractious, and the collectors realized that there were bargains to be had.

Today, finding an unabused Garand of the standard makers is challenging for under $2,200 or even $2,500. If you have your heart set on a Winchester, be prepared to fork over $3,000 for one that you could use. (When you shoot it, a Winchester collector will shed a tear with each round fired.) Whenever I see a re-weld or a "Tanker" built from an altered Garand, I weep.

If you think that's crazy, you have best not even look at the M1 Carbine market. When I was cruising gun shows every weekend (yes, I know, it was the disco era, and we used stone axes as backup weapons. I'm old, so what?), people bought M1 Carbines as "car guns." You bought one, checked the zero and function, and put it in your car's trunk or behind your truck's seat against future need. If it got beaten up or a little rusty, so what? It was "just" an M1 carbine, after all. Sure, gun collectors in those days would fight over the rarities, but the show was full of tables with many Inland carbines (the biggest maker, by far) on them. You could take your pick. The "pretty" ones might be $20 more. Now? The collectible M1 Carbines are as expensive as Garands. And the others are almost as pricey.

So, the simple advice is this: do your homework, and have all the data in your head before you look over Garands in a shop, at a show, or on an auction site. Because everyone else in the same arena will have, and they won't be of a mind to show you any mercy.

Why?

We made almost six-million Garands during a total world war and a police action, plus those produced overseas in Italy. Where did they all go? Well, for one, many got used up, left behind, blown up or otherwise lost during the wars. Dropped in the surf when the soldier or Marine carrying them was shot during a landing and

Photo: CMP Archives

The author doing his part to ensure the M1 Carbine is represented on the range. They are sturdy but won't last forever. Still, the last one will be working someplace at the beginning of the 22nd century.

not recovered? Gone. Dropped in the jungle, the same reason? Gone. Blown up, sank, used up, and scrapped. Then there are all the ones "loaned" to our various "allies" over the decades. The numbers are not so great for the next one. The Garands recovered in various law enforcement situations and then subsequently scrapped are lost to us since many jurisdictions require "crime" guns to be destroyed instead of auctioned off. (There's something almost maniacal about the official response to a firearm used in a crime: The knee-jerk reaction to scrap it, as if the inanimate object used must be punished — an almost medieval outlook.)

And then, there were the drill rifles. Used for close-order drills, ceremonial use, and those converted to blanks only for use in memorial services, those Garands have to number in the thousands as well, perhaps tens of thousands. Units like the USMC Silent Drill Team use Garands, instead of M14s or M16s, due to their balance. The ceremonial guards at many palaces, parliaments, tombs and tourist sites carry Garands for the same reasons.

So, millions of Garand have ceased to exist or have been so altered that they cannot be readily restored to service. Once the collectors turned their eyes toward them, the iron law of economics stepped in: If there is a limited supply of something, and the demand increases, the price/value of it will go up. Open economics will eventually result in manufacturers stepping in to gather some of those profits, stabilizing or bringing down the price.

With Garands now fetching the prices that they do, it might come to pass that someone begins to manufacture them again. Springfield Armory Inc. might be one, but there could be others. After all, all the dimensions are known, and it is simply a matter of getting them codified in a CNC machine and going from there.

We've seen that with the M1 Carbine. Collectors have pushed the prices of those up to absurd levels, and Inland Manufacturing is now making new ones, exact copies, because, well, if the collectors are asking $1,500 for an original, and you want one to shoot, buying a new one for less than the collectors' price becomes attractive.

Here's another reason Garands have disappeared. Decades ago, when hunters were looking for rifles, it was popular to "sporterize" military bolt-action rifles. Why spend the $80 a new Remington would cost when you could buy a surplus Mauser for $30, cut off the extra wood and ditch the extra weight, and have a rifle you could bag a deer with? Well, that happened to Garands, not as often as the Mausers, but it happened. And, as discussed, there

When he visited Greece, Sweeney went by the seat of government, and of course, there was a ceremonial guard. And to no great surprise, they were using Garands.

Since they went all around the world, it shouldn't come as too much of a surprise that they turn up wherever there are conflicts. This one, recovered in Iraq during the GWOT, was returned and placed in the display case of the unit that recovered it. Given the miserable holders of our elected posts, it was more likely destroyed. That would have been a shame.

was the "Tanker" Garands that got chopped to make them shorter and perhaps more "collectible." I've got one. It came into the shop long ago, and the owner could not be found after that. It was buffed and given a blued finish, the gas system altered, and stock changed, and it serves as a cautionary tale — a tale of what can happen when we lose sight of why something was made and try to make it into something it isn't.

Sigh.

THERE'S SOMETHING ALMOST MANIACAL ABOUT THE OFFICIAL RESPONSE TO A FIREARM USED IN A CRIME: THE KNEE-JERK REACTION TO SCRAP IT, AS IF THE INANIMATE OBJECT USED MUST BE PUNISHED — AN ALMOST MEDIEVAL OUTLOOK.

ENTERTAINMENT AND THE GARAND

Regarding the Garand's role on the silver screen, we have two categories: entertainment produced during the Garand era and entertainment set in the Garand era. All movies and TV shows with a military setting before about 1960 will have Garands in them because that was what there was.

One of the first flicks featuring the M1 Garand was *Battleground*, filmed in 1949, about the Battle of the Bulge and the 101st Airborne. What's amazing to viewers today, who do some research, is that combat veterans are in the cast. In this modern era of actors who are the products of one or another acting school and who have little or no real-life experience, the idea of grown men who did the deed, starring in a story about it, is a blast from the past. Veterans of the 101st who had been at Bastogne were hired to train the actors and worked as extras on-screen. While it was filmed on the U.S. West Coast, the screenwriter, Robert Pirosh, had even gone to the places he had been in Europe in 1944, where his unit relieved those inside the Bulge and found the exact spots he had fought from back then. Of course, "back then" had only been two years before.

If we take 1960 as the cut-off line — the M14 would have been an issue item by then, even if not common — I count no less than 35 movies the Garand stars in. However, I know there are many more, as I could come up with a bunch off the top of my head. (What can I say, I watched many war movies on TV back in the 1950s and 1960s as a kid.) Another 36 get listed in the next decade, up to *Patton*, in 1970. Then we get to movies with nothing to do with the military, like *Jaws*, with the Garand in it. Or, the under-rated *Go Tell the Spartans* with Burt Lancaster, where the ARVN troops carry Garands. You'd think that a rifle as old as the M1 Garand would hardly be seen on TV or the big screen, but it seems to be everywhere, even if it's only seen in racks of choices the latest video hero can choose from.

Saving Private Ryan is a more recent movie, but set in 1944. An interesting detail I learned about was

The actual Garand used in the Clint Eastwood movie *Gran Torino* in the vault of the prop house ISS. The author did not get to shoot it, but he did shoot the actual Dirty Harry .44 Magnum, so the trip was a resounding success, he reports.

that an auction house had offered one of the prop rifles used in the movie for sale. It was a rubber casting and was so detailed that you could even make out the serial number of the original.

And finally, one that wasn't set in the Garand era, but used a Garand as a main prop, was *Gran Torino*. Here, Clint Eastwood is a Korean War vet and retired assembly line worker living his last days in Detroit. One of the guns from his weapons stash in the movie is a Garand (the famous "Get off my lawn" scene), and when I visited the prop master, ISS, in southern California, I got to handle that rifle. Yes, it was fun, and yes, I got chills. And no, it was not rubber, but the real deal — a 100% genuine M1 Garand. •

The author and editors would like to thank the Civilian Marksmanship Program (CMP) for the use of many excellent images in this book. The CMP continues to keep M1 Garand collecting and shooting alive and is a premier source for today's military rifle shooters. To learn more, visit thecmp.org. Photos: CMP Archives

Gun Digest would also like to thank Rock Island Auction Company (rockislandauction.com) for additional images and information on the Garand.